Tacitus' Annals

OXFORD APPROACHES TO

Classical Literature

SERIES EDITORS
Kathleen Coleman and Richard Rutherford

Ovid's *Metamorphoses*
ELAINE FANTHAM

Plato's *Symposium*
RICHARD HUNTER

Caesar's *Civil War*
WILLIAM W. BATSTONE
CYNTHIA DAMON

Polybius' *Histories*
BRIAN C. McGING

Tacitus' Annals

RONALD MELLOR

UNIVERSITY PRESS

2011

OXFORD
UNIVERSITY PRESS

Oxford University Press, Inc., publishes works that further
Oxford University's objective of excellence
in research, scholarship, and education.

Oxford   New York
Auckland   Cape Town   Dar es Salaam   Hong Kong   Karachi
Kuala Lumpur   Madrid   Melbourne   Mexico City   Nairobi
New Delhi   Shanghai   Taipei   Toronto

With offices in
Argentina   Austria   Brazil   Chile   Czech Republic   France   Greece
Guatemala   Hungary   Italy   Japan   Poland   Portugal   Singapore
South Korea   Switzerland   Thailand   Turkey   Ukraine   Vietnam

Published by Oxford University Press, Inc.
198 Madison Avenue, New York, New York 10016

www.oup.com

Oxford is a registered trademark of Oxford University Press

Library of Congress Cataloging-in-Publication Data
Mellor, Ronald.
Tacitus' annals / Ronald Mellor.
p. cm. — (Oxford approaches to classical literature)
Includes bibliographical references.
ISBN 978-0-19-515192-3—ISBN 978-0-19-515193-0
1. Tacitus, Cornelius. Annales. 2. Tacitus, Cornelius—Criticism
and interpretation. 3. Rome—Historiography. I. Title.
PA6705.A9M45   2010
937'.07—dc22   2009047671

1 3 5 7 9 8 6 4 2

Printed in the United States of America
on acid-free paper

Nepoti Carissimo
Eric Abraham Mellor

Et Parentibus Suis
Nancy Balter et Blake Mellor

Editors' Foreword

The late twentieth and early twenty-first centuries have seen a massive expansion in courses dealing with ancient civilization and, in particular, the culture and literature of the Greek and Roman world. Never has there been such a flood of good translations available: Oxford's own World Classics, the Penguin Classics, the Hackett Library, and other series offer the English-speaking reader access to the masterpieces of classical literature from Homer to Augustine. The reader may, however, need more guidance in the interpretation and understanding of these works than can usually be provided in the relatively short introduction that prefaces a work in translation. There is a need for studies of individual works that will provide a clear, lively, and reliable account based on the most up-to-date scholarship without dwelling on minutiae that are likely to distract or confuse the reader.

It is to meet this need that the present series has been devised. The title *Oxford Approaches to Classical Literature* deliberately puts the emphasis on the literary works themselves. The volumes in this series will each be concerned with a single work (with the exception of cases where a "book" or larger collection of poems is treated as one work). These are neither biographies nor accounts of literary movements or schools. Nor are they books devoted to the total oeuvre of one author: our first volumes consider Ovid's *Metamorphoses* and Plato's *Symposium,* not the works of Ovid or Plato as a whole. This is, however, a question of emphasis, and not a straightjacket: biographical issues, literary and cultural background, and related works by the same author are discussed where they are obviously relevant. Authors have also been encouraged to consider the influence and legacy of the works in question.

As the editors of this series, we intend these volumes to be accessible to the reader who is encountering the relevant work for the first time; but we also intend that each volume should do more than simply provide the basic facts, dates, and summaries that handbooks generally supply. We would like these books to be essays in criticism and interpretation that will do justice to the subtlety and complexity of the works under discussion. With this in mind, we have invited leading scholars to offer personal assessments and appreciations of their chosen works, anchored within the mainstream of classical scholarship. We have thought it particularly important that our authors be allowed to set their own agendas and to speak in their own voices rather than repeating the *idées reçues* of conventional wisdom in neutral tones.

The title *Oxford Approaches to Classical Literature* has been chosen simply because the series is published by Oxford University Press, USA; it in no way implies a party line, either Oxonian or any other. We believe that different approaches are suited to different texts, and we expect each volume to have its own distinctive character. Advanced critical theory is neither compulsory nor excluded: what matters is whether it can be made to illuminate the text in question. The authors have been encouraged to avoid obscurity and jargon, bearing in mind the needs of the general reader; but, when important critical or narratological issues arise, they are presented to the reader as lucidly as possible.

This series was originally conceived by Professor Charles Segal, an inspiring scholar and teacher whose intellectual energy and range of interests were matched by a corresponding humility and generosity of spirit. Although he was involved in the commissioning of a number of volumes, he did not—alas—live to see any of them published. The series is intended to convey something of the excitement and pleasure to be derived from reading the extraordinarily rich and varied literature of Greco-Roman antiquity. We hope that these volumes will form a worthy monument to a dedicated classical scholar who was committed to enabling the ancient texts to speak to the widest possible audience in the contemporary world.

Kathleen Coleman, Harvard University
Richard Rutherford, Christ Church, Oxford

Acknowledgments

My thanks for this book must first go to Kathleen Coleman and the late Charles Segal for convincing me that I could write for this series a book unlike anything else I have written. After Charlie's death, Richard Rutherford stepped in as coeditor, and he and Kathleen have contributed far more than anyone could expect from series editors. Their learning, stylistic sensitivity, and attention to detail were all enormously helpful and much appreciated. Stefan Vranka, classics editor at OUP, has been patient and helpful, and his staff at OUP greatly expedited the production of the volume.

Some sections of the book have been given as papers at various venues. I spoke about Tacitus' visual representation of history at the University of Southern California and the University of Pennsylvania; on his ethnic prejudices at Tel Aviv University and the University of Maryland; and on Isaac Dorislaus and seventeenth-century English reactions to Tacitus at Yale, Harvard, and the University of Haifa (Israel Classical Association). I am grateful for the good advice (and well-founded doubts) expressed by colleagues at those universities, as both have helped to sharpen my ideas.

Anyone who works on the *Annals* necessarily owes the greatest debt (among living scholars) to Tony Woodman. His books, commentaries, and close readings of individual passages are an enormous help in understanding what Tacitus said and what he meant. Woodman's excellent translation, published by Hackett in 2004, provides a more accurate sense of the epigrammatic and asymmetrical Latin of Tacitus than does any other version in English, and I have used it in this book. Other translations, unless otherwise stated, are my own.

The excellent maps were prepared under the direction of Brian Turner of the Ancient World Mapping Center at the University of North Carolina, Chapel Hill. I am grateful to my friend Richard Talbert of UNC for facilitating that project. The genealogy of the Julio-Claudian dynasty was kindly prepared for me by my son, Blake Mellor. As a professor of mathematics, he is overqualified for such menial work, but I am grateful that he uncomplainingly allowed his underqualified father to exploit his skills.

My wife, Anne, who understandably thought that Tacitus had left our marriage, has once again been a good soldier and cast her professorial eye over every word in this book. If I have not made every change she requested, she above all will understand my stubborn streak. The book is dedicated to my grandson, Eric, who, being only two years old, is not under any obligation to read it . . . yet.

Contents

Tacitus' Annals

Introduction

"Your histories will be immortal."

—Pliny the Younger

Cornelius Tacitus was the greatest historian that the Roman world produced. Almost two millennia ago he drew on his rhetorical and literary training, his career in the law courts, and his experience in politics to create in his book, the *Annals*, the most penetrating indictment of the Roman Empire and its rulers. He believed that history should be important—for both moral and political reasons—and so he set himself up as judge:

> It will be apposite for these matters to have been assembled and transmitted, because few men have the proficiency to distinguish the honorable from the baser, or the useful from the harmful, whereas the majority are taught by what happens to others. (4, 33, 2)

But he was hardly a dispassionate judge. He joined to his private training and public experience a burning passion driven by an intimate knowledge of imperial tyranny. He was determined not only to avenge himself on what he saw as political monsters but to

3

provide lessons for future generations. In his own lifetime he wrote for the practical use of the political and literary elite, that is to say, a small group of other Roman senators and their descendants. He would certainly have been astonished to learn that his books have been read through twenty centuries in dozens of languages and on continents unknown in his own lifetime. We can presume that he would be delighted that his ideas have had such an influence.

Tacitus thus followed a long Roman tradition in believing that the examples of history would be better than the difficult logic of philosophers in determining worthy guides to behavior. Cicero was no historian, but he affirmed that history was the *magister vitae*, the guide of life (*De Oratore* 2, 36). Like all politicians, Tacitus wished to control the story of the past, but he was chiefly concerned with its ability to inspire good and deter evil in the future:

> I deem to be a principal responsibility of annals, to prevent virtues from being silenced and so that crooked words and deeds should be attended by the dread of posterity and infamy. (3, 65, 1)[1]

Yet, from antiquity to modern times, Tacitus has remained in the shadow of his more genial predecessor, Titus Livius. Livy, whose immense history of the Roman Republic was spread over 142 books—which, had it survived in its entirety, would fill about 35 modern volumes—presented in his surviving books uplifting themes of Roman virtue and Roman triumphs in an agreeably leisurely style.[2] (Though only about one quarter of his history survives, it is still more than six times longer than the *Annals*.) His characters live on in drama, music, art, and the popular imagination: Romulus and Remus, Tarquin and Lucretia, Horatius and Lucius Brutus, Coriolanus and Cincinnatus, Hannibal and Scipio. Livy

1. On this passage and the use of historical exempla for moral teaching, see Turpin (2008).

2. The lost books, covering the period from 167 to 9 B.C.E., must have presented the much more disheartening picture of the civil wars of the last century of the Roman Republic.

took both legends and historical accounts and wove them into his own prose epic of Roman majesty. The rhetorician and grammarian Quintilian referred to Livy's "milky richness" (*lactea ubertas*) and called his style "sweet and open and flowing" (*dulcis et candidus et fusus*). Nothing could be more different from the style or the content of Cornelius Tacitus. That imperial historian—though born only four decades after Livy's death—describes another world. He chooses to use a rapid, epigrammatic, asymmetrical Latin in the *Annals* to tell his depressing story of the progressive loss of freedom under the Julio-Claudian emperors. His education and intellectual formation took place during the literary experimentation of Flavian Rome, and he exulted in the witty ambiguity and grammatical freedom of his writing. The decline of traditional values is mirrored in the bold stylistic innovations in his text. Tacitus thus created one of the most remarkable works of Latin literature, not by the traditional literary devices of comfortable prose and pleasing digressions, but through a psychological penetration, acute political analysis, moral judgment, and literary genius that have dazzled his readers for the five centuries since his rediscovery in the Renaissance.

Every Roman writer in any genre aspired both to entertain and to teach his readers—Tacitus wished his book, as the poet Horace suggests, to be *dulce et utile* ("pleasurable and useful"). We must therefore examine how Tacitus might bring pleasure to his reader through his bleak picture of imperial Rome. The lessons are, on the surface, easy enough: one-man rule begets tyranny, corruption, the betrayal of traditional Roman values, and the pernicious distortion of language by its political (mis)use. Tacitus requires his reader to cast aside any rose-colored view of Rome and confront the darkness at the heart of a despotic empire. If Livy taught morality by holding up examples of virtue, Tacitus looks at the dark side of public life and the loss of that ancient *virtus*, while he analyzes the intertwining of political and personal evil. In the *Annals* we see his horror as senators of his own class whose ancestors had brought Rome to world power now abase themselves to gain favor with the corrupt despots who rule the empire. His passionate judgments and devastating portraits of the monsters of the imperial court can be every bit as entertaining as Livy's repetitive sketches of courageous soldiers, selfless politicians, and virtuous matrons. Readers in our own time, who can appreciate the portrayals of existential and interpersonal despair in the plays of Samuel Beckett and Harold Pinter, will also find pleasure in reading Tacitus' ironic portraits of the emperors and courtiers of imperial Rome.

This book will examine Tacitus' last and greatest work. The *Annals* remains the central historical source for understanding the events of the early Roman Empire, since it provides the best narrative material for the reigns of Tiberius, Claudius, and Nero, as well as a probing analysis of the imperial system of government. But the *Annals* must also be seen as far more than a historical source; it is not merely a chronicle from which to extract the facts for the reconstruction of Roman history. The *Annals* is indeed brilliant history, but it is also a superb work of literature that has become an important text in the Western literary, political, and even philosophical traditions. In this brief volume I hope to increase the reader's understanding of Tacitus' *Annals* in its multiple facets as history, literature, and political theory, and to explore the range of its implications as a seminal text.

It may seem surprising to a contemporary reader to regard a book of history as a literary text. In 1896 Friedrich Leo, the greatest Latinist of his time, called Tacitus "one of the few great poets" of the Roman world, but through the twentieth century the writing of history has been regarded as the province of scholars rather than literary artists.[3] Scholars prize "accuracy" above all else and tend to be somewhat condescending toward gentlemen historians like Will Durant or purveyors of popular biographies. They have often preferred narrowly focused historical monographs, "microhistories" of "ordinary people," or even "social science history" (relying heavily on quantitative data), since in all those modes the academic historian believes he or she can achieve greater precision in treating a limited

3. Leo's oration on Tacitus is printed in English translation in Mellor (1995), 218–229.

amount of material. This is the way young historians are trained to write their dissertations. But occasional scandals—plagiarism, faked sources, bogus memoirs—show that even the academy is capable of its fictions. The only professional historian to win the Nobel Prize for Literature was Theodor Mommsen, who received it in 1902—the second year it was given—for his four-volume *Roman History*, published in 1854–1856. (When the politician-historian Winston Churchill was awarded the Nobel Prize for Literature in 1953 for *A History of the English-Speaking Peoples*, it was commonly thought that it was, in the absence of a Nobel Prize for War, being given to him for his role in the defeat of Hitler and Fascism.) Despite the fact that Mommsen was the greatest classical scholar and most learned historian of the nineteenth century—even Mark Twain was impressed by him at dinner in Berlin—his *Roman History* was a passionately sweeping survey of the entire Roman Republic (without footnotes) that grew out of his despair at the failed political movements of 1848. He showed withering contempt for the talkers (Cicero and most senators) and deep admiration for the doers—especially for the dynamic Julius Caesar. Mommsen was hoping for a German version of Caesar, who would unify and modernize the German principalities—and he lived to see it accomplished by Otto von Bismarck. Mommsen, like Gibbon a century earlier, was exceptional in being a meticulous scholar who could successfully write popular, and best-selling, history. But he was at a turning point in the development of historical writing. From antiquity until the nineteenth century, history remained more the realm of writers than of researchers, so we must be careful in applying contemporary expectations of the modern discipline of history to its practitioners in earlier eras.

Before the nineteenth century, it was relatively rare for prose works to have a lasting literary impact. Though we can think of Plato, Thucydides, Cicero, and a handful of others, it has usually been poetry that has had the greatest influence outside its own era; we need only consider Homer and the Greek tragedians, Vergil and Ovid, Dante, Shakespeare, and love poetry through the ages. Prose is more detailed and less universal, not least because, in a pre-Gutenberg age of limited literacy and limited access, poetry could be recited aloud and memorized by a wider audience. Thus poetry leaves a lasting effect on the very language in later ages. Only the Bible (also memorized in English in the wonderful King James translation) has given as much to our language and our storehouse of metaphor as has poetry. It is only during the last two centuries that readers have turned increasingly from poetry to fiction for individual pleasure-reading and even collective reading at family gatherings. As the great novels of the nineteenth century reached for universality, characters from Mary Shelley, Austen, the Brontës, Trollope and Dickens, Hugo, Flaubert and Balzac, Dostoyevsky and Tolstoy, Hawthorne and Melville became the sort of models for human behavior or avoidance that epic and tragic heroes had played in earlier times.

But what of historians? Their characters were drawn from real life and rarely had the compelling personality of an Odysseus, Oedipus, Hamlet, or Faust. A historian was, and is, the captive of his or her material, and only someone very creative can infuse those characters with sufficient universality to bring them off the page for future generations. Even great historians might not be as interested in personalities as was the moral biographer Plutarch, instead focusing on wars or politics. For example, we can hardly assert that Thucydides "created" Pericles and Alcibiades—other sources also show that these were remarkable men. But there can be little doubt that our image of the pathological emperor Tiberius is the creation of the historian, Tacitus. That character dominates the first six books of the *Annals* in a way that would surprise us if we had read the other sources about Tiberius first. Tacitus could take real historical characters—Tiberius as well as many others—and transform them into personalities that leap off the page. He did not just tell a story, but evoked it for his reader through a creative depiction of personalities and dramatic moments.

It is for this reason that Tacitus has had a resonance and influence usually reserved for "creative" artists. Livy also inspired poets and artists, but for a different reason. He provides the classic versions of many fascinating stories, including those of Lucretia, the

Tarquins, and the Horatii. It is the uplifting content of his history that appeals to his readers, whereas with Tacitus it is more than the specifics of his stories. It is rather his irony and his acerbic perspective that come down through the centuries when his characters are re-created in literature, music, and art: Shakespeare's diabolical Richard III (drawn by Thomas More from Tacitus' portrait of Tiberius); Monteverdi's image of Nero's cruel exile of his wife, Octavia, and the enforced suicide of his teacher Seneca before the emperor sings drunkenly with his friends and amorously with his new empress, Poppaea, in *L'incoronazione di Poppea*; or Poussin's great deathbed scene in his painting *The Death of Germanicus*, which not only tells the story but is pervaded with a Tacitean sense of the betrayal of the young prince. We shall see in the final chapter of this book that the Tacitean influence also pervades the political and philosophical writings of the sixteenth, seventeenth, and eighteenth centuries: Machiavelli, Montaigne, Francis Bacon, and Montesquieu.

· 1 ·

The Creation of a Political Historian

Since Romans regarded the writing of history as a political act usually undertaken by senators, the political as well as the intellectual formation of Tacitus becomes an important aspect in assessing his work. We know almost nothing of him save what we find scattered in his own writings, especially his biography of his father-in-law, Julius Agricola. There are almost no contemporary references to him, except in the letters of his friend Pliny. We cannot even be certain whether his praenomen—a Roman's personal name—was Gaius or Publius.

It was soon after the accession of Nero in 54 C.E. that Cornelius Tacitus was born in heavily Romanized southern Gaul, Gallia Narbonensis, often called the *provincia* (now called "Provence"). His father was a financial official in the northern province of Gallia Belgica and belonged to the "equestrian" order. The equestrians were socially respectable administrators, but they were a large step below the political and military elite, who were members of the higher senatorial order. (Perhaps the most famous equestrian in history was Pontius Pilate, governor of the rather minor province of Judaea.) Even though Tacitus himself became a senator at an early age, he retained a pride in his upright provincial ancestors, whom he considered far more virtuous than the corrupt senators who had prospered under the despotic emperors Caligula and Nero. At the same time, his pride in his free Gallic origins was accompanied by a visceral contempt for his perceived ethnic inferiors: easterners and freedmen.

When Vespasian (69–79 C.E.) came to the imperial throne after the terrible civil war of 69, the new emperor brought increasing numbers of Spaniards and Gauls into high office and thus into the Senate. In fact, the ancestors of such later emperors as Trajan, Hadrian, and Marcus Aurelius first rose to high office under him. The adolescent Tacitus was among the ambitious provincials streaming into Rome to study rhetoric, the traditional education for the Roman elite. Tacitus soon achieved success in the law courts, and he advanced quickly after his marriage to the daughter of the well-connected Gallo-Roman senator Julius Agricola. The young advocate received minor honors from Vespasian and, during the brief reign of Vespasian's son Titus (79–81 C.E.), was "elected" quaestor. Though the quaestorship was a junior official who served on the staff of provincial governors or higher officials at Rome, it brought with it membership in the Senate. At the age of twenty-five, Tacitus had joined the political elite.

The future historian held higher office under Titus' successor and younger brother, the unstable Domitian (81–96 C.E.), for whom he probably served as a legionary commander during the years 89 to 93. When that paranoid emperor began a bloody persecution in 93 C.E., Tacitus kept clear of public life. Soon after the murder of Domitian in 96, he reached the consulship.[1] For the provincial Tacitus to become consul at the minimum age of forty-two was an indication of his political and administrative competence and his good connections. Tacitus had served Domitian loyally for more than a decade and had been rewarded well, yet he was deeply affected by Domitian's persecutions of friends and senatorial colleagues, and in the *Agricola* he claimed that fifteen years of his life were erased by the

---

1. During the Roman Republic two annually elected consuls were the highest officials. Though they had little of that authority under the empire, the office still carried great prestige.

emperor's tyranny. While we cannot know how Tacitus actually spent the three years of Domitian's terror, he saw his own complicity in senatorial hands "stained with innocent blood." Both guilt and political frustration drove him to the study of history.

Like most ancients, Tacitus believed that political experience was necessary for an historian. He certainly had that as well as other necessary qualifications: psychological insight, political acumen, access to sources, and literary skill. Over two decades he wrote five books, beginning with short monographs and then showing increasing sophistication and stylistic virtuosity in large annalistic histories. The early monographs were less ambitious, but they were in fact a necessary apprenticeship for the writing of his masterpiece. In them Tacitus first developed the narrative techniques and political attitudes that form the heart of the *Annals*.

★ ★ ★

It may be useful to look briefly at Tacitus' early books to examine the development of the aspiring historian as well as the origins of themes that will reappear in the *Annals*.

1. *Life of Julius Agricola*—Gnaeus Julius Agricola was a highly Romanized Gallo-Roman, born in 40 C.E. in Forum Julii (modern Fréjus) on the southern coast of Gaul. His father held office in Rome and was murdered by Caligula. Agricola joined Vespasian's army during the civil war of 69 C.E., and over fifteen years became the leading general of his time. He served for an extraordinary three terms as governor of Britain, winning victories in both Wales and Scotland. In 84, at the height of his career, the new emperor Domitian recalled him, and the general—still only forty-four years old—was consigned to private life until his death in 93. What we know of his life we owe to the brief biography published by his son-in-law.

Tacitus was extremely fond of Agricola, to whom he owed his political advancement and whom he also admired as an example of old-fashioned values. Roman aristocrats traditionally delivered a public speech (called a *laudatio*) at the funeral of a distinguished relative in which the *laudator* glorified the entire family by praising the achievements and character of the deceased. This book is Tacitus' *laudatio* of Agricola, and it was not published until several years after his death because, as Tacitus says, under tyranny all praise of individual virtue was regarded as subversive. Only after the murder of the detested Domitian could Tacitus write and publish this book; only then could he become an historian.

The *Agricola* is, however, much more ambitious than a traditional spoken *laudatio*. In addition to the facts of Agricola's life, the book contains geography, ethnography, historical narrative, and even speeches. In it Tacitus produces a prototype for his later historical masterpieces. In the *Agricola* we see the apprentice historian's personal resentment, his political agenda, and his literary techniques. The *Agricola* contains the genesis of his moral, political, and psychological ideas.

In his narratives of Agricola's campaigns against the Druids on Anglesey and against the rebels in Scotland, Tacitus subordinates military details to the dramatic and psychological elements of the battle. Here we see the beginnings of the cinematic approach that he perfected later in the grand military tableaux of his *Annals* and *Histories*. From the time of Herodotus, all Greek and Roman historians had composed speeches for the characters in their histories. Though the speeches were invented, they were supposed to be appropriate to the occasion. Tacitus includes in the *Agricola* extended speeches for both Agricola and his principal British antagonist, the rebel chieftain Calgacus. Calgacus delivers a powerful oration to thirty thousand British troops gathered before the decisive battle at Mons Graupius in Scotland. In this declamation, Tacitus uses his own rhetorical training to create in Calgacus an opponent worthy of Agricola. The speech echoes familiar accusations of Rome's greed, cruelty, and arrogance which earlier Roman writers had attributed to their enemies, as Sallust did to King Mithradates 150 years earlier. Calgacus concludes with perhaps the most famous denunciation of Roman imperialism:

> To robbery, to slaughter, and to theft they give the false name of "Empire"; where they create desolation, they call it "peace." (*Agricola* 30)

Throughout the *Agricola* Tacitus maintains the serious tone that Romans thought appropriate to history. Ancient biographies often contained casual conversations, trivial details, jokes, and even coarse anecdotes such as those that Suetonius included in his *Twelve Caesars*. Tacitus prefers rather to adumbrate the political themes which he would develop later in greater detail in the *Annals*: censorship and the loss of political freedom; the insidious maneuvers of imperial freedmen; and the corruption of both language and values. The central theme of the *Agricola* is one close to the heart of Tacitus: "Even under bad emperors men can be great." Under tyrannical government, the compromise (*moderatio*) of an Agricola is more effective than the dramatic resistance of self-appointed martyrs. Tacitus is probably defending his own acquiescence under Domitian as well as praising Agricola.

This laudatory biography is not a mere political tract; it shows genuine warmth for its subject. Agricola is praised for his military skill as well as for his deep family affections. Though the final paragraph abounds with rhetorical commonplaces—"great souls do not perish with the body," "your spirit will live forever," and so on—Tacitus invests these clichés with a sincerity that makes the conclusion a personal farewell. The book is an act of piety, but it also heralds the arrival of a great new historian and provides a blueprint for his future program.

2. On the Origin and Land of the Germans (Germania)—From the time of Homer, poets and historians had incorporated into their books material on the geography, local customs, political organization, and religious beliefs of foreign peoples. Tacitus followed that tradition in his *Germania*, which is the only complete ethnographic monograph surviving from antiquity. The *Germania* briefly describes the geography and customs of Germany before providing a historical account of the various tribes. Unlike many other ethnographers, Tacitus undertook no personal research in Germany and relied entirely on earlier books. In fact, some of his sources were more than a generation old, and there is little that reflects the actual conditions in Germany in Tacitus' own time. Ancient writers often generalized when describing barbarian peoples, and Tacitus was no exception in attributing to the Germans characteristics of other tribes. Nevertheless, much that is contained in the *Germania* has been confirmed by archaeology—if only for a somewhat earlier era.

But Tacitus did not really write the *Germania* to inform the Romans about a foreign land and its peoples. For example, he passes much too quickly over the geography of Germany. His paramount aim is to pursue another central theme of ancient ethnography—the contrast with the author's own society. Tacitus wished to critique Roman morality and political life through the implied comparisons. His anger at the fashionable immorality of contemporary Rome leads him to idealize German life: "No one there laughs at vice, or calls it fashionable to seduce or be seduced" (*Germania* 19). Young Germans are eager to prove their valor as warriors, not as lovers.

The *Germania* idealizes the political freedom of the Germans, who, unlike the Romans, make their important decisions collectively. When Tacitus describes the power of kings as subordinate to the will of their people, he shows that Rome remains an absolute monarchy, even in the happy reign of Trajan when he is writing. Amid his critique of Rome's moral and political condition, Tacitus also warns of the threat that a united Germany could pose to Rome in the future. This is a challenge to the new emperor to return to Julius Caesar's (and Agricola's) aggressively expansionist foreign policy and fulfill the destiny of the empire.

Since the rediscovery of the *Germania* in the fifteenth century, Germans have viewed it as an affirmation of their noble past and lost national independence. Its picture of chaste Germans and corrupt Romans became enormously popular during the Reformation, when the papacy was regarded as the successor of the corrupt and tyrannical Roman emperors. But the greatest impact flowed from Tacitus' observation that

> I agree with those who consider the peoples of Germany, free of all stain of intermarriage with other nations, to be a distinctive and pure race, like no other but themselves. (*Germania* 4)

Looking back after World War II, the great Italian Jewish historian Arnaldo Momigliano concluded that the *Germania* was among the "most dangerous books ever written."[2]

3. *The Dialogue on Orators*—Soon after his first two books, Tacitus turned his hand to an intellectual dialogue in the tradition of Cicero. The *Dialogue* records an imaginary conversation among four historical orators that supposedly took place in Rome in 75 C.E. at the house of Curiatus Maternus. Tacitus skillfully draws the personalities of Maternus and his friends Vipsanius Messala and Marcus Aper, and he provides some indication of their ideas on literature and politics. Maternus has turned from oratory to the writing of poetic tragedies, and Aper chides his friend for wasting time on poetry. Wouldn't he prefer to defend a friend in the present than to glorify long-dead Cato in a tragedy? Aper also sees oratory as the path to fame and fortune, and he cannot understand why his friend fritters away his time in such an unrewarding and idealistic pursuit as writing poetry. Maternus, for his part, believes that the political tyranny of the empire has corrupted oratory; he will not prostitute his rhetorical skills. The late-arriving Messala livens up the discussion. He criticizes the contemporary reliance on rhetorical technique and exercises and prefers the deeply humane moral and literary education of earlier orators like Cicero. The decline of literature from the earlier golden age is a persistent theme in the writing of the time, just as, in his 1946 essay "Politics and the English Language," George Orwell argued that decadent civilization produces decadent language.[3] Though no single speaker serves as a mouthpiece for Tacitus, he certainly sympathizes with Maternus, who forsook oratory for poetry, as Tacitus himself had rejected oratory for history.

The Latin style of the *Dialogue* is unexpected: its Ciceronian amplitude once led many scholars to reject it as a work of Tacitus, or to see it as a work of his youth. But Tacitus was a highly trained

2. Momigliano (1966), 112. This lecture, "Some Observations on the Study of War in Ancient Historiography," was originally given in Copenhagen in 1954.

3. Reprinted in Orwell (1954), 162–177.

rhetorician, who could write Ciceronian Latin when appropriate—as it certainly was in a Ciceronian dialogue. Most scholars now date the *Dialogue* to 102 C.E., since it is dedicated to the consul of that year, Fabius Justus. Tacitus incorporates into this essay on literature his historical analysis of the effects of tyranny. The lasting lesson of the *Dialogue* is that art and society are intertwined, and neither can escape the pressures of political life.

4. Histories—After the completion of his two short historical monographs, Tacitus began his first major annalistic work, the *Histories*. (This title was attached to the manuscript by a Renaissance editor; the original name is lost.) The work contained twelve books and covered the period from 69 to 96 C.E.—the entire period of Flavian rule. Annalistic history proceeded consular year by consular year, like the official *annals* kept by the high priest during the Roman Republic. But only four complete books of the *Histories* and part of a fifth survive. The year 69 C.E. saw four emperors reach the imperial throne—Galba, Otho, Vitellius, and Vespasian—and Tacitus' treatment of that year is the most detailed narrative in any work of Greek or Roman historical writing.

When young Tacitus came to Rome soon after 69 C.E., he met many of the important political figures in Flavian Rome. He had seen and heard much, but he supplemented memory with the *Acts of the Senate*, the records of senatorial deliberations and decisions. In addition to using histories and memoirs, he asked friends for eyewitness accounts, as when he asked Pliny to describe the eruption of Mt. Vesuvius that he witnessed from Misenum on the northern tip of the Bay of Naples in 79 C.E. Though Tacitus followed the annalistic method of organizing his history—hence Book I begins with January 1, 69 C.E.—he sometimes followed a thematic thread across several consular years, since he understood that the consuls were now of little importance.

Tacitus begins the *Histories* with a personal prologue that addresses the difficulty of writing the history of tyrants: there is only flattery in their lifetime and, most often, hostility after their death. He confesses how much his career owes to Vespasian, Titus, and Domitian, yet he asserts that he can write "without affection and without hatred" (*Hist.* 1, 1). After a brief description of the causes of the civil war and of the state of the empire, the narrative begins with the last two weeks of Galba's reign and of his life. Galba is the right man at the wrong time; his unquestionable integrity becomes an anachronistic priggishness unsuited to a corrupt and selfish age. In one of the historian's notable epigrams, he pithily describes the emperor as being "thought capable of ruling, if only he had not had the opportunity to rule." The Latin—*capax imperii nisi imperasset*—is even pithier and more barbed. (*Hist.* 1, 16). Galba stubbornly refused to appease the troops, and his murder led to the acclamation of Otho by the praetorians and of Vitellius by the German legions.

The second book opens with a brief glance at the Roman commander in the East, Vespasian, who was destined to emerge as the ultimate victor in the civil war. But he was still far offstage; the looming conflict was between the forces of Otho and those of Vitellius. Not since Augustus fought with Mark Antony a century earlier had Roman armies engaged in civil war, but at least those earlier rivals fought in Greece and Egypt, and thus avoided devastation within Italy. Otho and Vitellius had no such compunction. Neither had much military distinction, but Vitellius' command of the experienced German legions enabled him to defeat Otho and take control of Rome.

Book 3 is truly epic in scope. Though Vespasian remained in Judaea, the armies under his brother's command defeated the Vitellians in northern Italy, where they pillaged the ancient city of Cremona. Tacitus depicts the conflicting moods as the Flavian army approached Rome, before the desperate Vitellians put the imperial capital to the torch. Words and images from Vergil's account of burning Troy in the *Aeneid* are used by the historian in describing the appalling destruction of both Cremona and Rome itself. This dramatic book closes with the murder of the disgraced Vitellius.

The final complete book turns from Rome to a rebellion of the Batavians in the Low Countries. The generals give long speeches defending their political stance: the rebel leader Julius Civilis' denunciation of Roman imperialism and the Roman general

Cerialis' justification of the empire are especially important. While Vespasian and his elder son Titus remained in Judaea, his younger son Domitian represented him in Rome. The brief fragment of book 5 begins with a confused and hostile account of the Jewish people and their religion. The *Histories*, as we have it, breaks off in midsentence as Tacitus returns to the Batavian revolt.

The historian tells his story with striking rapidity. Despite the shifting focus of the action from Rome to Judaea to Cremona to Germany, the narrative is brisk and tightly organized. Tacitus' compressed style contributes to the swift progress of the story. Dramatic vignettes, character sketches, and digressions enliven the inexorable march of armies. These events were largely acted out in public, with scenes of armies, mobs, and provincials being addressed in public speeches. Later, in the *Annals*, Tacitus would turn to the secret activities within the imperial palace.

Tacitus regarded the civil war of 69 as the greatest calamity ever to befall the Roman people. It destroyed military discipline and allowed provincials to rebel; it brought scoundrels like Otho and Vitellius to power; and it resulted in the sacrilegious burning of the temple of Jupiter on the Capitol. The theme of moral decline is ever-present. The legions had become cowardly, insubordinate, and corrupt; they even sacked Roman cities. The senators and common people were little better; the senators cravenly gave up their freedom of speech, and the Roman mobs were so corrupted that they cheered on Roman soldiers fighting each other in the streets as though they were in the arena.

In the *Histories* Tacitus first shows his understanding of imperial politics and the "secret of power": that real power lay not with the Senate or the constitution, but with the army. In 97 C.E. Tacitus had seen the elderly emperor Nerva shrewdly adopt an outstanding general, Trajan, as his heir, and the historian understood that adoptive monarchy could be the means of avoiding hereditary despots like Caligula, Nero, and Domitian. He even puts such ideas into his version of the futile speech that Galba delivered on the occasion of his adoption of Piso. Despite its inability to save Galba, the speech articulates well the new theory of succession by adoption which in fact did ensure competent government at Rome from 96 C.E. until the accession of Commodus in 180.

The *Histories*, published about 108 C.E., is a masterpiece. Tacitus showed himself to be a mature historian capable of telling a powerful story in an individual style. On reading it, Pliny told his friend, "Your histories will be immortal."[4]

5. Annals—During Tacitus' twenty years as a writer, he remained active in political life under what he called the "happiest age" (*Agricola* 3) of the good emperors Nerva and Trajan. His public career continued and was crowned when he held the prestigious governorship of the province of Asia in 112 C.E. He is thought to have died soon after 117 C.E.

Tacitus even announced in the preface to the *Histories* that in his old age he would write the happier history of the reigns of Nerva and Trajan. Yet he never did so; he chose to look further into the past, finding in Tiberius the dark origins of imperial tyranny. The *Annals*—we do not actually know the ancient title of the work—is a penetrating exposé of Julio-Claudian politics that represents the pinnacle of Roman historical writing. During the decade when he worked on his masterpiece, Tacitus progressed from excellence to genius. The *Annals* has survived in two separate blocks (books 1–6 and 11–16). The first block—from which most of book 5 is lost— treats the reign of Tiberius (14–37 C.E.); the second begins about halfway through that of Claudius (41–54 C.E.), and covers the reign of Nero until 66 C.E., when the text breaks off. The treatment of Caligula (37–41 C.E.) is unfortunately completely lost. Tacitus probably concluded the *Annals* at the end of the year 68 C.E., since his *Histories* begins on January 1, 69 C.E. We cannot be certain, however, that the work was in fact completed.

Tacitus probably shaped the *Annals* into three hexads—blocks of six books. The first six books cover the reign of Tiberius, and the second hexad also closes with the death of an emperor, Claudius. Tacitus marks the entrance of Tiberius in the following way: "The first crime of the new regime was the murder of Postumus Agrippa"

4. Pliny *Letters* 7, 33.

(1, 6). A clear reminiscence accompanies the accession of Nero at the beginning of the third hexad: "The first death of the new regime . . ." (13, 1). The lost account of the accession of Caligula in book 7 may well have echoed the same theme. Tacitus so focused the *Annals* on the imperial tyrants that, in the fifth century, St. Jerome actually referred to the book as *The Lives of the Caesars*. Though Tacitus did not write biographies, Jerome was perceptive in seeing that Tacitus' interest never wandered very far from the imperial palace or from Rome itself.

·2·

The Historian and His Sources

When a historian provides an account of the past, the critical reader naturally wishes to know how accurate that version is. Of course that raises a series of further questions: where the historian found the information, how accurate that source was, how closely the historian followed the source, and the reasons for any deviations. It is not very different from the situation when we ask a friend who spreads a rumor: "Where did you learn that? How did they know? Do you really believe it?" With the exceptions of barroom arguments, talk radio, and the Internet, most people regard information as no more reliable than its source. When we question the veracity of a history, we naturally examine the historian's sources. In recent years we have seen these questions of source criticism transformed from a subject of academic debate among historians into bitter political controversies over the use (and misuse) of military and political intelligence information from dubious sources. The examination of sources remains a central element in our judgment about the reliability of any historian.

I have already mentioned that an ancient Roman writer of history was more interested in style than a twenty-first-century historian, and he was less interested in unearthing new material in archives. Yet Tacitus makes it clear that he did indeed do research, and, regarding accuracy as important, he distrusts many of the written sources. He also recognizes that some imperial historians feared a repressive regime, others tried to curry favor with the emperor in a servile manner, while still others spewed venom on the memory of dead emperors. For that reason Tacitus begins the *Annals* with his famous boast that he writes "without anger or partiality, any reasons for which I keep at a distance" (1, 1). In this he follows Cicero and Sallust in their pious but often empty protestations that truth must be the highest goal for an historian. Of course, even though Tiberius and Nero were long dead, Tacitus shows considerable animosity toward them. So when we indeed find hostility and favoritism throughout his writings, we must assess whether they come from Tacitus' own biases or from those of his sources.

A modern historian provides guidance to the reader in footnotes. There the scholar deploys primary sources and the scholarly interpretations of those sources that are employed in the narrative. But an ancient historian, not unlike a modern popular biographer, provides much less information about conflicting sources, since that was rarely of great interest to the ancient reader. This does not mean that the historian did no research or did not care about accuracy, but rather that the ancient reader wanted a clear, well-written story, just as modern readers who choose to read "popular history" do not want to be "confused" by footnotes and alternative explanations. So it is very much the exception when Tacitus, despite his innate skepticism about any story, details varying sources, but he occasionally does so, even self-consciously commenting on his method, as when he reports on the various versions of Nero's plan to murder his mother:

> For myself, with my intention of following an authorial consensus, I shall transmit under their own names any diverging accounts they have handed on. (13, 20, 2)

That is hardly satisfactory to a modern historian, since we want to know not only what he includes but what he omits, but Tacitus goes further than did his predecessors in critically evaluating sources.

On the rare occasions when Tacitus mentions specific sources, they are earlier writers or people recorded in oral reports. But there were other sources as well. Tacitus had met many of the important political figures in Julio-Claudian and Flavian Rome, and, though he obviously learned much from these personal conversations, he found some of the rumors incredible:

> In transmitting Drusus' death I have recorded what has been recalled by most authors and those of the greatest credibility; but I am not inclined to neglect from those same times a rumor so effective that it has not yet abated. (4, 10, 1)

He details at length a scurrilous rumor that implicated Tiberius in the poisoning of his own son Drusus. Then he dismisses it:

> This was bandied about in public, but beyond the fact that it is affirmed in no reliable author, you can readily refute it. (4, 11, 1)

After a detailed rebuttal of the illogicality of such an accusation, Tacitus concludes:

> In my case the reason for transmitting and criticizing the rumor was that on the basis of a resounding example I might dispel false hearsay and ask of those into whose hands my work comes that they should not be hungry to accept well publicized incredulities nor prefer them to what is genuine and uncorrupted by the miraculous. (4, 11, 3)

Of course we recognize that, despite the historian's pose of historical rigor, he does manage to report the unreliable slander to add to his unflattering portrait of Tiberius. He was trained as an advocate, and, like his famous predecessor Cicero or modern attorneys, he knew how to slip "irrelevant" or "untrue" material into his continual indictment of Tiberius.

In addition to the eyewitness accounts the diligent historian demanded of such friends as Pliny, he also mentions (5, 4) the records of the Senate (*acta senatus*), and he almost certainly made use of those records as well as the collection of decrees kept in the state archives. Many inscriptions—carved versions of laws and senatorial decrees—had long been publicly preserved on the Capitoline Hill, but we have few that can be compared with Tacitus' histories. Few stone inscriptions survived the multiple destructions, notably the fire of 69 C.E., and, even without natural disasters, nearly all Roman bronze texts were eventually melted down for their intrinsic value. For example, Augustus' *Record of Achievements* (*Res Gestae*), once set up in bronze outside his mausoleum in Rome and throughout the provinces, is now known only from stone copies found in Asia. Despite all this destruction, scholars have rediscovered a number of important bronze tablets containing inscriptions concerning the death of the imperial prince Germanicus and its aftermath. The first group of texts—primarily the *Tabula Hebana* and the *Tabula Siarensis*, found in Italy and Spain between 1947 and 1982—provide an extensive list of the honors (decrees, statues, arches, buildings, etc.) voted to Germanicus after his death in 19 C.E. For example, the anniversary of his death was to be celebrated each year on October 10. These accounts are more detailed than is the list provided by Tacitus (2, 83).

A half-dozen fragmentary texts have been discovered more recently in Spain and published as the "Senatorial Decree Concerning the Elder Piso" (*Senatus Consultum de Pisone Patre*, hereafter *SCPP*).[1] They concern the trial and suicide of Germanicus' antagonist and possible murderer, Calpurnius Piso, in the year after the prince's death. (Piso is described as "father" because his two sons were also charged.) Those texts, written and sent to the provinces by order of the Senate and with the approval of the emperor Tiberius, have been subjected to close scholarly scrutiny during the past decade, and they provide an alternative version to one of the most dramatic episodes in Tacitus' *Annals*. A comparison of these versions permits us to contrast these "official" reports and Tacitus' account written ninety years later, and to appraise the purpose and accuracy of each.

1. Eck, Caballos, and Fernández (1996). For a collection of papers discussing this text, cf. Damon and Takács (1999).

Germanicus, nephew of Tiberius, is the only heroic figure in the first two books of the *Annals*. Tacitus records his military triumph in Germany and his death in Syria against the background of a brooding and hostile Tiberius in Rome. Augustus had regarded his young step-grandson (father of that emperor's only great-grandchildren) as an ideal future emperor, and thus forced his own designated successor, Tiberius, to adopt his nephew Germanicus as coheir with his own son Drusus II. (Drusus II is to be distinguished from Drusus I, Tiberius' brother and Germanicus' father, who died in 9 B.C.E.) The aloof Tiberius always remained deeply suspicious of the charming and beloved Germanicus. The emperor's disquiet led to his recall of Germanicus from Germany, when he gave him a consulship, because, in Tacitus' opinion, he was fearful that the young commander would achieve even greater triumphs (2, 26).

Even in Tacitus' sympathetic portrayal of Germanicus, there is ample justification for Tiberius' uneasiness about this emotional young man, who was prone to quite unmilitary theatrical gestures with his troops: weeping, threatening suicide to quell a mutiny, and displaying his wife and children to the troops to win sympathy as though he were in a Roman law court. He was perhaps a competent general—though Tacitus' account of his triumphs is somewhat confused by having to rely on very flattering sources written in the reigns of his relatives Caligula, Claudius, and Nero. In fact, Germanicus' army suffered heavy losses in the German campaign, and his fleet also underwent considerable damage on its return voyage. It was at that point that Tiberius recalled him to Rome, though Germanicus wished to stay for another campaign. Later, he broke with imperial policy by visiting Egypt without permission "to see the antiquities," and while there he grandly opened the warehouses and distributed free grain. Despite being reprimanded for that visit, Germanicus also behaved haughtily toward Calpurnius Piso, a long-time confidant of Tiberius sent to assist him in Syria. Germanicus' arrogance—based on the fact that his wife and children were the only surviving direct heirs of Augustus—must certainly have annoyed Tiberius and added to the good reasons he had to restrain this rash young man.

Things in Syria turned out very badly. There was personal antagonism from the start between Germanicus and Piso, and their sycophantic retinues did little to help, especially the entourage of Germanicus:

> His friends, astute at inflaming his sense of offense, let fly with the truth, heaped up falsehoods, and in various ways incriminated Piso, Plancina [Piso's wife], and their sons. (2, 57, 2)

Their differences concerning Roman policy toward Parthia brought them close to open conflict. After Piso finally left his province, Germanicus became ill and died. At that time, to the horror of Germanicus' supporters, Piso returned to Syria until he was recalled to Rome by Tiberius. Germanicus himself suspected that somehow Piso and Plancina were causing his death, though neither Tacitus nor the senatorial decrees take this accusation seriously.

Perhaps the young prince was incited by his even more headstrong wife, Agrippina, who was eventually to assail Tiberius and, as a result, be murdered with two of her sons by the emperor's men. Tacitus seems to acknowledge this in the death scene of Germanicus, who calls on his friends for revenge against Piso but warns Agrippina to repress her pride:

> "If I were succumbing to fate, my indignation even at the gods would be justified, nor snatching me—in my youth, by a premature departure—from my parents, children, and fatherland. As it is, I have been cut off by Piso's and Plancina's crime, leaving these as my last prayers in your hearts: relay to my father and brother the embitterments with which I have been tormented, the snares by which I have been surrounded, as I end my most pitiable life with the worst of deaths. Anyone who was moved by my hopes, by kindred blood, even by resentment toward me during my lifetime—they will shed tears that a once flourishing survivor of so many wars has fallen to womanly foul play. But it is you who will have the

chance of complaining before the senate, of invoking the laws. It is not the principal responsibility of friends to serve the deceased by means of idle complaints but to observe his instructions. Germanicus will be wept for even by strangers; but it is you who will avenge him, if it was me rather than my fortune that you befriended. Show to the people of Rome the granddaughter of the Divine Augustus, who is likewise my wife; count out our six children. Pity will be on the side of the accusers; and those fabricating criminal instructions will either not be believed by men or not forgiven." His friends, touching the right hand of the dying man, swore that they would sooner give up breath than revenge.

Then, turning to his wife, he begged her by the memory of him, by their mutual children, to cast aside her defiance, to submit her spirit to the savagery of fortune, and not, on her return to the City, to goad her superiors in power by rivaling them for it. These words openly; others were in secret, by which he was believed to have shown dread of Tiberius. And not long afterwards his life was extinguished, to the mighty grief of the province and its surrounding peoples. (2, 71–72)

It is not precisely clear why Tacitus regards Germanicus as such an example of ancestral virtue, but he does. He probably inflated the qualities of Germanicus to provide a moral contrast to Tiberius. Tacitus reports the preposterous accolades made at the prince's funeral by his entourage, who compared him to Alexander the Great, the conqueror of Asia as far as India:

The funeral, though without images and procession, was well attended by the praise and remembrance of his virtues. And there were those by whom his good looks, age, and manner of death were matched—on account of the proximity too of the place of his demise—with the lot of Alexander the Great: each of graceful physique and illustrious family, and not long after exceeding his thirtieth year, had fallen to the snares of his own people among foreign nations. But this man, they said, had been gentle toward his friends, moderate in his pleasures with only one marriage and his children certain. Nor was he any less a combatant, even if he lacked temerity and had been prevented from pressing the Germanies, though pounded by so many victories, into servitude. If he had been the sole arbiter of affairs, they said, with royal prerogative and name, he would have achieved military glory more readily, just as he excelled in clemency, restraint, and the other good qualities. (2, 73, 1–3)

But it was not Tacitus alone who put Germanicus on a pedestal. The biographer Suetonius and the later historian Cassius Dio also praise him extravagantly, and both believe that he was indeed poisoned by Piso. The elaborate funeral honors recorded in contemporary documents demonstrate that this was not merely later rhetorical inflation of Germanicus; there must have been genuine popularity, which Tiberius was careful to appease after his death.

But what had Germanicus done to merit such extraordinary admiration? Admittedly, he was handsome, charming, and married to the only living grandchild of the great Augustus. His father, Drusus, Livia's older son and Tiberius' brother, had also been much beloved at his early death in 9 B.C.E., perhaps because he was thought by some senators to harbor a secret affection for the Republic. The Roman people seemed to have felt particular affection for princes who died prematurely, as Tacitus suggests in a famous epigram about Drusus: "Brief and unpropitious were the loves of the Roman people" (2, 41, 3).

Germanicus did have some talent for writing poetry in both Greek and Latin, and he translated a learned astronomical book from Greek into Latin. His interest in history took him sightseeing to the site of Varus' defeat in Germany, the site of Actium, and the Egyptian pyramids.[2] But his popularity with his troops was the most likely cause of Tiberius' suspicion, despite the fact that Tiberius himself had been quite popular with the legions he had led in

---

2. Augustus defeated Antony and Cleopatra at Actium in 31 B.C.E. As governor of Germany, Varus led three Roman legions into a devastating ambush in 9 C.E. On Germanicus as a "reader" of history, cf. O'Gorman (2000), 46–56.

Pannonia along the Danube and Germany. So Tacitus and other Roman writers believe that, despite an outward show of support, Tiberius concealed a deep hatred for his adopted son. Of course they relied on sources written in the reigns of Germanicus' son (Caligula), brother (Claudius), and grandson (Nero). We might be understandably skeptical of any such evidence deriving from the "House of Germanicus," which ruled Rome from 37 to 68 C.E.

In book 2 of the *Annals* Tacitus casts Gnaeus Calpurnius Piso as the brutal henchman of Tiberius during the illness and death of Germanicus, calling him "temperamentally violent and a stranger to compliance, with the innate defiance of his father" (2, 43, 2). But the historian provides little background information about Piso's father, a member of the old Republican aristocracy. We learn from other sources that Piso's father had joined the conspiracy against Julius Caesar in 44 B.C.E. but was later pardoned by Octavian. The elder Piso took no part in the new regime until 23 B.C.E., when he was named consul by Augustus. It was a critical time, when the emperor was seriously ill, and Piso was entrusted with military and financial records. The son was also favored by Augustus, who named him consul for 7 C.E. with the heir-apparent Tiberius as his colleague. Piso served as governor of Africa and a legionary commander in Spain before Tiberius named him as governor of Syria under the overall authority of Germanicus as "commander of the East." So Piso had genuine service under Augustus and had served as the consular colleague of Tiberius; he had every reason to be proud of his connections and his career.

Although Piso was a haughty Republican aristocrat, he was also personally loyal to Tiberius, and a competent general. His first appearance in the *Annals* showed him to be a shrewd courtier able to rescue his leader in an embarrassing moment. During one of the early trumped-up "treason" trials, Tiberius was goaded into imprudently prejudging the case:

> At this Tiberius flared up to such an extent that, shattering his taciturnity, he announced that he too would express an opinion in the case, openly and on oath, so that the same

constraint should apply to the others. Even then there remained traces of dying freedom: so Cn. Piso said, "In what place will you vote, Caesar? If first, I shall have something to follow; if after everyone else, I am afraid lest I dissent improvidently." Shaken by these words, and passive from penitence at having boiled over too incautiously, he allowed the defendant to be released from the charges of treason; the question of extortion went to the recoverers. (1, 74, 4–6)

Hence it becomes rather difficult to envision Piso as a rogue administrator who sought to undermine the emperor. More likely, he saw his role as providing "adult supervision" to the impetuous Germanicus, whom Tiberius had already had to rein in. It is even implied by Tacitus that such orders were given to him in writing by Tiberius. Tacitus also reports that Piso's wife was very close to the dowager empress, Livia. So conflict was inevitable between the proud, experienced senior senator and the headstrong young prince surrounded by a sycophantic entourage. Tacitus even reports that Piso was confident enough to insult Agrippina and Germanicus. The illness and death of Germanicus—which Tacitus does not attribute to Piso except in Germanicus' fevered deathbed accusations—elevated this political turf battle into the realm of melodrama and tragedy. During Piso's confident return to Rome in Book 3, he even stopped to visit the emperor's son Drusus II on the way. But in Rome he was confronted with a groundswell of outrage at Germanicus' death, for which he would become the most convenient scapegoat. So Tacitus changes his rhetorical portrait of Piso from a suspected murderer to the sacrificial victim of the historian's favorite target, Tiberius.

2 | The Tacitean Version of Piso's Trial

The five-page account that Tacitus devotes to the Piso episode falls into two parts: the return of Piso to Rome amid growing anger at the death of Germanicus, and his trial before the Senate. It becomes clear that Piso, who took several months to make the journey back to Rome, was confident of Tiberius' support, but the emperor was becoming nervous at the continuing unrest among the Roman masses after Agrippina's dramatic return with her husband's ashes. When the crowds complained that insufficient honor was shown to Germanicus, Tiberius attempted to calm them by issuing a proclamation that said in part:

> There was no need of examples from more olden times, such as when the Roman people had borne steadfastly the disasters of armies, the demise of leaders, and noble families utterly lost. Principes were mortal; the state eternal. (3, 6, 3)

That final aphorism—*principes mortales, rem publicam aeternam*—sounds as though it might well be a direct quote from the emperor. But if the masses were temporarily calmed, Tacitus makes the overconfident return of Piso the cause of revived rumor and anger:

> He moored himself at the tomb of the Caesars—and in daylight too, the bank crowded, and himself with a great column of clients and Plancina with a company of women; and it was with eagerness on their faces that they strode on their way. Among the incitements to resentment were his house looming over the forum and its festive decoration, his party and banquet; and, given the crowdedness of the place, nothing was concealed. (3, 9, 2–3)

Such an ostentatious arrival in the city would have been normal for a Republican aristocrat, but it was very foolish in the current circumstances. The next day senatorial flatterers vied with Germanicus' friends to bring charges against Piso and his family. After taking counsel with his closest advisors, Tiberius chose not to hear the case privately, as Piso had hoped, since that would doubtless give rise to further suspicions. The emperor referred the case to the Senate for trial amid rumors about "whether Tiberius would manage to contain and repress his own feelings" (3, 11, 2).

In fact, Tiberius opened the trial by delivering a remarkably evenhanded introductory speech, in which he made clear that the senators were consulted on the appointment of Piso:

On the day of the senate Caesar delivered a speech with considered balance: Piso had been his father's legate and friend and had been given by himself, on the senate's authority, to Germanicus as his helper in the administration of affairs in the East. Whether he had there stung the young man by his truculence and tussles and had been merely delighted at his departing, or whether he had extinguished his life by some crime, must be judged with a open mind. "If the legate cast aside the boundaries of his office and his compliance toward his commander and was delighted at his death (and at my grief too), I shall reject him and bar him from our house and thus it will not be as princeps that I shall avenge a private antagonism; but, if a deed is uncovered which in the case of the killing of any mortal whatsoever would require vengeance, you for your part must visit both the children of Germanicus and us his parents with the consolation we deserve. And at the same time reflect on this: whether Piso handled his armies disruptively and mutinously, whether the soldiers' affections were acquired by corrupt methods, whether the reclamation of the province was by arms, or whether there were falsehoods, publicized with exaggeration by his accusers.

"It is the excessive enthusiasms of the latter to which I rightly take exception. What was the point of stripping his body and permitting its handling by the eyes of the public of spreading abroad, even among foreigners, that his life had been cut short by poison, if those matters are still uncertain and require examination? Of course I lament my son and will always lament him; but I am not preventing the defendant from producing everything by which his innocence can be bolstered or by any irregularity of Germanicus' confirmed. And I pray that you should not regard the connection between the case and my pain as a reason to receive the proffered charges as proved. Those who have become his advocates because of kindred blood or individual loyalty, help the imperiled man as effectively as each of you can with your eloquence and concern. In only one respect shall we have placed Germanicus above the laws, namely that the investigation into his death is being held in the curia rather than in the forum. Before the senate rather than before the judges; let everything else be handled with equal restraint. No one should have regard for the tears of Drusus, no one for my sorrowfulness, nor for any hostile fabrications against us." (3, 12, 1–7)

This speech seems to have certain stylistic quirks peculiar to Tiberius, and Tacitus probably read it in the archives of the Senate. Of course he would not have copied a speech *verbatim*. But it is clear that Tiberius emphasized Piso's political crimes rather than Germanicus' death.

In typical Roman fashion, the trial was rapid: two days of prosecution followed by a six-day hiatus before three days of defense arguments. Tacitus' view was that there was no real evidence of murder but ample indication of tampering with the army. When Piso saw that Tiberius was not going to save him, he seemingly committed suicide or at least was found with his throat cut. Tacitus reports rumors he had heard in his youth, and adds a considerable degree of ambiguity to his narrative:

> (I remember hearing from my elders that a document was
> often seen in Piso's hands, which he himself did not publicize; but his friends had insisted that it contained a letter
> from Tiberius and instructions against Germanicus, and the
> intention had been to produce it before the fathers and to
> accuse the princeps, had he not been outwitted by [praetorian prefect] Sejanus with empty promises; also that his life
> had not been extinguished of its own accord but after an
> assailant had been sent in. Neither of these would I be
> inclined to assert; nevertheless I have no right to conceal
> what was told by those whose lives lasted into my own
> youth.) (3, 16, 1)

According to Tacitus, Tiberius read to the Senate a letter written by Piso claiming his own innocence and pleading for the acquittal of his sons. After the Senate imposed penalties on the sons, Tiberius mitigated them and allowed Piso's property to be retained by his family. One son even became consul in 27 C.E.—a mere seven years after his father's trial—and a grandson was consul in 57 C.E. This letter of Piso is not mentioned in the *SCPP*, since his plea of innocence would complicate the clear assumption of guilt in the Senate's decree.

3 | Decree of the Senate Concerning the Elder Piso (*SCPP*)

In fact, the *SCPP* provides a much less complex version of this entire episode—one suitable for the regime to disseminate throughout the empire as the official account of these events. The long decrees concerning the death of Germanicus and the trial of Piso exist in multiple, if fragmentary, copies from which scholars have been able to re-create virtually the complete decree. It is one of very few senatorial decrees from the Roman Empire to survive. In fact, more surviving inscriptions treat Germanicus' death and Piso's trial than any other historical event in Roman history, so it was obviously of great importance to the imperial government at the time. The *SCPP* was intended to be read by as wide a public as possible:

> It is the Senate's pleasure . . . that this decree of the Senate, inscribed on bronze, should be put up in the most frequented city of each province and in the most frequented place of that city; and likewise, that this decree of the Senate should be put up in the winter quarters of each legion, at the standards. (*SCPP* 170–172)[3]

The inscription makes clear that Tiberius had referred the case of Piso, his wife, and his son to the Senate, and it records the

---

3. For the translations of the *SCPP*, I have used Rowe (2002). Greg Rowe's interpretation of this and the other Tiberian texts is an excellent guide to these problems.

decree the Senate issued on December 10, 20 C.E. Since Germanicus died on October 10, 19 C.E., and the trial of Piso took place in May of 20 C.E., it seems likely that it was the public celebration of the anniversary of Germanicus' death in October of 20 C.E. that once again aroused popular discontent and compelled the government to make a public statement. Hence the Senate begins by thanking the immortal gods and Tiberius for protecting the state from unrest, and puts a great deal of emphasis on Tiberius' devotion to duty. The decree also compliments Tiberius for his fairness in insisting on a proper defense of Piso—even after his suicide. It likewise praises

> the exceptional patience and restraint of Germanicus Caesar, overcome by the savagery of Piso senior, and that on that account, when he was dying, Germanicus Caesar, who himself bore witness that Cn. Piso senior had been the cause of his death, not without good reason renounced his friendship with a man who—when he ought to have remembered that he had been assigned as an aide to Germanicus . . . (*SCPP* 26–30)

But there is no further mention of the charge of murder. The emphasis is on disruptions caused by Piso as he stirred up war with the Armenians and Parthians and, even more seriously, tried to provoke civil war by corrupting the soldiers. He gave out bonuses in his own name from the imperial treasury so that some soldiers called themselves "Pisonians" as opposed to "Caesarians." This was the focal point of the accusation against Piso, and the rhetoric recalls the terrible decades of the civil wars in which Republican generals bribed soldiers to follow them into battle against other Romans. All that civil strife had been ended by Augustus fifty years earlier with his victory over Antony, and the Senate warns that only loyalty to the imperial family can preserve the peace at Rome.

The *SCPP* totally blackens the character and political loyalty of Piso, and the rhetoric of the text casts Tiberius in the role of the betrayed victim. Piso's suicide was not punishment enough. The Senate decreed that his family could not mourn him, that his statues and portraits be removed and not be used in future family marriages or funerals, that his name be eliminated from inscriptions, and that his property be confiscated. It may seem ironic that a text ostensibly published for the purpose of decreeing the official obliteration of Piso's name in fact kept his treachery so vividly alive throughout the empire. Of course, that was precisely the purpose. Earlier senatorial decrees would only have been set up in Rome itself, but in this case the government thought it imperative to publicize Piso's crime—particularly among the armies where his name was known and respected—while at the same time insisting that his name should be forgotten at Rome.

The question of expurgation of someone's name (known by the modern term *damnatio memoriae*—"condemnation of one's memory") had previously been regarded as a private family issue, but in the case of Piso the state intervenes for the first time. The extraordinary sanctions have a moral and ideological tone and imply that Piso, his freedmen, and slaves had long been troublemakers. But this implication runs counter to his appointment by Tiberius to the crucial position of governor of Syria—an appointment endorsed by the Senate itself only three years earlier. While there is no contradiction in the Senate's official decree, which does not mention senatorial involvement in Piso's appointment, the Tacitean account shows that there were uncertainties and rumors about his actual assignment in the East. In some ways the *SCPP* may be responding to some of those questions, though it does not articulate them very clearly.

Perhaps the most delicate issue was what to do with Piso's wife, Plancina. Here the Senate defers to Tiberius and, through him, to Livia:

> As regards the case of Plancina, against whom a great many extremely serious charges were brought, because she admits that all her hope resides in the mercy of our princeps and the Senate, and because our princeps has often and zealously requested from this order that the Senate, content with punishing Cn. Piso senior, spare his wife as it is sparing his son

Marcus, and himself pleaded for Plancina at the request of his mother and accepted the very just reasons that had been put to him by her for his mother wanting to secure her request, the Senate thinks that support and indulgence should be accorded to Julia Augusta—who has served the state supremely not only in giving birth to our princeps but also through her many great favors toward men of every order, and who, although she rightly and deservedly ought to have supreme influence in making a request of the Senate, yet uses that influence most sparingly—and to the supreme devotion of our princeps toward his mother; and it is [the Senate's] pleasure that Plancina's penalty be waived. (*SCPP* 109–120)

This elaborate sentence, with several levels of subordination and two dozen clauses in the Latin, shows the care with which the senatorial rhetoricians composed it. Plancina is not pronounced to be innocent, but her punishment is waived as a favor to Livia. Why Livia should be so sympathetic to the possible murderer of her grandson is carefully avoided; that she had reasons is mentioned, but those motives are not revealed. Livia's intervention saves Plancina, just as Tiberius' mercy spares Piso's sons and the family property. It seems a bargain had been struck for the family's silence, which, of course, did not find its way into the official account.

4 | Tacitus versus the Decree

Tacitus provides a more complex account of the Germanicus-Piso episode than that of the "official" version in the decree. Even within Tacitus' report, the emphasis changes as he moves from rumors about the death of Germanicus, disseminated by his entourage, to the death of Piso, associated with a different sort of gossip. It was to control the gossip concerning the possible murder of Germanicus and the scapegoating of Piso that the official decree had to be widely disseminated. The *SCPP* attributes Tiberius' implacability toward Piso to his abhorrence of disloyalty and the possibility of civil war, whereas Tacitus implies that Piso was Tiberius' creature in the persecution of Germanicus and that there might even have been written evidence to prove it.

Tacitus is more overtly hostile to Plancina. Though the *SCPP* does not spell out the charges against her, the *Annals* makes clear that she was accused of inciting Piso's arrogance, reviewing troops, openly insulting Germanicus and Agrippina, and being close friends with a certain Martina, a woman known in Syria for her skill with poison. After the death of her protectors Livia and Sejanus, Plancina was herself accused in 33 C.E. and, like her husband, chose suicide:

> Formerly wedded to Cn. Piso and openly delighted at the death of Germanicus, when Piso fell she had been defended by the pleas of Augusta and no less by the antagonism of Agrippina. But as hatred and influence ceased, justice came into effect; and, now the target of accusations by no means unfamiliar, with her own hand she exacted a late rather than an undeserved reprisal. (6, 26, 3)

Tacitus' treatment of Plancina makes clear that he knew far more than the *SCPP* reveals. He must have read senatorial speeches of the time as well as later historians. If Tacitus does not repeat the official version of the trial, he also avoids the simplistic smear of Piso contained in the pro-Germanicus historians. He provides at least some insight into the behavior of all the actors and admits to doubt about certain facts, whereas the official *SCPP* admits no doubt. Official documents rarely do. From the Tacitean version we can see not only that Piso is "evil" but that a serious clash of personalities drove the conflict in Syria. The historian was less interested in the spurious "certainty" expressed in the legal formulas and proclamations in the *SCPP*, instead bringing hearsay and rumor into his account. He certainly did not bother to detail every honor posthumously voted to Germanicus, nor to repeat the claim in the decree that Tiberius was the model of civic virtue. His conclusion emphasizes the continuing ambiguities surrounding the entire episode, whereas the *SCPP* blithely asserts that its widespread circulation will make everything clear. As in any despotism, genuine transparency was far too dangerous to be permitted. As always, Tacitus was groping through the political verbiage toward the underlying reality.

★ ★ ★

What light do these newly discovered inscriptions shed on Tacitus' accuracy? Modern historians of antiquity (and of many other eras) give significant weight to contemporary testimonia—especially inscriptions, papyri, and coins that contain what the Romans "really" intended to record for the present and future. Hence we greet the news of a newly discovered inscription with the hope that we will get closer to "the real story." After all, the Greek and Roman writers of history looked back decades, or even centuries; they were often less "primary sources" for history than "interpreters" of history. And yet, in antiquity as in the twenty-first century, the official document or press release is likely to be far more self-interested than the distanced historian. Every new release of diplomatic or presidential papers reveals the obvious truism that governments (mis)use information to their own advantage.

A primary source, like Augustus' autobiographical *Res Gestae* or the *SCPP*, ought to be telling us "what really happened," but we know that it often does not. So we rely on the historian, ancient and modern, to excavate the truth from the documents just as archaeologists do from the ground. Tacitus uses rumor and gossip—much as a journalist might do—to see beyond the official interpretation. The Piso episode shows how very perceptive he was at cutting through the official verbiage of decrees, the records of the Senate, and even preserved speeches. The senatorial decree is exciting to scholars, because for once we have the "official story." But is it accurate? Does it represent political reality? Instead, the decree confirms that the official story is less reliable than the incisive and skeptical interpretations of a historian who wrote a century after the events—Cornelius Tacitus. His ambiguous picture of a deluded and betrayed Piso is more credible than the decree's simplistic notion of a formerly loyal henchman of Tiberius who seems to give in to innate, and irrational, savagery against Germanicus. Far from undermining

Tacitus' credibility, the contradiction between his version and the *SCPP* buttresses our respect for his political acuity. Of course he is far from "impartial"—no one who had lived under tyranny could view another tyrant with complete equanimity. Every historian of any era has political, ethnic, religious, or economic views that shape his or her thinking; the central issue is whether those views result in dishonest history. In the case of Piso, far from being dishonest, Tacitus presents a more accurate account than does his sources. It is a topic to which I will return in chapter 9 when discussing Tacitus' version of Claudius' speech concerning the Gauls.

·3·

Ethnic Prejudice in Tacitus

At the beginning of book 5 of the *Histories*, Tacitus offers a confused and hostile description of the Jewish people on the eve of the destruction of Jerusalem. It is often regarded as the *locus classicus* of Roman anti-Semitism, but it is best to place Roman prejudice against Jews within a larger context. A. N. Sherwin-White regarded Roman hostility to Germans, Britons, Jews, Greeks, and Parthians all equally as manifestations of "racial prejudice."[1] Yet, in our own era, we tend to use "racism" somewhat more selectively, so that prejudices between English and Irish, or Indians and Pakistanis—however acrimonious—are attributed to religious, cultural, or historical antagonisms. Thus Benjamin Isaac, in his recent magisterial treatment of ancient racism, is careful to differentiate the concern with appearance or with culture and the hostility toward strangers from what he terms "proto-racism."[2] In the same way, we must

---

1. Sherwin-White (1967).

2. Isaac (2004); on these general issues, cf. especially his introduction, pp. 1–51, and "Ethnic Prejudice, Proto-Racism, and Imperialism in Antiquity," pp. 503–516. Isaac's book is extensively annotated and contains a comprehensive recent bibliography on Roman views of various foreign groups.

historicize and contextualize Roman forms of ethnic prejudice that we find in Tacitus.

1 | Roman Views of Foreigners

While Roman writers were usually contemptuous of non-Romans, there are many instances of Roman admiration for Greek culture, British courage, or German love of freedom. That mixture of distrust and admiration appears throughout the works of Tacitus. Some later Romans realized that Romulus' gang of followers needed foreigners—and especially foreign (Sabine) women—if their embryonic settlement was going to survive. Amid all the later patriotic jingoism directed against foreigners, it is useful to return to the emperor Claudius' impassioned speech to the Senate in 48 C.E. on behalf of a policy allowing Roman citizens of Gallic descent to serve in the Senate. He points out that many distinguished Roman families were themselves immigrants:

> "My ancestors, of whom the most ancient, Clausus of Sabine origin, was assumed into Roman citizenship as well as into the families of the patricians, encourage the use of similar counsels in political life, namely the transferring hither of whatever proves to be exceptional elsewhere. For I am not unaware that the Julii were summoned into the senate from Alba, the Coruncanii from Camerium, the Porcii from Tusculum." (11, 24, 1–2)

As Rome expanded into central Italy, conquered peoples, such as the neighboring Latins, were granted full or partial Roman citizenship. But that early, and necessary, generosity toward conquered peoples was by the second century B.C.E. overwhelmed by the arrogance of Roman military dominance. Even the Italian allies who fought as part of the Roman armies had to rise in revolt in the Social War (90–88 B.C.E.) to compel the Roman Senate to extend full citizenship throughout the peninsula. Overseas, Roman generals treated both enemies and allies with a contempt that they described as *nova sapientia*—a "new wisdom" that we might call

Realpolitik. In 168 B.C.E. Rome's ambassador Popilius drew a circle around Antiochus, the Syrian king, and told him to agree to the Senate's demand that he withdraw from Egypt before leaving the circle. It was an indication of the contempt that Rome felt for peoples whom the Romans regarded as weaker than themselves. Yet even the super-patriot Cato the Elder bemoaned Rome's arrogant mistreatment of its longtime allies the Rhodians. Roman military domination of the Mediterranean encouraged dreams of an imperial destiny best expressed when Vergil has Jupiter bestow power on Aeneas and his descendants: *imperium sine fine dedi* ("I give you empire without limit"; *Aeneid* 1, 279).

But the Roman assumption of divine favor was seriously challenged by the recurring civil disturbances that marked the decline of the Republic and the establishment of the Roman Empire. Tacitus is acutely aware of the fragility of Roman domination. He manifests his own provincial origins when he points out that Rome's foreign subjects had little love for the old Republican system and even welcomed Augustus' transformation of the state into a virtual monarchy:

> Nor did the provinces reject that state of affairs, the command of the senate and people having become suspect owing to the contests of the powerful and the greed of the magistrates (there being no effective assistance from the laws, which had been disrupted by violence, intrigue, and finally money). (1, 2, 2)

Yet Tacitus knows well what hereditary monarchy would bring: mad rulers like Caligula and Nero, court intrigues, and finally the civil war of 69 C.E. as the only alternative to hereditary succession.

Every great imperial power must create tools, usually accompanied by an ideology, to secure the loyalty of its subjects. In modern times European powers have used Christianity and asserted their cultural superiority to justify their control and exploitation of native peoples from New England, Mexico, and Peru to Africa, India, and Polynesia. So the Romans argued for their own superiority as a civilizing power; the governor of Germany, Dubius Avitus, warned a restless tribe in 58 C.E. that they should tolerate the commands of their betters, he said; what the gods whom they were imploring had decided was that any verdict should remain with the Romans as to what was granted and what taken away. (13, 56, 1)

But the Romans' view of their "civilizing mission" emphasized their political and military contributions to a chaotic and corrupt world. Everyone knew that Greece was the home of an older and more respected civilization, but even the Greek philosopher Plutarch recognized that Rome's political genius had restored peace and order to the world. The Greek orator Aelius Aristeides delivered before the emperor Antoninus Pius in 143 C.E. a panegyric in praise of Rome: "There is one world; a federation of free cities under the presidency of Rome."[3] Aristeides primarily valued the Roman contribution to effective administration and peace, and the Roman emperors were delighted to see their empire so described.

One of the complications in examining Roman prejudice toward other peoples is the function of ethnographic writing. Contemporary ethnographers write to describe the customs of other peoples or groups, while ancient writers were primarily concerned to show differences from their own society. For example, Tacitus emphasizes the positive virtues of barbarian peoples— most famously in his monograph *Germania*—to criticize Roman morality and political life. But if Tacitus wishes to lavish praise on Roman commanders, he must create worthy opponents. In his biography of Agricola, Tacitus gives to the British chieftain Calgacus a powerful speech to rouse his troops on the eve of battle by denouncing their Roman enemies:

> They are the plunderers of the world; now that the earth lacks booty for their indiscriminate looting, they look to the sea. A rich enemy arouses their greed, a poor one their desire for power. Neither East nor West has satisfied them. (*Agricola* 30)

3. For translation and commentary on Aristeides' oration, cf. Oliver (1953), 871–1003.

In the *Annals*, Tacitus portrays another British leader, Queen Boudicca, castigating the Romans for treachery after she had been beaten and her daughters raped, despite her late husband's loyalty. She showed her defiled daughters to the Britons and concluded with a challenge to the men:

> If they weighed up within themselves their resources in armed men and their reasons for war, they must conquer in that line or fall. That was the design of a woman; the men could survive—and be slaves! (14, 35, 2)

The most successful of the barbarian tribal chiefs was Arminius, who in 9 C.E. destroyed three Roman legions in an ambush in the Teutoburg Forest. Seven years later he too reminds his troops that the choice is between freedom and slavery:

> They themselves had only to remember the enemy's greed, cruelty, and haughtiness; did they have anything else left except to hold on to their freedom or to die before servitude? (2, 15, 3)

For Tacitus, with his jaundiced view of Roman acquiescence under tyrannical rule, the principled defiance of the barbarians was less about their actual values (or their actual words) than about his own nostalgia for the more courageous Romans of the Republic.

Yet, despite his admiration for their courage, Tacitus shows little real interest in the cultures of Rome's barbarian subjects. Like other Roman writers, he sometimes transfers qualities from one ethnic group to another, since there was only a vague sense of the differences among the northern barbarians. Of course, this tendency to homogenize one's enemies has continued through history with ethnically and religiously diverse Africans (Hutu and Tutsi in Rwanda), South Asian Muslims (Urdu and Bengali speakers in Pakistan in 1947), or peoples of Ottoman Mesopotamia (Kurds, Sunni and Shia Arabs) placed together in artificial nation-states with continuing consequences. Tacitus has the deep prejudices of an imperial race that insists on contempt, or at least condescension, toward the conquered. Since they lost, they must be inferior or at least have less powerful gods. They were lesser beings, and so their treatment could be morally justified.

2 | Northern Barbarians

In contrast to the negative views of the Greek geographer Strabo, Tacitus had a greater affinity for the northern barbarians than for any other conquered peoples. Though he was himself from southern Gaul, that area had been highly Romanized since 120 B.C.E.—almost two centuries before his own arrival in Rome. Thus his sympathy for the Gauls and Germans may stem less from a personal connection than from his recognition of their valor and their love of liberty that found parallels in the heroic tales in Livy. Many of their leaders, like Arminius, had fought bravely as part of the Roman army before they turned into freedom fighters, and the Romans repeatedly emphasized the large size of Gauls and Germans. On the other hand, Tacitus was much harsher toward the Greeks, Jews, and other easterners—probably because those peoples seemed to him to display a smug sense of cultural or religious superiority.

In 68 C.E. Julius Civilis, a well-connected local aristocrat and a Roman citizen, led the Batavians—a Germanic people living near the lower Rhine—in a revolt against Roman legions distracted by civil war. Tacitus gives him a rousing speech:

> "Let Syria, Asia, and the Orient accustomed to kings, be slaves; in Gaul there are many living who were born in the days before tribute. . . . Nature has given liberty even to dumb animals while courage is a special gift of men. The gods favor those who are braver." (*Histories* 4, 17)

Despite the eventual defeat of Civilis, his were not empty boasts, since the German annihilation of Varus' legions was the greatest Roman defeat in living memory. The loss of the sections of the *Annals* containing Tacitus' account of the British revolt of 43 C.E. (probably book 9) and the German and Gallic revolts of 68 C.E. (book 18) deprives us of his interpretation of these barbarians at their most dangerous.

Tacitus provides an analysis of the courageous **Britons** to buttress his panegyric of Agricola's exploits in defeating them. Although he acknowledges the similarities between the Britons and their Gallic cousins across the English Channel—which he attributes more to heredity than to environment—he tries to point out the differences as well:

> The Britons, however, exhibit more spirit, being a people whom long peace has not yet softened. Indeed we understand that even the Gauls were once outstanding in war; but soon a laziness stemming from peace crept over them, and they lost their courage along with their freedom. This too has happened to the long-conquered tribes of Britain; the rest are still what the Gauls once were. (*Agricola* 11)

Tacitus extols the Britons' dynamism, vitality, pride, love of war. He refers to their earlier *virtus* (courage) positively, whereas his later term, *feritas* (wildness), is more negative. But the Britons had not been emasculated like their Gallic cousins by the long years of peace, which was evident in their willingness to revolt against the cruelty of some Roman centurions.

Agricola is of course presented by Tacitus as a brilliant administrator who manages to seduce the Britons into baths, togas, and even the use of the Latin language in an attempt to take away their virility.

> Moreover he educated in literature the sons of the chieftains, and he preferred the natural talent of the Britons to the hard work of the Gauls so that those who had recently scorned Latin now became eager to acquire eloquence in it. Hence our dress became popular and the toga was often worn. Gradually the Britons slipped into the charms of vice: porticos for strolling, baths, and the elegance of banquets. In their innocence they called this "civilization" (*humanitas*) when it was really part of their subjugation. (*Agricola* 21)

But, despite the veneer of Roman civilization, Tacitus believed that the Britons remained morally and culturally inferior and that they were, like other barbarians, capable of every kind of cruelty. This was the innate characteristic of northern barbarians, and it was the reason they could never be trusted. During Boudicca's revolt, reported in the *Annals*, the Britons savaged Roman settlements such as Verulamium:

> It has been agreed that about seventy thousand citizens and allies fell in the places which I have recalled. There was neither capturing nor selling or any other feature of the trade of war, but they speeded up their slaughtering, gibbets, fire, and crosses—as though destined to pay in reprisals, but in the meantime preempting revenge. (14, 33, 2)

Yet the double standard is remarkably clear when, a few paragraphs later, Tacitus presents the Roman slaughter of civilians and women as a glorious victory:

> And the [Roman] soldiery did not refrain from the execution even of women; and baggage-animals too, transfixed by weapons, had enlarged the heaps of bodies. Brilliant was the praise acquired that day, and the equal of ancient victories. There are those who transmit that a little less than eighty thousand Britons fell, with roughly four hundred Roman soldiers killed and not many more wounded. (14, 37, 1–2)

Tacitus understandably had more complicated ideas about the **Gauls**, since he understood that Gaul contained quite distinct populations.[4] His own homeland of Gallia Narbonensis had become so highly Romanized that Julius Caesar regarded it as decadent (*Gallic War* 6. 24). Pliny the Elder wrote a century later that it was "more truly Italy than a province" (*Natural History* 3, 31: *Italia verius quam provincia*). It had a cosmopolitan mixed population of Gauls, Romans, and even some Greeks in their former colonies of Massilia (Marseilles) and Nicaea (Nice); there was no memory of war or insurrection.

---

4. Woolf (1998); Isaac (2004), 411–426.

Yet Tacitus had a general sympathy to Gallic lands that extended beyond his own province.[5] When Julius Caesar famously wrote, "All Gaul is divided into three parts," he referred to the three provinces of "long-haired" Gaul (*Gallia Comata*), which he subjugated during the 50s B.C.E. In the century after Caesar, the Gauls had become rather tranquil, with only some local tax rebellions in 21 C.E. Tribal chiefs now held estates and manors, and the Druid priestly caste had virtually disappeared, although many of their beliefs remained. Local aristocrats often held priesthoods in the imperial cult, which then gave them and their descendants' Roman citizenship.

And yet, unlike the Narbonese Gauls of the south, the northerners were excluded from the Senate, and they resented the second-class citizenship. The emperor Claudius saw that intermarriage and military service were producing a common way of life across Gaul, and we will see in chapter 9 how he argued to bring the northern Gauls into the Senate. How Romanized some then had become we see from the case of Julius Vindex, descended from a king of Aquitania and son of a Claudian senator, who was governor of a Gallic province in 68 C.E. He rose in revolt against Nero and, although his largely Gallic troops were soon suppressed by armies loyal to the emperor, it was Vindex who began the process that drove Nero from the throne. Once again, the loss of Tacitus' account in the eighteenth book of his *Annals* is especially sad, since he must have given there a more extensive portrait of Vindex. One problem is that Vindex's revolt was accused in Flavian propaganda (as it has been in some modern scholarship) of being a nationalist rebellion, when it was no more "nationalist" than Galba's or Vespasian's revolt against the sitting emperor. The Flavian suspicion of Vindex is yet another indication of prejudice (and even paranoia) against a highly Romanized northern Gaul, and Tacitus' missing interpretation would be invaluable, since he might well have represented Vindex as a heroic Romanized provincial (like Agricola or himself) embodying the old values now lost in Rome.

5. Syme (1958), 623–624.

When Vespasian began after 70 C.E. to replace the depleted Senate with deserving provincials—almost 20 percent of his newly appointed senators were of provincial origins—he drew from Gallia Narbonensis and Spain rather than from the north. New senatorial families from these provinces later produced Trajan and Hadrian, Antoninus and Marcus Aurelius, while the prejudice against northerners continued among the Roman elite even into Tacitus' own time.

Tacitus' most extensive treatments of a barbarian people are his detailed discussions of the history and customs of the **Germans** in the *Annals* and in his ethnographic monograph, *Germania*.[6] He writes more about the Germans than did any other ancient writer, despite the fact that he never visited Germany and that his principal source—Pliny the Elder's now lost *History of the German Wars*—was almost forty years old. He provides both complicated and contradictory pictures of the people whom he saw as the greatest danger to the Romans. In *Germania* 37 he points out that the Romans had been fighting with the Germans for more than two centuries, since the Cimbri invaded Roman Gaul and Italy around 110 B.C.E., and he details their battles with Julius Caesar, Varus, and Germanicus, down to the recent reign of Domitian. Roman commanders may have celebrated triumphs, but the Germans were never truly conquered. In this they were the most resilient of all Rome's enemies—neither Gauls, Parthians, nor Carthaginians had threatened Rome for two centuries. Tacitus understood that, unlike Hannibal or the Parthian kings, the Germans were fighting for their own freedom.

But the *Germania*, written in 98 C.E. soon after the assassination of Domitian and amid danger of another civil war, was less about the real Germans than an idealized picture to contrast with the moral failings of Rome. Thus the Germans are a pure-blooded people of martial virtue and moral rigor: strong family ties, a love of freedom, courageous and loyal women, and an avoidance of luxury. Intermarriage or contact with Romans saps their native strength. There is little place for nuance in this idealized world.

6. Isaac (2004), 427–439.

But when Germans appear in Tacitus' *Annals* and *Histories*, they are far less sympathetic, as we see instances of cruelty, hypocrisy, and torture. They lack culture or even humanity when they resort to drunkenness, gambling, and uncontrolled destruction. Their courage and boldness are fearsome, but can quickly fade in adversity. When the Roman general Cerialis warns the Gauls not to be taken in by the German call to fight jointly for their "freedom" from Rome (*Histories* 4. 73–74), he shrewdly reminds them how often the Germans had invaded Gaul. Despite the idealized image in the *Germania*, in real life the Germans are not a people to be trusted.

And yet Tacitus in the *Annals* repeatedly shows his admiration for the Germans' courage and pride. On one occasion, when German leaders came to Rome to appeal to the emperor Nero against the Frisians who had taken their lands, they went as tourists to look at the enormous theater of Pompey.

> While they idled away their time there (in their ignorance they took no delight in the entertainment), they inquired about the assembly in the auditorium, the distinctions between the ranks, which the equestrians were, where the senate—and they noticed some people in foreign dress in the senators' seats. When, on asking who they were, they were told that that was an honor given to the legates of those people who excelled in courage and in Roman friendship, they exclaimed that no mortals were ahead of Germans in arms or loyalty, and they went down and sat among the fathers—an action received affably by its observers as typical of a primitive impulse and a fine rivalry. Nero presented them both with Roman citizenship—and ordered the Frisians to withdraw from the territory. (13, 54, 3–4)

Likewise the historian believes that the Greeks and Romans have much to learn from Germans such as Arminius. Although he was a traitor who lured three legions into an ambush and annihilated them, he deserves remembrance. As Tacitus says in his obituary of Arminius:

(He) is still sung among barbarian races, though unknown to the annals of the Greeks, who marvel only at their own, and not celebrated duly in the Roman, since we extol the distant past, indifferent to the recent. (2, 88, 3)

With considerable prescience Tacitus saw that the free Germans, if they could unite, would pose the greatest future danger to the Roman Empire. Not that this was a new idea—Velleius Paterculus and Seneca had already made this point—but the Germans combined their native ferocity with a certain craftiness that came from long interaction with Roman troops and traders along the Rhine. The Romans must hope that the Germans will continue to fight among themselves, as when sixty thousand Bructeri were slaughtered by other tribes. "Fortune can offer us nothing better than discord among our enemies" (*Germania* 33).

Farther to the east the Romans also confronted the still less civilized **Thracians**. The inhabitants of Thrace, a country north of Greece, lived rather wildly in the Balkan mountains. It had long been a recruiting territory for strong slaves (among them, Spartacus) to serve as gladiators, and during the empire the Romans also "recruited" men for their auxiliaries there. Unsurprisingly, Tacitus tells us with some sympathy, the Thracians rebelled against this in 26 C.E.:

The reason for the turbulence, apart from the people's temperament, was that they scorned to endure levies and to give all their most effective men to our service, being accustomed to obey not even their kings except at whim or, if they sent auxiliaries, to appoint their own leaders and not wage war except against their neighbors. And then a rumor had spread that, dispersed and merged with other nations, they would be dragged off to different and distant countries. (4, 46, 1–2)

Although Tacitus admired the Thracians' resistance to being unwillingly drafted into the Roman army and sent far from home, he is less sympathetic to their wild singing and dancing, drunken orgies, greedy pursuit of plunder, and dereliction of duty when sated with food and drink. Once again, he is torn between admiration for freedom and disapproval of license.

3 | Tacitean Attitudes toward Easterners

There is no question that Tacitus is much more hostile to Roman subjects in the eastern Mediterranean: Greeks, Jews, and Egyptians. It seems likely that he is deeply defensive regarding their assertions of superiority and claims to great antiquity. Greek culture, Jewish morality, and Egyptian religion were widely admired by other Mediterranean peoples, and Tacitus resents such pretensions in what were to him peoples who were inferior because they had been conquered.

The Romans first encountered the **Greeks** and Greek civilization in the cities of southern Italy and Sicily.[7] Many elements of Greek culture—the Olympian gods, the alphabet, and literature— had been adapted into Roman life even before Roman armies crossed the Adriatic into Greece itself. Late in the third century B.C.E., the senator Fabius Pictor wrote the first Roman history *in Greek*, to celebrate the Roman past among non-Romans; soon afterward the arch-nationalist Cato the Elder taught his son Greek. Waves of Hellenization swept to Rome as statues, books, philosophies, and even entire libraries were brought in among the spoils of conquest. Roman intellectuals such as Cicero and Horace regarded a sojourn in Greece as an essential element in their education. After his defeat by Caesar in 46 B.C.E., Cato the Younger killed himself with his sword after having read in Greek Plato's account of Socrates' suicide. In the famous words of Horace, "Graecia capta ferum uictorem cepit / et artis intulit agresti Latio" ("Captured Greece overcame its fierce conqueror, and brought the arts to rustic Latium").[8] The deathbed words of both Caesar and Augustus were Greek, and Caesar and Antony made love to Cleopatra (it was said) in Greek. It

---

7. Petrochilos (1974); Isaac (2004), 381–405; Lomas (1993); Mellor (2008), 79–126.
8. Horace *Epistles* 2, 1, 156.

would seem that by the time of the empire the Roman intellectual elite had accepted the synthesis of Greco-Roman civilization.

Yet we find bitter hostility to Greeks running through Tacitus—much more than in the biographies of his contemporary Suetonius. But it was not the Greek culture of the past that Tacitus opposes; he doubtless studied Athenian tragedy, historiography, and oratory as part of his rhetorical training. In fact, while describing the tortured soul of Tiberius, he refers directly to a passage in Plato's *Gorgias* in which Socrates (called the "greatest teacher of philosophy") warns of the effects of cruelty on a despot's soul:

> Not without reason did the most outstanding man of wisdom customarily affirm that, if the minds of tyrants could be opened up, mutilations and blows would be visible, since, just as bodies were mauled by lashings, so was the spirit by savagery, lust, and evil decisions. In Tiberius' case neither his fortune nor his solitude protected him from admitting the tortures of his own soul and his own punishments. (6, 6, 2)

But Tacitus believes ancient Greece and its noble values had been lost. The contemporary Greeks create fictions of their past, and, as he mentions in his obituary of Arminius, they have no interest in the achievements of others. The ancient Athenians existed no more, since "Greeks" now referred to all kinds of easterners. He obviously approves of the words he gives to Piso in his criticism of Germanicus:

> He had, with excessive affability, paid court not to Athenians, who after so many disasters were extinct, but to that famous cesspit of nations. (2, 55, 1)

Tacitus is especially angered by the pernicious influence of Greeks at the imperial court over the previous century. Although Greek exiles and freedmen had long been an accepted part of Roman life, under the Julio-Claudians they became identified with sycophancy and despotism. Perhaps the presence of Greeks as Roman consuls under the tyrant Domitian—Julius Celsus of Ephesus (cos. 92 C.E.) and Julius Quadratus of Pergamum (cos. 94

C.E.)—made the historian even more jealous of the Greek presence in government. The *Annals* depicts a growing Greek influence at court, and that influence was all to the bad. From his long exile on Rhodes to his final withdrawal to Capri, Tiberius was surrounded by an entourage of ambitious Greeks. He gave high honors to his Alexandrian astrologer Thrasyllus, whose son Balbillus was later the astrologer to Nero and prefect of Egypt.

The continuity of Greek influence could best be seen among the descendants of Mark Antony: Caligula, Claudius, and Nero. Caligula and Claudius grew up surrounded by eastern princes such as Herod Agrippa. Tacitus narrated the reign of Caligula in the lost books of the *Annals*, so we rely on other sources, including Suetonius, for stories of the emperor's extravagant demonstrations of philhellenism. Claudius relied heavily on Greek freedmen (whom Tacitus despised), including the avaricious and arrogant courtier Marcus Antonius Pallas, who had pretensions to royal lineage. When Nero went on his Greek concert tour to seek the craven approval of his subjects, Tacitus felt only contempt and shame.

In his own time Tacitus saw the increasing prominence of expatriate Greeks in the circle around Hadrian, the nephew and eventual heir of Trajan.[9] Some were rhetoricians who claimed descent from old royal and priestly families. Tacitus understood that the Greek freedmen and intellectuals who had populated the imperial court during the past century were now being replaced by Greeks of a higher status, who came closer and closer (in the view of an anxious Gallo-Roman) to controlling the destiny of the empire.

In any examination of Tacitus' view of the **Jews,** it is of course difficult to separate completely the past from the present.[10] The sixteenth-century rediscovery of Tacitus laid bare his pagan anti-Semitism; in fact his hostility to Jews in the *Histories* led the scholar Guillaume Budé to call Tacitus "the most depraved of all writers."

9. Syme (1958), 517–519, argues that Tacitus' jibes at earlier Hellenizers are in fact aimed at Hadrian.

10. For Roman views toward the Jews, cf. Feldman (1993); Schäfer (1997); Isaac (2004), 440–491.

Later, in the nineteenth century, modern anti-Semites looked to antiquity for texts to buttress their opinions. Although Christians of antiquity (Tertullian; Orosius) were upset by Tacitus' brief dismissal of their religion in his account of the fire in Rome in 64 C.E., the passage in question is really more anti-Semitic than anti-Christian, since Tacitus knew so little about the Christian sect:

> There was no getting away from the infamous belief that the conflagration had been ordered. Therefore, to dispel the rumor, Nero supplied defendants and inflicted the choicest punishments on those, resented for their outrages, whom the public called Chrestiani. The source of the name was Christus, on whom, during the command of Tiberius, reprisal had been inflicted by the procurator Pontius Pilatus; and, though the baleful superstition had been stifled for the moment, there was now another outbreak, not only across Judaea, the origin of the malignancy, but also across the City, where everything frightful or shameful, of whatever provenance, converges and is celebrated. . . .
>
> Hence there arose—albeit for culprits who deserved the ultimate exemplary treatment—a feeling of pity, as though it were not in the public interest, but for one man's savagery, that they were being eliminated. (15, 44, 2–3; 5)

Most of the pagan anti-Semitic tradition stems from the conflict in Hellenistic times between Greeks and Jews. This anti-Semitism consists of either a reaction against monotheism and Jewish social separatism or a political antagonism resulting from conflicts between Jews and other peoples. Tacitus' most comprehensive treatment of the Jews and their religion is contained in his prelude to the fall of Jerusalem in book 5 of the *Histories*. Although the actual military events were in the part of the text that is now lost, Tacitus does provide a traditional ethnography: the origins, customs, and geography of the Jewish people, with a sketch of their history. There is no evidence that Tacitus had at this point visited the East; he served as proconsular governor of Asia only after the *Histories* were finished. His knowledge came entirely from books. So Tacitus' excursus is important not for his own views, but as a synthesis of anti-Jewish tradition. Through him the mainstream Alexandrian Greek anti-Semitic prejudice enters the Western tradition.

In his discussion of Jewish origins, Tacitus is more moderate than earlier authors in providing six different explanations taken from the Egyptian and Greek tradition. There is a certain sympathy for the remote antiquity of the Jewish people—the age of Isis and that of Saturn are mentioned—and the account of Assyrian origins via an invasion of Egypt is the closest to the biblical version. But if the account of origins is less judgmental, Tacitus' report on Jewish customs is much more hostile; there he uses such scornful superlatives as *taeterrima* ("basest") and *despectissima* ("most despised") to describe the low status of Jews among other Eastern peoples (*Histories* 5, 8). He believes that their sacrifices of the ram and ox are aimed at mocking Egyptian belief (*Histories* 5, 4–5).

Although there are many positive elements in Tacitus' description of the Jews—and he is more positive than Plutarch and other Greek authors—those aspects are often embedded in a negative context. The Jews' prohibition on infanticide is presented as merely part of their passion for propagating their "race." The historian correctly points out their conception of God as nonphysical and their unwillingness to worship images; he does not mention charges of human sacrifice often leveled against the Jews. In that way the Jews should be more sympathetic than Egyptians, whose worship of animals revolted the Romans. But he notes that the Jews do not pay tribute to Roman emperors, even though we might expect Tacitus to feel sympathy toward people who would not worship Caligula and Nero. When he criticizes a Jewish hatred of other peoples, he acknowledges that they were the most persecuted people of the Near East. He also acknowledges their rigorous honesty and their compassion toward other Jews. Tacitus even blames Roman maladministration for the Jewish revolts against Roman authority.

Perhaps there was a genuine fear of the Jews in Tacitus—not only of a successful military rebellion, but of cultural and religious success throughout the empire. Jews were thought to be proselytizers;

in fact, there was an expulsion of Jews from Rome for proselytization as early as 139 B.C.E. Tacitus was far more tolerant of what he regarded as "ancestral religion," but conversion took new adherents away from the religion of their forefathers. As a member of the priesthood charged with the supervision of religion (*xv viri sacris faciundis*), Tacitus was concerned with the religious turmoil during the first century. He reports that in 19 C.E.

> There was discussion also about banishing Egyptian and Jewish rites, and there was passed a fathers' decision that four thousand of the freedmen class, who had been tainted by such superstition and whose age was suitable, should be transported to the island of Sardinia to curb banditry there, and, if they died owing to the oppressiveness of the climate, it was a cheap loss; the rest should withdraw from Italy, unless before a certain day they had discarded their profane ceremonies. (2, 85, 4)

Later, under Nero, a Roman matron, Pomponia, was tried for "foreign superstitions"—probably for having adopted Jewish practices (13, 32). Though she was acquitted by her husband in a family trial, Tacitus seems to see a growing danger.

There was certainly evidence of the increasing influence of Jews in the Near East. Since Tacitus was familiar with Greek anti-Semitic texts, he was nervous at what he saw. Vespasian's son Titus had a well-known romance with the Jewish princess Berenice, and the apostate Jew Julius Alexander was the prefect of Egypt whose troops first acclaimed Vespasian as emperor. Tacitus must also have been familiar with the Jewish historian Josephus at the court of the Flavian emperors. The high moral standards and philanthropy of the Jewish communities in Asia Minor attracted admiring adherents, called "god-fearers," who formed part of a growing pagan interest in monotheism. Of course, Tacitus might well have seen the incipient spread of Christianity as another example of a growing acceptance of Jewish ideas. There were even Jewish revolts in Cyrene during the reign of Trajan—precisely the period when Tacitus was writing the *Annals*.

While Tacitus scorns the despotism of eastern monarchs in Cerialis' speech on eastern servility, he elsewhere shows admiration for the martial courage of the **Parthians**.[11] When these equestrian Iranian warriors, originally nomads from Central Asia, made the prince Vonones their new king in 16 C.E., they were appalled that during his years as a hostage in Rome he had become "degenerate." He was no longer interested in hunting or horsemanship and was even carried around in a litter. Tacitus is sympathetic to their outrage:

> Where was that glory of the butchers of Crassus, of the evictors of Mark Antony, if a menial of Caesar, having endured slavery for so many years, took command of the Parthians? (2, 2, 2)

Scholars may rightly question how much Tacitus really knew of Parthian attitudes, but it is interesting that he attributes such warlike pride to them. Here is an admiration that he never shows toward Greeks.

4 | Prejudices toward Barbarians

Tacitus displays a set of diverse, and even contradictory, attitudes toward non-Roman peoples. At its simplest level, the barbarian is "the other"—the opposite of Rome. Trajan's Column, erected at the same time that Tacitus was writing history, is the greatest visual record of the contrast between the disciplined Roman soldier and wild barbarian. But that simplistic dichotomy can hardly account for the differences that he reports between the culturally sophisticated (but cowardly) Greeks, the heroic Britons, and the brutal Germans.

The writers of the empire retained romantic ideas of the barbarians' "freedom," and even Vergil's melancholic admiration of conquered peoples appears in Tacitus. He wishes Rome to co-opt the martial energy of European barbarians, even to use them as

11. Isaac (2004), 371–380.

models for Roman behavior. But Tacitus is also well aware of the danger of training barbarians like Arminius, Calgacus, and Civilis; all three used their experience of the Roman army to lead rebellions against Rome.

Aside from their courage and love of freedom, non-Romans exhibited many behaviors that Tacitus found contemptible: drunkenness, fickleness, emotionalism, lustfulness, cruelty, lack of discipline, and adherence to strange religions (*superstitio*). Of course, such vices appeared in different combinations among barbarous peoples: Germans were drunken but sexually chaste; Jews were highly moral but superstitious and lascivious; and so on. Of even greater concern was the increasing barbarization of the Romans themselves—especially the Hellenized members of the imperial court. Tacitus saw these un-Roman traits in the laziness of Tiberius at Capri, the sexual abandon of Messalina, the cruelty of the younger Agrippina, and the capricious philhellenism of Nero. When Claudius gave advice to the new Parthian king, he told him

> that he should think, not in terms of domination over slaves, but of being a guide for citizens, and he should embrace clemency and justice, their unfamiliarity among barbarians making them all the more welcome. (12, 11, 2)

It would certainly have seemed ironic to Tacitus to report such advice coming from a member of the Julio-Claudian dynasty. But even worse was Vitellius (in *Histories* 2, 73), who managed to combine the worst traits of northern European barbarians (cruelty) with the sloth and despotism of the East.

Perhaps more striking is the way in which Tacitus transfers the terminology of barbarian behavior to the Roman armies. During the civil war of 69 C.E., the armies behaved like barbarians in their pitiless sack of Roman cities and burning of the Temple of Jupiter on the Capitoline Hill in Rome. In defeat the emperor Otho's army fled like a disorganized mob—Tacitus uses the word *vulgus*—with a lack of Roman discipline. The troops follow rumor and superstition, more than the chain of command. They have lost all resemblance to a Roman army.

Tacitus both scorns and fears the non-Romans. Like many xenophobes through the ages, he worries about both military conquest and the more insidious barbarization of his own society. The contemporary satirist Juvenal makes the simple case that the scum of the East is flooding into Rome. But Tacitus is more subtle; he sees that Roman emperors and armies are taking over the worse characteristics of barbarians. Rome is becoming, in his view, "barbarous." In addition to this contempt, there is also a genuine fear of the inexorable military rise of the Germanic peoples in the West and the spread of the Jewish religion throughout the East and even to Rome. And Tacitus, it seems to us now, was more prophetic than paranoid. The coming centuries would see Germans sweep repeatedly across the frontiers until a Gothic king replaced the Roman emperor in 476 C.E. And, by the fourth century C.E., the Judeo-Christian "superstition" would have forever displaced traditional Roman religion.

·4·

Ut Pictura Poesis: The Visual Representation of History

Every historian or biographer must include some visual material in his or her account of the past. Writers of contemporary history, like Thucydides, or Tacitus in his *Histories*, or modern biographers, can rely in part on their own memories, but most historians are dependent on earlier descriptions, or artistic representations (portraits, busts, or, in more recent times, photographs, film, and videotape). But they vary widely in how, and how much, they use visual material. We often hear of "characters that leap off the page," but does that come from realistic description or psychological penetration? We have learned in the twentieth century that short actors can be impressive heroic figures, that large sopranos can be persuasive as consumptive operatic waifs, that a brilliant mezzo-soprano singing Julius Caesar (replacing the *castrato* for whom Handel wrote) can transform suspicion into conviction. Art is not reality, but . . . artifice. Yet, we expect historians to be more straightforward, less "literary" in their deployment of the evidence, more "realistic" in their depiction of the past. How did Tacitus the artist deal with visual material?

In 1614 Baltasar Alamos de Barrientos, who translated the *Annals* into Spanish for the first time (for which he was imprisoned by King Philip II), described Tacitus through the metaphor of the visual arts, when he said that the historian wrote "as in a painting."[1] Later in the same century the playwright Jean Racine, after referring to his "painting" of the court of Nero in his tragedy *Britannicus*, acknowledged his model to be Tacitus, "the greatest painter of antiquity."[2] The image of historian as painter continues in unexpected places. The emperor Napoleon I, who hated Tacitus for "having slandered the emperors whom the Roman people loved," grudgingly praised the historian's skill as a painter but criticized his palette: he painted everything in black.[3] Even twentieth-century scholars used the same metaphor, as when Gaston Boissier called Tacitus a great painter of men, who vividly depicted great scenes and "darkened the colors" of his pictures.[4] And, in his great book *Mimesis*, the comparatist Erich Auerbach identified Tacitus, along with Petronius, as an example of the successful cultivation of the visual and sensory in ancient literature.[5]

At first glance, this should be no great surprise. We know that graphic descriptions were highly prized in ancient poetry, as in Homer's description of the shield of Achilles, Vergil's of the shield of Aeneas, and Simonides' saying that painting is mute poetry and poetry is a speaking picture. Aristotle was concerned with *mimesis*, how the artist represents reality, and Horace's ambiguous phrase *ut pictura poesis*—"a poem like a painting" is a possible meaning—has provided grist for centuries of commentators. Even the artists themselves are misled, as the Enlightenment critic G. E. Lessing pointed out in his preface to *Laocoön*. He said that poets add descriptions to their poetry to make it more "visual,"

---

1. *Tacito Español* (Madrid, 1614): *como en una pintura.*

2. "Second Preface" to *Britannicus* (1676) in Racine's *Théâtre Complet*, ed. J-P Collinet (Paris, 1982), 305: *J'avais copié mes personages d'après le plus grand peintre de l'antiquité, je veux dire d'après Tacite.*

3. *Mémoires du Prince de Talleyrand* (Paris, 1891), 442–446.

4. See Boissier (London, 1906), 68–94, on the "artist in Tacitus." On Tacitus' darkening of color, see 109.

5. Auerbach (Princeton, N.J., 1953), 46.

while painters turn to allegory to make their work more "poetic."[6] The late first century C.E. brought a particular reflorescence of the visual imagination: Nero's fantastic Golden House, the elaborate Fourth Style of Pompeian painting, and "Flavian baroque" sculpture. The degree of interchange between art and literature is extraordinary: Pompeian walls contained not just myths, but specific Ovidian versions, while the poets of the time used much of the pictorial. This was soon followed by great narrative friezes; during the very years in which Tacitus was at work on his histories, the emperor Trajan recorded his Dacian victories in the great historical relief on the column standing in his new Forum, to be "read" from the adjoining Greek and Roman libraries like a vast unrolling papyrus scroll.

Earlier Roman historical writers deployed vivid pictorial elements. Livy had scenes of extreme realism of the sort that some art historians have regarded as characteristic of Roman popular culture. Livy's revolting image of a Roman who had chewed at his enemy's face in his final death throes inspired imitations in Statius and even Dante's *Inferno*.[7] Julius Caesar's narratives also abound with careful descriptions of landscapes and battlefields. Tacitus' friend Pliny the Younger responded to the historian's request for a firsthand report on the eruption of Vesuvius with two extraordinarily detailed letters (Pliny *Letters* 6, 16; 6, 20) which provide the only contemporary account of the mushroom cloud rising over the bay of Naples in 79 C.E.—the first surviving written eyewitness account of a natural disaster in world history. It is particularly unfortunate that Tacitus' reworking of that material was contained in the lost books of his *Histories*. Tacitus' contemporary Suetonius uses vulgar realism in his biographies to describe each of the emperors; especially graphic are Caligula (*Caligula* 50: goatlike body hair, spindly legs, bald head, and sunken eyes) and Nero (*Nero* 51: squat neck, malodorous body, and bulging belly to accompany his "pretty" face).

6. Lessing (Baltimore, 1984), 5.

7. Livy 22, 51, 5; Statius' Tydeus at *Thebaid* 8, 751–766; Dante's story of Ugolino at *Inferno* xxxii, 127–129.

What, then, are examples of naturalistic descriptions that we might look for in Tacitus? Landscape (Caesar and Livy); detailed visual description of troops and armor (Caesar; Trajan's Column); realistic portraits of individual characters (Suetonius)? In fact, despite Tacitus' considerable reputation as a "painter" and his creation of memorable dramatic spectacles, there are few picturesque details and little purely decorative language in his writings. It is through dramatic construction, psychological engagement, or a quick image of movement that the historian brings his tableaux to life. Just as Tacitus is interested in the ideas and intentions that lie below the surface of words, of political stances, of personalities, he is likewise more concerned with conveying the moral force of a scene than providing specific details.

Tacitus uses few similes and, unlike Caesar, gives only sketchy descriptions of cities, rivers, and mountains. The only genuine landscape in the *Annals* would seem to be the brief sketch of the beauty of Capri (4, 67), intended to contrast with the loathsome Tiberius, who had retired there. Tacitean *gravitas* demands that the trivial and the sordid be avoided; one can hardly expect to find in annalistic history the crude stories or images that Suetonius provides. But Tacitus' restraint goes much further: picturesque details were included not for amusement or diversion (as was common in nearly all ancient writers), but only for their emotional, moral, or psychological effect. This is particularly clear in the historian's sparing use of the decorative appeal of color. It has led some scholars to speak of his "sculptor's palette," or how his scenes are like a bas-relief. When Napoleon said Tacitus paints everything in black, his comment was literal as well as metaphorical: Tacitus' preferred color is indeed black.

Darkness is the predominant atmosphere, or rather the contrast of night and sporadic light. The crucial events in Tacitus' histories usually take place in dark, torch-lit rooms of the imperial palace or the Senate house. Lights blaze only to reveal scandalous behavior in the surrounding darkness, as in the chiaroscuro style of painting by Caravaggio. Firebrands flare at the praetorian prefect Tigellinus' extravagant orgy on the shores of the artificial lake built by Agrippa, on which the ships "glittered with gold and ivory":

Already the gestures and movements were obscene; and, after *darkness* had started to come on, every adjacent copse and the surrounding houses resounded with singing and *shone with lights*. (15, 37, 3)

The orgy reaches its culmination when Nero marries his freedman Pythagoras:

There was a dowry, a marriage-bed, and *wedding torches*. Everything, in short was observed which even in the case of a female is covered by *night*. (15, 37, 4)

These scenes immediately precede Tacitus' description of the great fire (rumored to have started on Tigellinus' estate) that all but destroyed Rome in 64. But even this fire never really brightens the city. Outdoor scenes of battle rarely occur in the bright sunshine that we find in Livy. Battles are often nocturnal, with even the moon covered by clouds. Even in daytime battles, the sun is mentioned less often than the literally ominous clouds or storms that darken the field of combat. The few scenes of daylight festivity are heavily ironic. For example, Tacitus uses Bacchic imagery and maenads to lend an air of oriental depravity when the empress Messalina celebrates her bigamous marriage to Silius in the context of a feigned Dionysiac harvest festival while Claudius is away in nearby Ostia (11, 31). One celebrant climbs a tree and predicts "a frightful storm from Ostia." The dancing stops as the oncoming storm foretells the return to "normality"—the arrival of Claudius and the execution of Messalina. The agricultural abundance of Italy, often used by Augustan poets and artists as a metaphor for the moral and political regeneration of the Roman people, is here inverted by Tacitus.

Although black and white predominate throughout Tacitus' descriptions, there is one other color that returns: red. There is frequent mention of blood, which sometimes stains the ground, sometimes the water, or even, after the murder of Galba, the Forum itself (*Histories* 1, 47). The sky becomes red; the rebel Julius Civilis dyes his hair red and lets it grow until he conquers a Roman legion

(*Histories* 4, 61). The ominous quality of the use of red is hardly subtle; it rather shows that Tacitus had little interest in the realistic use of color per se, any more than in description per se. Visual details serve only as part of his emotional message.

Visual passages can in fact be found more often in Tacitus' *Histories* than in the more masterly *Annals*, as though the historian were moving toward a more intense emotional narrative which he no longer wished to interrupt for leisurely description. But, even there, as in the descriptions of armor and soldiers in the civil war battles in the first three books of the *Histories*, the detail is often less decorative than ironic. The triumphant procession of Vitellius' army into the city along the via Flaminia is schematically described—although the only specific color is white—until Tacitus performs the concluding twist against the hapless leader:

> In front of the eagles marched the camp prefects, the tribunes and the senior centurions dressed in *white* robes. Each other centurion marched beside his own unit, who *glittered* with armor and decorations. The breastplates and neckchains *gleamed*: it was a splendid sight and an army worthy of a better emperor than Vitellius. (*Histories* 2, 89)

But it takes only a few pages to discover that the description of the glorious German legions would soon be ironically expunged by the historian's picture of the same troops, ragged and dispirited, leaving the city to confront in the north the invading Flavian army—loyal to the future emperor T. Flavius Vespasianus.

The most graphic pages in all of Tacitus occur in the third book of the *Histories*, which begins with the horror of the siege of Cremona—the first destruction of a Roman city by a Roman army. The magnificent conclusion of the book is breathlessly dramatic and continuously ironic—from the burning of the Capitol, heavily dependent on Vergil's poetic description of the sack of Troy, to the pursuit and murder of the pitiful Vitellius. Although the detailed descriptions in this book are hardly a decorative digression for the pleasure of the reader, Tacitus here slows the narrative flow to allow that reader (or, at an oral presentation, the listener) to grasp the full horror of the civil war and the sack of Rome by Roman armies within their own lifetime.

In the *Annals* we also find numerous scenes of considerable dramatic power. Despite Tacitus' evident contempt for Nero's stage performances, readers through the centuries have recognized in the historian himself an accomplished dramatist who moves his extraordinarily vibrant characters across the grand stage of the Roman Empire. Tacitus resembles Charles Dickens in being the master dramatist of his age without actually writing for the theater. Like Dickens, Tacitus created characters who demand to be transported onto the stage, and so they have been from Ben Jonson (Sejanus and Tiberius), Monteverdi (Nero, Poppaea, and Seneca), and Racine (Agrippina, Nero, and Britannicus) in the seventeenth century to the BBC *I, Claudius* television miniseries in the twentieth. Although no Roman dramas survive from Tacitus' own maturity, he grew up in a theatrical age in which the dramatic had permeated much of art, architecture, and literature. Tacitus followed the taste of his time, and his work was, in the words of his sixteenth-century editor Justus Lipsius, "like the theater of everyday life."

It may be illuminating to examine several of the memorable dramatic tableaux from the *Annals* to see if graphic embellishment or decorative detail plays a role in the author's effects. An excellent example is the opening of book 3, which describes the moving arrival of Agrippina in Brundisium with the ashes of her husband, Germanicus, who, as we have seen, had died in Syria under mysterious circumstances. Since Agrippina was the last surviving grandchild of Augustus, and Germanicus was popular with the Roman masses, the description is filled with emotion and political meaning:

> And, the first moment the fleet was seen out at sea, not only the harbor and the inshore waters but the walls and roofs and wherever afforded the furthest view up with a crowd of the sorrowful, asking one another repeatedly whether to receive her disembarkation in silence or with some utterance or other. And there was still no sufficient agreement as to what suited the occasion, when the fleet gradually neared—not

with eager rowing, as is customary, but with everything composed for sadness. When, on disembarking from the ship with her two children and holding the funeral urn, she cast her eyes downward, there was the same groan from everyone and you could not distinguish relatives from others, the breast-beating of men or women, except that Agrippina's company, exhausted by its long sorrow, was outstripped by those meeting her and fresh to the pain. (3, 1, 3–4)

Despite the crowds of mourners along the shoreline, the fleet coming into view, the loud groan when Agrippina appears carrying the urn with the ashes of Germanicus like Electra with the remains of her brother Orestes, little pictorial detail appears in this passage.[8] There is no description of the mourning garb, the funeral offerings, the milling mobs, or the cries of grief. There are virtually no descriptive adjectives. Here, as elsewhere in the *Annals*, drama, that is, action, is all pervasive. Individual books often begin or end like an act of a play. Here the reader needs little detail to set an emotional stage: the younger Agrippina returning to Italy with her children and the ashes of her husband, with the crowds surging along the dock (and commenting on the events) as the flotilla sailed into port, and the cortège then begins its march to Rome.

★ ★ ★

In 61 C.E. the Roman governor of Britain, Suetonius Paulinus, attempted to conquer the island of Mona (modern Anglesey) near the coast of Wales. Mona was a stronghold of the Druids, and Tacitus infuses this attack with the terror of the Roman legionaries seeing wild women alongside men on the field of battle:

> There stood along shore a diverse line, dense with arms and men, and with females running in between: in funereal clothing and with tumbling hair, they were flourishing

8. Santoro L'hoir (Ann Arbor, Mich., 2006), 61–70, discusses Tacitus' use of Greek drama to depict Agrippina.

firebrands after the manner of Furies; and Druids around about, pouring forth ominous prayers with their hands raised to the sky, stunned the soldiery by the strangeness of their appearance, so that, as if their limbs were stuck fast, their bodies presented a stationary target for wounds. Then, after exhortations from their leader and goading themselves not to panic at a womanly and fanatical column, they advanced the standards, lay low those in their way, and engulfed them in their own fire. After this a garrison was imposed on the conquered and their groves were extirpated, consecrated as they were to savage superstition: They held it right to grill captive gore on their altars and to consult their gods with the entrails of men. (14, 30, 1–3)

Once again Tacitus works with images of crazed women in a passage in which the modifiers are usually participles, and even the few adjectives—*dirus* (ominous); *fanaticus* (fanatical); *immobilis* (stuck fast); *saevus* (savage)—convey mood or action rather than visual details. The overall effect is unmistakably vivid, but the historian has created that illusion through action rather than by detailed physical description.

★ ★ ★

In the following scene from the German wars, Germanicus is shown the night before the battle wandering through his camp disguised in an animal skin and listening to the soldiers praising him:

At the start of the night, leaving his augural tent by secret ways unknown to the watches, with a single companion and his shoulders covered with a wild-animal pelt, he approached the roads of the camp, stopped at the pavilions, and had the pleasure of hearing reports about himself, as one man extolled the leader's nobility, another his demeanor, many his tolerance, affability, and equal attentiveness in gravity and jest; and they declared that they must express their gratitude in the line of battle, likewise that the disloyal breakers of the peace should be sacrificed to vengeance and glory. (2, 13, 1)

A few sentences convey the drama inherent in the situation, with the "wild beast's skin" (*ferina pellis*) the only specific visual detail. In their nervousness on the eve of battle, Tacitus shows the soldiers bolstering their confidence by praising their general. Shakespeare recognized the scene as a brilliant theatrical idea, embellished it with dialogue that brought out the humor, and thus raised it to its full dramatic potential when Henry V goes in disguise through the English camp to test his men on the eve of Agincourt in *Henry V*. There he encounters the swaggering and boastful soldier Pistol:

> Pistol: The king's a bawcock, and a heart of gold,
> A lad of life, an imp of fame;
> Of parents good, of fist most valiant:
> I kiss his dirty shoe, and from heart-string
> I love the lovely bully. What is thy name?
> Henry: Harry le Roy.
> Pistol: Le Roy! A Cornish name: art thou of Cornish crew?
> (IV.i.44–50)

★ ★ ★

The most extraordinary of the dramatic tableaux in the *Annals* is Tacitus' extended account of the mutinies that followed the death of Augustus. For almost twenty pages he provides a tour de force of narration. Nevertheless, it is not a static painting, but a cinematic drama into which individual scenes and characters are brilliantly interwoven; menacing darkness sets the mood. Amid the grand movements, gestures, and emotions of the crowds of angry soldiers, Tacitus, like a director of grand historical films (e.g., D. W. Griffith, Sergei Eisenstein, David Lean), shifts his focus from the sweeping panorama of a faceless mob to glimpses of individual faces and brief close-ups until the camera's restless eye settles on particularly telling images: an eloquent mutineer rouses the troops with a fiery speech, and rapacious centurions are humiliated and even murdered by the rebellious troops. In the following passage, Germanicus melodramatically threatens to commit suicide until a cynical soldier offers his own "sharper sword"; and the commander is dragged to safety as other officers flee into hiding.

> Subsequently, hearing of the legions' turmoil, he set off hurriedly and confronted them outside the camp, their eyes cast down toward the ground as if in remorse. After he had entered the rampart, however, discordant complaints began to make themselves heard; and some men, grasping his hand in a show of effusive kissing, inserted his fingers so that he would feel mouths devoid of teeth; others displayed limbs twisted with old age. (1, 34, 1–2)

After Germanicus demanded that the soldiers fall into formation, they reluctantly began to listen to him until he touched on their mutiny:

> They bared their bodies as one man and remonstrated about the weals from their wounds and the marks of their beatings. Then, in indistinguishable utterances they censured the price of exemptions, of their straitened wages, the hardness of their work and specifically the ramparting, ditches, and haulings of pasturage, fuel and wood, and anything else which was required out of necessity or merely to combat inactivity in camp. A particularly frightening shout arose from the veterans, who, counting out their thirty or more years of service, begged both that he should cure their exhaustion and for an end to such grueling soldiering and for a not impecunious retirement, not for death amid the selfsame toils. There were those too by whom the money bequeathed by Divine Augustus was demanded as their right, along with words of auspicious omen for Germanicus; and, if he wanted the command, they demonstrated their readiness.
>
> At that, as if contaminated by their crime, he leapt headlong from the tribunal. They blocked his departure with their weapons, threatening if he did not go back; but he for

his part, shouting repeatedly that he would rather die than cast aside his loyalty, snatched the sword from his side, brought it upward, and was on the verge of bringing it down into his heart, had not those nearest grasped his hand, holding it fast by force. The farthest section of the meeting, clustered together as it was, and (scarcely credible to say) some individuals who came up nearer urged him to strike; and a soldier by the name of Calusidius offered his own drawn sword, adding that it was sharper. Even to the madmen that seemed savage and a sign of evil behavior, and there was an interval for Caesar to be snatched away by his friends into his pavilion. (1, 35, 1–4)

As the long description of the mutiny continues, natural surroundings set the mood: soldiers confront each other in the darkness and panic at the omen of a waning moon; rebels are driven into their tents by rainstorms; and as Germanicus turns his troops against the Germans, they find in the ghostly Teutoburg Forest Roman bones from Varus' slaughtered legions still lying unburied in the marshy land:

In the middle of the plain there were the whitening bones, scattered or piled up, exactly as men had fled, or resisted. Nearby lay fragments of weapons and horses' limbs, and also, on the trunks of trees, skulls were impaled. In the neighboring groves were barbarian altars, at which they had sacrificed tribunes and first-rank centurions. And survivors of the disaster, who had slipped away from the fight or their bonds, reported that here the legates had fallen, there the eagles had been seized; where Varus' first wound had been driven home, where he had met his death by a blow from his own luckless right hand; from which tribunal Arminius had harangued; how many gibbets there had been for the captives, and which were the pits; and how in his haughtiness he had mocked the standards and eagles. (1, 61, 2–4)

Through these pages Tacitus rapidly changes focus and tone with the speed and skill with which Shakespeare and Verdi shift from monologue or aria to chorus: mass movement intermixed with individual suffering; swift changes from light to darkness, with melodrama elevated to the level of tragedy. Near the end of the mutiny the commander's wife Agrippina and their little son, the soldier's pet Caligula, accompany a group of weeping officers' wives who leave the camp to seek the protection of Rome's Gallic allies. A contrived scene, and surely a melodramatic one, as is the final image of Germanicus' weeping over the massacres that he had intentionally incited. These vivid scenes in their entirety form what is one of the most graphic dramas that ancient Rome produced.

And yet, to what degree is this a realistic picture? If Tacitus is a painter, he is an impressionistic one. There are once again relatively few descriptive adjectives; the narrative is carried by the dramatic energy of verbs and participles. One of the most specific images is the eerie scene amid the bones and skulls of Varus' army, but Tony Woodman has shown that these details were taken from Tacitus' earlier description of the battlefield at Cremona.[9] Here, as elsewhere, Tacitus is content to draw on a bank of stereotypical images, as a rhetorician describes a virgin, or the sculptors of Trajan's Column or Roman sarcophagi look to visual master texts for their battle scenes. They are all certainly vivid, but they may not be very specific. Literary critics sometimes suggest that detailed description stops the narrative flow, and Tacitus preferred the rapidity of the darting phrase or the passing image. The historian looks to a psychological and emotional reality: the walls and temple of Jerusalem are not intended as a verbal picture as much as an evocation of impregnability. The appeal of Tacitus' "paintings" is to the brain and the heart—not to the eye.

Such is also the case with the portraits of individuals. Despite some brief descriptions of secondary characters, the portraits of such central figures as Tiberius and the elder and younger Agrippina are

9. Woodman (Cambridge, Mass., 1988), 168–178. Since 1987 archaeologists have been excavating the remains of a defeated Roman army at Kalkriese; most scholars have identified it as the site of Varus' defeat. Now cf. Wells (2003) for bibliography on this controversy.

developed indirectly. The striking exception is a single sentence describing the depraved old Tiberius living on Capri:

> There were those who believe that in old age his physical appearance too had been a source of shame (he had a spindly and stooping loftiness, a summit denuded of hair, and an ulcerous face, generally patched with cosmetic medications). (4, 57, 2)

Although of Tacitean brevity, these unpleasant details seem more Suetonian than Tacitean. We might ask why Tacitus now suddenly presents them. The answer can be found in the following rhapsodic evocation of the beautiful island to which Tiberius had retired:

> I am inclined to believe that it was its solitude which most appealed to him, because the sea around is harborless and there are scarcely refuges even for modest craft; nor could anyone have moored there without the knowledge of the guard. The climatic conditions in winter are mild owing to a mountain barrier which fends off any savage winds; its summer faces Westerlies and, with the open main all around, is exceptionally attractive; and it used to have the prospect of a very fine bay until the fires of Mt. Vesuvius altered the area's appearance. (4, 67, 2)

Hence, the deformity of the corrupt emperor is presented primarily as a counterpoint to the beauties of Capri; neither the imperial portrait nor the island landscape serves a decorative so much as a rhetorical and dramatic purpose.

★ ★ ★

The literary artist (including the ancient historian) can provide picturesque details to engage or amuse the reader, or he can provide a full report of the lands and peoples of whom he writes. And yet, in his descriptions, as elsewhere, Tacitus is not, at his core, that which appears on the surface. At the conclusion of his *Agricola* the historian addresses the subject of that laudatory biography, his own father-in-law:

I would also recommend this to a daughter and a wife—to honor the memory of that father, that husband by pondering all his words and deeds in their hearts, and to embrace the form and features of his character rather than of his person. I do not think one should reject the likenesses carved in marble or bronze, but as the faces of men, so the images of the face are weak and perishable but the form of the mind is eternal which you cannot hold or express in some foreign substance or in art, but in your own behavior. Whatever we loved in Agricola, whatever we admired, survives and will survive in the hearts of men, in the eternity of time, in the reputation of history. (*Agricola* 46)

Tacitus likewise is not overly concerned with the representation of physical reality. He conjures up pictures; he does not describe. Character is more important than a physical likeness. His cinematic, evocative, quicksilver style is not concerned with color, visual texture, or ornamental descriptions; he aims at a psychological, political, and moral truth. Despite centuries of scholars and artists regarding him as the supreme historical "painter," he is in fact less concerned with the traditional painterly skills than are many other historians. His goal is not a picture but a deeper impression, to which the picture is only a means.

In fact, it is only incidentally that Tacitus gives us any picture at all.

· 5 ·

Freedom and Censorship

One of the principal themes in the *Annals* is freedom, or, perhaps more specifically, the loss of freedom as the inevitable consequence of the growth of political tyranny at Rome. Tacitus had written about the "freedom" of barbarians in his earlier books: in his *Agricola* and *Germania* he suggested the Britons' and Germans' desire for freedom and hatred of slavery, and in the *Histories* he portrays the rebel leader Julius Civilis as accusing the Gauls of passively confusing their wretched "servitude" with "peace." In the *Annals* the historian continues this theme in his obituary of the German general Arminius at the conclusion of book 2, where he chides Greek and Roman authors for giving him less than his due. For Tacitus, Arminius was the true "liberator of Germany" when his victory over Varus drove the Romans back across the Rhine, which remained into Tacitus' own day, a century later (and into ours almost exactly two millennia later), the permanent division between Roman and Germanic Europe. But when Tacitus broadcasts this quest for freedom by native rebels against Roman domination, does he identify himself as an opponent of imperialism? Almost certainly not! He is merely, by putting these words into their imagined speeches, lamenting that Rome's barbarian enemies are more committed to *libertas* than are the Romans themselves.

Tacitus is here skillfully fusing the lost freedom of conquered barbarians with the lost freedom of the Romans themselves. Despite all the drama of Tacitus' statements, his conception of the "loss of freedom" does not come from his concern for the Roman provincials or the masses, much less for the conquered peoples of East and West, but only for his few hundred comrades in the senatorial order. He is of course primarily concerned with the Roman elite, whose loss of freedom of speech was closely tied to their loss of political power.

In the opening paragraph of the *Annals* Tacitus calls his readers' attention to what he sees as the very beginning of the process.

> The Roman people of old, however, had their successes and adversities recalled by brilliant writers; and to tell of Augustus' times there was no dearth of deserving talents, until they were deterred by swelling sycophancy. The affairs of Tiberius and Gaius, as of Claudius and Nero, were falsified through dread while the men themselves flourished, and composed with hatred fresh after their fall. (1, 1, 2)

His vivid accounts of those political persecutions have made the *Annals* a central text in many discussions of freedom from the Renaissance to the Age of Revolutions.

But what did Tacitus really mean by freedom (*libertas*)?[1] In modern times political freedom can have one of several meanings: independence from foreign domination, a legal system that secures civil and human rights, and the democratic right to have a voice in the political system. These ideas have many sources; democracy, for example, stems from Athenian political life (which created the word), in which free men could all speak and vote in the assembly. But the Romans did not have a word for democracy; even during the Republic the rights of the people were far more restricted than in Periclean Athens, since there was no open discussion at meetings

1. On *libertas*, cf. Wirzubski (1950).

of the assembly. Tacitus lived in a world in which masters controlled every aspect of their slaves' lives, women had restricted civil liberties and no political rights, election to office and admission to the Senate required the approval of the emperor, and sixty million conquered men and women around the Mediterranean were subject to Roman imperial rule. So his conception of freedom was in almost every way far narrower than our own.

At the beginning of his earliest book, the *Agricola*, Tacitus made it clear that he saw in freedom of speech the lynchpin of all political liberty, although of course he is interested only in the political and intellectual elite. He expressed bitterness at the loss of fifteen years of his life under the tyranny of Domitian, and is angry that he must ask permission to write this biography of Agricola, "which I should have not had to ask." He especially bemoans the persecution of philosophers who disagreed with the regime, and the suppression of adulatory biographies about them:

> We have read that when panegyrics were pronounced by Arulenus Rusticus on Thrasea Paetus, and by Herennius Seneco on Helvidius Priscus, it was a capital crime: cruelty was not only visited on the authors themselves but on their books and the task was given to the executioners to burn those works of genius in the place of assembly and the forum. In that fire they thought that the voice of the Roman people, the freedom of the Senate, and the conscience of the human race would be destroyed. At the same time the teachers of philosophy were banished and every intellectual pursuit was driven into exile, so that nothing virtuous might remain. (*Agricola* 2)

But this suppression of free speech was hardly new to the age of Tacitus. For centuries Roman political leaders had exercised "censorship" over what they regarded as impermissible language and unacceptable ideas.

Censorship began in the Roman Republic. In our own time some form of censorship exists in many countries in the control of the press, minimum-age limits on film audiences, restrictions on pornography, removal of books from school libraries, or blocks on access to Internet Web sites. In other words, censors are moral arbiters or political police officers. Censor is the title given to a Roman official whose most important duty was to conduct the census. The censor was also in time empowered to expel members of the Senate for immorality, and the elder Cato (234–149 B.C.E.) used his censorship to attempt to raise the moral tone in Roman life, even trying to restrict the dress and jewelry of women. The word "censor" in our modern sense does not occur in Latin, and it first appears in English (according to the *Oxford English Dictionary*) in John Milton's *Areopagitica*—an essay written to the British Parliament in 1644 in support of the freedom of unlicensed printing. In what follows I am using "censorship" in this modern sense.

Tacitus makes clear that the Romans themselves knew that they were less tolerant than the Greeks of free speech. The Greek word *parrhesia*, which usually carried the positive meaning of "freedom of speech" for the Greeks, was translated into Latin as *licentia* (license)— a word that had negative overtones. The earliest Roman Law Code—the *Twelve Tables*, compiled about 450 B.C.E.—prohibited slanderous songs on penalty of death. In the third century B.C.E., the poet Naevius, whose epic poem on the First Punic War and historical dramas constitute the earliest historical writing in Latin, was cast into prison after his attack on a powerful family. Should we see this as the first instance of a Roman historian punished for plying his trade? Probably not. More likely, Naevius was punished under the Twelve Tables for writing songs mocking the prominent family of the Metelli. Rome was still an oral culture in which few were literate, and written histories posed little danger to individuals or political groups.

In the succeeding centuries there are more instances of banned speech than banned books. In 155 B.C.E. three Athenian ambassadors who were waiting in Rome to argue a legal appeal began to lecture about philosophy to young Roman noblemen. Cato the Elder and other conservatives became alarmed that such ideas were being spread, and the philosophers were soon expelled—but no one protested the vast number of Greek books that flooded into Rome at the same time. Sixty years later, rhetoricians who were teaching young Romans how to use Greek rhetorical techniques in Latin were also banned. They must have provoked the same anxieties that those Greek philosophers and rhetoricians called Sophists caused among conservative Athenians four centuries earlier, ultimately leading to the execution of Socrates. It seems that the Romans were initially far more frightened by the spoken word than the written word, given that the former could be diffused more widely in a semiliterate society. The Roman elite wished to prevent agitation by the masses.

While there was complete freedom of speech in the Roman Senate, senators spoke in order of seniority, so there was minimal opportunity for an impassioned young man with radical ideas to have a significant effect on the deliberations. Meetings of the public assemblies included Romans—only men, of course—from all levels of society, but there were no discussions at those formal meetings, only votes. However, the magistrates held informal gatherings, called *contiones*, in which all could air their opinions, but without voting, and the presiding official had great discretion over who could speak and what could be said. On rare occasions, foreign ambassadors and even women were called upon to speak.

The ferocious give and take in the political debate of the late Republic is exemplified in Cicero's aggressive speeches in the Senate and law courts. He had a sharp tongue—we need only recall his hilarious suggestion of incest against his enemy Clodius in the *Pro Caelio* and his vicious speeches against Mark Antony, called *Philippics* after Demosthenes' bitter denunciations of Philip of Macedon three centuries earlier. After Cicero was killed by Antony's order, his wife, Fulvia, was said to have stuck her hairpin in the orator's tongue as his head and hands were displayed at the rostrum in the Forum. But his books were not burned. Decades later, the elder Seneca, who had actually seen emperors destroy books, tells us that schoolboys debated, as a rhetorical exercise, whether Cicero ought to have consented to the burning of his books, had Antony allowed him to live in return. But that is all schoolroom fantasy: the rhetoricians were intellectuals who took books seriously, perhaps too seriously. It was only the spoken word that posed a threat to the aristocratic rulers of the Roman Republic. Books of history would not arouse the plebs, would not damage the loyalty of the legions, would not divide the senators from the equestrians. So the most effective forms of censorship were exile or political oblivion, not book burning. When Caesar dominated Rome he made his peace with Cicero; Cicero would retire to his study and write, but not engage in public politics. And, when Julius Caesar's opponents wrote pamphlets attacking him (*libelli*, from which our term "libel" comes), he merely answered with his own pamphlets. The pen was not yet mightier than the sword.

So we turn to Tacitus. The historian said that the freedom of historians ended when Augustus became the single master of Rome.[2] While there had earlier been many authors writing freely about Roman history,

> after the battle of Actium, when it became necessary that all power devolve on one man for the sake of peace, these great geniuses faded away. At the same time truth was damaged in many ways: first by ignorance of this unfamiliar state, then through a passion for flattery or on the other hand a hatred toward the rulers. Between hostility and servility, neither group was concerned with posterity. But while we easily turn from a writer's idolization, detraction and spite find ready ears, since flattery earns the disgraceful accusation of subservience while bitterness appears as a false show of freedom. (*Histories* 1, 1)

Yet, in most ways, the first emperor seemed tolerant of intellectual dissent, as long as it did not grow into political opposition. Tacitus admits in the *Annals* that Augustus brought the end of civil war so that "the people were seduced by grain, the soldiers by pensions, and all with the sweetness of peace." So, he continues, there was little opposition,

2. On the suppression of dissent under Augustus, cf. Raaflaub and Samons (1990), 417–454.

since the most defiant had fallen in the battle line or by proscription and the rest of the nobles, each in proportion to his readiness for servitude, were being exalted with wealth and honors and, enhanced by the revolution, preferred the protection of the present to the perils of old. (1, 2, 1)

In a famous story, Augustus directed a good-humored jibe at his friend, the historian Livy, when he referred to the Republican sympathies in Livy's writings by calling him a "Pompeian." The biographer Plutarch (*Cicero* 49) records the sentimental story of Augustus coming upon his grandson hiding a copy of Cicero's works in the folds of his toga. Glancing at the book and handing it back to the boy, the emperor is supposed to have said, "A learned man, and one who loved his country!" And this of a writer in whose murder he had once acquiesced! Suetonius (*Augustus* 51–56) portrays the emperor as a grand old man above such petty brutality, who pardoned former enemies and punished with a short exile Cassius Patavinus, who openly boasted at a dinner that he would enjoy killing Augustus. The emperor even once hurried from the Senate house in the face of shouted criticisms, but did nothing about them. Though Suetonius' rose-colored view is perhaps exaggerated, Augustus was assuredly less despotic than his successors.

Nevertheless, other sources do report cases of political opposition and literary censorship. At least six or eight "conspiracies" are mentioned, although none were the serious threats to the regime that later occurred under Caligula and Nero. Under Augustus tyranny was disguised, and most writers were controlled through self-censorship, although there is some evidence that intellectuals were suppressed. The orator and historian Titus Labienus— nicknamed "Rabienus" for his rabid attacks—was a Republican sympathizer whose books were burned by a senatorial decree; the author then committed suicide. But he was attacked by his enemies, rather than by the emperor. A better-known episode is more closely linked to Augustus: the devil-may-care poet Ovid was forced into exile in 8 C.E. for, as he himself said, "a poem and a mistake." He spent the rest of his life in a town on the remote Black Sea writing letters to the emperor begging for his return to Rome. Scholars still debate the precise cause of Ovid's exile, although the most plausible suggestion is that the poet satirized the behavior of Augustus' promiscuous daughter, Julia, who was herself exiled. So Augustus certainly was known to have ultimate power to control free speech, and on occasion he did so. But the punishment was a fine or book burning or exile, rather than execution.

While Tacitus wishes us to understand that the suppression of truth had already begun under Augustus, he believes it was greatly expanded under Tiberius.[3] Some ancient sources report a less tyrannical Tiberius, as when Suetonius remarks that "he would often say that the liberty to speak and think as one pleases is the test of a free country" (*Tiberius* 28). But it is Tacitus' very hostile picture of Tiberius that has survived through the centuries. For example, the emperor relied on a minor Augustan precedent for his much crueler suppression of dissent. In Tacitus' account of the first trials for treason, he points out that they were based on the ancient law (c. 100 B.C.E.) which allowed prosecution of anyone who harmed the *maiestas populi romani* ("majesty of the Roman people"). Augustus first allowed that law to be used not to punish actions but to enforce censorship, but in 15 C.E. Tiberius extended that law:

> He had brought back the law of treason. This had the same name in the time of the ancients, but different matters came to court, such as the impairment of an army by betrayal or of the plebs by sedition, or in fine, of the sovereignty of the Roman people by the maladministration of the government. Actions were prosecuted, talk had impunity. Augustus was the first to handle a trial of defamatory documents under the category of that law, being roused by the passion with which Cassius Severus had defamed illustrious men and women in provocative writings; subsequently Tiberius, consulted by the praetor Pompeius Macer, on the question whether legal proceedings would be allowed in cases of

3. Rutledge (2001).

treason, replied that the laws should be enforced. He too had been stung by the publication of poems, of uncertain authorship, against his savagery and haughtiness and his disaffected relations with his mother. (1, 72, 2–4)

Although Tiberius urged that the laws be enforced, in his early years he pardoned many who were accused by the senatorial prosecutors, each eager to outdo one another in trying to ingratiate themselves with the emperor. He thereby established that there were earlier laws against free speech, but only the emperor could show mercy. Speech and books were prosecuted under the charge of having diminished the majesty of the Roman people—*laesa maiestas*—a charge that has reappeared in other tyrannical regimes as the *lèse majesté* of the French monarchy and as "antistate activity" in the former Soviet Union and contemporary China.

Tacitus shows Tiberius as deeply devious in hiding his real desires and allowing informers and prosecutors to enforce harsh laws while distancing himself from them. This has become a tactic of tyrants through the ages—today we call it "deniability." In 21 C.E. Clutorius Priscus, despite having been rewarded by the emperor for a moving poem on the death of Germanicus, was denounced for having prematurely written a dirge for Tiberius' ailing son Drusus—obviously hoping for another imperial gift. Prosecutors and senators quickly condemned and executed Clutorius:

> That was censured by Tiberius before the senate with his customary ambiguities, since he extolled the devotion of those keenly avenging the injuries (however limited) to a princeps, he deprecated such precipitate punishment of mere words. (3, 51, 1)

A few years later Tacitus attests that censorship went beyond words or books to images. Every aristocratic family preserved in the front hall of their home their *imagines*—the portraits of their ancestors—which would then be carried in family funerals. But if the display of *imagines* was the means by which families rewrote their place in history, these busts were likewise dangerous to their opponents.

In 23 C.E., when Junia—niece of Cato, sister of Brutus, and widow of the assassin Cassius—died at the age of 90, sixty-four years after her brother and husband at Philippi, her funeral was splendid:

> Twenty images from the most brilliant families were carried in front, the Manlii, Quinctii, and other names of similar nobility; but outshining all were Cassius and Brutus, for the very reason that likenesses of them were not on view. (3, 76, 2)

In 1859, in the midst of a political campaign in the City of London, Lord John Russell used the phrase "conspicuous by its absence." He then went on to say that he had taken the expression from "one of the greatest historians of antiquity."[4] Hence Tiberius' suppression of Caesar's enemies became a cliché in Victorian England and remains in our language today. If remembering is the function of historians, politicians often prefer to encourage forgetting.

The paradigm case of the loss of freedom of speech under Tiberius was the trial of the historian Cremutius Cordus in 25 C.E. Although Suetonius did not mention this trial, he attributed to Cremutius' history the story that Augustus wore a steel corset and sword under his clothing when he presided over the Senate and that senators were searched for hidden weapons (*Augustus* 35). That does not quite fit with the image of the much beloved father of the country, and may even have marked out Cremutius as an opponent of the new regime. Still, Cremutius wrote his history under Augustus, and the emperor even attended one of his readings—all without censure or punishment. But Aelius Sejanus, Tiberius' powerful praetorian prefect, brought charges against Cremutius, and Tacitus provides the compelling story of the trial, which took place in the presence of the emperor. Cremutius was accused of calling Brutus and Cassius "the last of the Romans," and he decided that, since he was doomed, he might as well mount a courageous defense:

> "It is my words, conscript fathers, that are criticized, so completely am I innocent of deeds; but not even they were

4. *Oxford English Dictionary* (s.v. "conspicuous," 2.b) cites Russell's *Speech at London Tavern* on April 15, 1859, for the creation of this idiom.

directed at the princeps or the princeps' parent, whom the law of treason embraces. I am said to have praised Brutus and Cassius, whose achievements, though many have compiled them, no one has mentioned without honor.

"Titus Livius, quite brilliant as he is for eloquence and credibility, first of all elevated Cn. Pompeius with such praise that Augustus called him 'a Pompeian'; and that was no obstacle to their friendship. Scipio, Afranius, this very Cassius himself, this very Brutus, nowhere did he name them as 'bandits' and 'parricides' (the designations which are now imposed) but often as distinguished men. Asinius Pollio's writings transmit an exceptional memorial of the same individuals; Messala Corvinus used to proclaim Cassius 'his command'; and each continued to thrive in wealth and honors. To the book of Marcus Cicero in which Cato was exalted to the sky, how else did the dictator Caesar reply than with a responding speech as if before a jury?

"Antonius' letters, Brutus' public addresses contain abuse against Augustus which is admittedly false but of much acerbity; the poems of Bibaculus and Catullus, packed with insults of the Caesars, can still be read; but Divine Julius himself, Divine Augustus himself bore and ignored them all—whether with more restraint or wisdom, I could not easily say: what is spurned tends to abate; but, if you become angry, you appear to have made an admission. (I do not touch on the Greeks, among whom not just liberty but license too went unpunished; or, if anyone took notice, he avenged words with words.)

"What was particularly exempt, and had no one to disparage it, was to publish about those whom death had removed from hatred or favor. For surely it is not the case that, by my having Cassius and Brutus armed and holding the plains of Philippi, I am inflaming the people in public addresses with civil war as my motive? Is it not rather the case that, slain as they were seventy years ago, they for their part not only come to be known by their images—which not even the victor abolished—but retain some part of their memory among writers in exactly the same way? Posterity pays to every man his due repute; and, if condemnation is closing in on me, there will be no lack of those who remember not only Cassius and Brutus but also myself." Then, leaving the senate, he ended his life by fasting.

The cremation of his books by the aediles was proposed by the fathers; but they survived, having been concealed and published. Wherefore it is pleasant to deride all the more the insensibility of those who, by virtue of their present powerfulness, believe that the memory even of a subsequent age too can be extinguished. On the contrary, the influence of punished talent swells, nor have foreign kings, or those who have resorted to the same savagery, accomplished anything except disrepute for themselves and for their victims' glory. (4, 34, 2–35, 5)

Cremutius was correct; he is remembered only for his persecution. And Tacitus takes the case as an opportunity to consider the futility of despotism and how it is especially foolish to create martyrs for freedom. His deep sympathy for Cremutius allows Tacitus to link his own historical writing with the achievement of his heroic predecessor.[5]

Tacitus closely linked the loss of freedom of speech with the decline of political liberty. Truth became a casualty of tyranny precisely because senators (and therefore historians) could not speak out. Since Roman historical writing was always deeply political, despotic emperors effectively suppressed history through much of the first century C.E. Tacitus' treatment of Caligula's reign (37–41 C.E.) is unfortunately lost; that account would doubtless have been marvelously entertaining. But Suetonius reports that the unstable emperor allowed the republication of the burned books of Labienus, Cremutius, and Severus, while he considered

---

5. For an interesting discussion of Tacitus and Cremutius, cf. Sailor (2008), 250–313.

suppressing Livy ("too wordy"), Vergil ("untalented"), and even Homer, since Plato had proposed doing so in his ideal Republic (*Caligula* 16; 34). He even suggested that the legal profession be abolished.

Claudius was the only Julio-Claudian emperor who imposed no censorship on writers. Perhaps that is because he himself was an historian. As a boy, he began writing a history of Rome beginning with the assassination of Julius Caesar, and even held public readings. But his mother, Antonia, and grandmother Livia made it clear that he would not be able to publish an honest account of the civil wars between his grandfather Mark Antony and his step-grandfather Augustus. So he wrote only two books on the immediate aftermath of Caesar's assassination in 44 B.C.E. and then, leaving a gap, recommenced with forty-one books beginning with the end of the civil wars in 30 B.C.E. Later he more cautiously wrote histories of the Etruscans and of Carthage to which no one would object, because no one cared very much.

Tacitus lived his first thirteen years in the reign of Nero (54–68 C.E.) and entered public life under Vespasian, so he knew well the censorship of those regimes. During the first eight years of Nero's reign there were few political persecutions—although he murdered his mother, Agrippina. After 62 C.E. so many senators were persecuted that it is difficult to regard the execution of distinguished writers as "censorship."[6] The epic poet Lucan was part of a genuine plot against Nero's life; Seneca's enforced suicide was more a result of his general disapprobation of his former pupil Nero's excesses than his philosophical treatises; and the philosopher Thrasea Paetus was persecuted for his sympathy to other dissidents. Though Tacitus reported them all as part of the decline of freedom, he brought a special dark humor to the death of the satirist Petronius—author of the *Satyricon*—who had once been Nero's "arbiter of elegance" but had fallen foul of the emperor's courtier Tigellinus.[7]

---

6. On the persecution of intellectuals under Nero, cf. Rudich (1993) and Rudich (1997).

7. For a further discussion of Petronius, see chapter 8 of this book.

The death of Nero brought a temporary respite from persecution—or so it might seem. Suetonius claimed that no innocent senator was ever punished by Vespasian, and even Tacitus recognized that he was perhaps the only emperor who improved *after* he came to office (*Histories* I, 50). Although he finally ordered the execution of Helvidius Priscus, no one denied that the curmudgeonly philosopher had repeatedly insulted the emperor in public. But the cruelty of Domitian—the despot under whom Tacitus served as praetor before withdrawing from Rome for three years—was a reversion to the days of Tiberius and Nero. In fact, we are told that that despot studied the workings of tyranny by reading the autobiography of Tiberius. It was the regime of Domitian that traumatized Tacitus and drove him to try to understand the origins of the harsh dictatorship of the early Roman Empire.

Tacitus clearly regarded the loss of freedom of speech on the part of senators and intellectuals as a central element in the history of the first century C.E.—perhaps even *the* central element. He proclaims in the preface to his *Histories* that he was living in blessed times "when we might think what we please and express what we think." Like all great historians he gave shape to an age and imposed his values on it. Since the Renaissance, the Julio-Claudian emperors have been seen through his eyes. Tacitus' focus on freedom is why he was loved by Ben Jonson, John Milton, and Thomas Jefferson and hated by popes, kings, and the emperor Napoleon. We today read him with admiration and delight, but we should be cautious about the narrowness of his conclusion. Tacitus thought the emperors gave a great deal of attention to snuffing out the freedom of senators, historians, and intellectuals. That did happen, but those autocrats usually regarded it as only one minor aspect of their desire for total control.

A century later, in his own autobiographical *Meditations*, the emperor-philosopher Marcus Aurelius emphasized the importance of freedom of speech and refers to writers such as Thrasea, who died under Nero, and his son-in-law Helvidius Priscus, as well as Brutus and Cato:

From my brother Severus, I learned to love my kin, and to love truth, and to love justice; and through him I learned to know Thrasea, Helvidius, Cato, Dio, Brutus; and from him I received the idea of a polity in which there is the same law for all, a polity administered with regard to equal rights and equal freedom of speech, and the idea of a kingly government which respects most of all the freedom of the governed. (*Meditations* 1, 14)

The emperor's book, although never published in his lifetime, presents the attitude toward freedom that Tacitus thought "good emperors" should adopt.

·6·

A Tiberian Narrative

I | The Long Shadow of Caesar Augustus

In his fifties, after great success as a lawyer, an administrator, a politician, and a writer, Cornelius Tacitus embarked on the project that is his own lasting memorial: a history of the emperors from Tiberius to Nero. In his earlier essay on Agricola he had promised his readers a "record of our former servitude and a testimony to our present good fortune." We might reasonably expect that he would write about Domitian's tyranny and the happy age of Nerva and Trajan, but that was not to be. After he completed the books that we call the *Histories*, ending with the death of Domitian in 96 C.E., Tacitus turned away from the expected treatment of his own time to trace in the *Annals* the origins of the imperial system. But his point of departure in 14 C.E. is puzzling, since he makes clear that it was Augustus, who took power four decades earlier, who established a monarchy.

The first paragraph of the *Annals* is remarkable in many ways. There is no formal prologue such as we find in Livy or in Tacitus' own *Histories*, but the first two words, *urbem Romam*, indicate the real focus of the senatorial historian. It is on the imperial capital, rather than its sprawling empire. The 250 years of the monarchy (753–509 B.C.E.) are dismissed in a mere twelve words. When Tacitus turns briefly to the Republic, he is most interested in emphasizing that none of the other dictators or dynasts or triumvirs who seized (or were voted) power during its five centuries had ever, until Augustus, established the permanent institution of monarchy. These sentences make it clear that the establishment of freedom with the first consuls of 509 B.C.E. had come to an end with the triumph of Augustus. That loss of political freedom is indeed the central theme of the *Annals*.

> The City of Rome from its inception was held by kings; freedom and the consulship were established by Lucius Brutus. Dictatorships were taken up only on occasion, and neither did the decemviral power remain in effect beyond two years, nor the military tribunes' consular prerogative for long. Not for Cinna nor for Sulla was there lengthy domination, and the powerfulness of Pompeius and Crassus passed quickly to Caesar, the armies of Lepidus and Antonius to Augustus, who with the name of prince (*princeps*) took everything, exhausted as it now was by civil dissensions, under his command.[1] (I, I, I)

Tacitus professes that he will pass on only a few details about Augustus' final period (*pauca de Augusto et extrema tradere*), but he does provide several paragraphs describing how Augustus successfully outmaneuvered his rivals, organized his new regime,

---

1. Tacitus here summarizes more than seven centuries of Roman history. Rome was founded by Romulus in 753 B.C.E., and seven kings ruled until Brutus established the Republic in 509. The Decemvirate (451–449) was charged with writing the first legal code, while the military tribunes held power from 408 to 367. Cinna held power 87–83, while Sulla was dictator 82–79. Crassus and Pompey were consuls in 70, and both were important political leaders (and members of the First Triumvirate with Julius Caesar from 60) until Crassus' death in 53 (fighting the Parthians) and Pompey's in 48 after being defeated by Caesar. Lepidus, Antony, and Octavian/Augustus formed the Second Triumvirate from 43 until Lepidus' loss of power in 36 and Antony's death in 30. Octavian then ruled as "Augustus" with the title of "princeps."

and struggled with the succession. He reduces the most crucial four decades of Roman history (31 B.C.E.–14 C.E.) to a few dense, cynical paragraphs which include this remarkable judgment:

> When he had enticed [*pellexit*] the soldiery with gifts, the people with food, and everyone with the sweetness of inactivity, he rose up gradually and drew to himself the responsibilities of senate, magistrates, and laws. (1, 2, 1)

Although bonuses, food, and peace hardly seem subversive, Tacitus' use of *pellexit* conveys a negative, almost sexual force as the new leader seduces one and all. Tacitus is not only a master of identifying the political (ab)use of language, but as a practiced professional orator he is himself a master of innuendo.[2] When he tells us in the opening paragraph that he writes *sine ira et studio* ("without anger and partiality"), he means that he has no personal grievance against the Julio-Claudian emperors (unlike the writers of their own times). But it is equally evident that his passion for Rome's lost freedom informs every page of the *Annals* and leads him, in the defensive and angry words of Napoleon, to make the emperors into the blackest villains.

Tacitus sees Augustus only as setting the stage for the new despotism. The historian, who in his early youth had seen Rome descend into civil war in 68–69 C.E., recognized that a century earlier Augustus had rescued Rome from a similar path toward self-destruction. He took Julius Caesar's name to establish his legacy, but he achieved dominance the same way as other Roman dynasts: through politics and force of arms. Yet Caesar received a kinder treatment in Tacitus, perhaps because his record of imperial conquest was greatly admired in the time of Trajan. Augustus preferred consolidation to conquest, and the succession of his stepson Tiberius in 14 C.E. brought to Rome the overtly hereditary monarchy that would produce Caligula, Nero, and Domitian. After the death of Augustus and even before his state funeral, Tacitus introduces the accession of the new emperor with the words:

2. Sinclair (1995).

The first act of the new principate was the slaughter of Postumus Agrippa. (1, 6, 1)

The insinuation that Tiberius (or his mother, Livia) ordered the murder of Augustus' last surviving grandson sets the dark tone of court politics and dynastic struggles that form the principal themes of the *Annals*. The great mythical family tragedy of the house of Atreus—Thyestes, Agamemnon, Clytemnestra, Orestes, and Electra—had been explored by all three great Athenian playwrights (Aeschylus, Sophocles, Euripides) and was reexamined in Roman tragedies.[3] So it was an obvious template for Tacitus to use in creating the cruel pathology of the Julio-Claudians. It was Tiberius himself who drew Tacitus back to the beginnings of what he saw as that murderous dynasty. Tacitus, who lived through the terror of Domitian, saw in the reign of Tiberius the clear foreshadowing of the horrors of the succeeding century.

Scholars have wondered why Tacitus did not begin his story earlier, perhaps when Augustus became *princeps* or when he moved toward institutionalizing hereditary rule by adopting his nephew Marcellus, his grandsons Gaius and Lucius, and his stepson Tiberius. Although Tacitus did mention all those things, his goal was to focus his odium on Tiberius:

> Not even Tiberius had been adopted as successor through any affection or any concern for the state, but, because he had insight into the man's arrogance and savagery, by the basest of comparisons he had sought glory for himself. (1, 10, 7)

When the brutish, long-imprisoned grandson of Augustus, Agrippa Postumus, was executed soon after the emperor's death, Tacitus undercuts Tiberius' claim that it was done on the secret orders of Augustus. He prefers to insinuate that it was arranged by Livia and Tiberius. Whatever the faults of Augustus, he functions here primarily to cast a shadow over Tiberius.

---

3. Syme (1958), 363, first refers to the parallels with the house of Atreus. More recently Santoro L'hoir (2006) provides an extensive examination of Tacitus' use of this material via allusions both to Greek literature and to such Latin tragedies as Accius' *Clytemnestra* and Seneca's *Agamemnon*.

In the age of Tacitus, there was no longer the opportunity for a Caesar or a Cicero to rouse the crowds or the Senate with political rhetoric. Rather, an accomplished orator plied his trade in the law courts and there perfected the literary tactics and emotional stratagems of a cynical advocate. In writing history, Tacitus was able to bring the formidable arsenal of a lawyer's expertise at last into the political arena. When he mentions the accession of Tiberius, his telegraphic language dispenses with connective conjunctions (a technique called "asyndeton" by grammarians) to portray the stampede of the Roman elite to outdo each other in flattering the new *princeps*; Woodman's translation (1, 7) does it justice:

> *At Romae ruere in servitium consules, patres, eques.*
> [But at Rome there was a rush into servitude from consuls, senators, equestrians.]

The rhetorical tour de force, however, is Tacitus' account of the funeral of Augustus.

There was, of course, no record of what people said in the streets on that momentous day, but a skillful orator (like a modern debater) can construct probable arguments from several viewpoints. Tacitus skillfully presents credible arguments by three groups: the foolish masses, the thoughtful supporters of Augustus, and (the longest and most detailed account) the critics of his reign. The masses have no genuine political awareness; they talk about how striking it was that Augustus died in the same room of his south Italian villa as his father, or that he died on the very anniversary of taking power. These and other coincidences were to Tacitus trivial; he turns quickly to the praise of the politically sophisticated (*prudentes*) in the crowd.

> Because of devotion to his parent and the requirements of the state, in which at that time there had been no place for law, he had been driven to civil war, which could be neither prepared for nor maintained by good behavior. . . . Yet it was neither on kingly rule nor dictatorship but on the name of "princeps" that the state had been based. The empire was

cordoned by the sea of Ocean or distant streams; legions, provinces, fleets, everything was interconnected; there was legality among citizens, restraint among allies; the City itself was magnificent in its apparel; just a few things had been handled by force to ensure peace for the rest. (1, 9, 3–5)

While this approval, along with the stated satisfaction of the provincials, the army, and the urban population, would seem to be a compellingly positive evaluation of Augustus' reign, Tacitus then proceeds to a more detailed and more powerful negative appraisal. Augustus' loyalty to Julius Caesar and his concern for the state were mere smokescreens to cover his unconstitutional personal ambition. The historian portrays unnamed critics in the crowd—the text simply reads *Dicebatur contra* ("It was said on the other side")—who assail Augustus' cruelty, deception, hypocrisy, and even call the Augustan peace "bloody" with military disasters abroad and persecutions in Rome. The first ten chapters of the first book of the *Annals* praise Augustus sufficiently to disparage Tiberius, but he is hardly allowed to escape Tacitean innuendo as the creator of a despotic political system.

2 | Tiberius and His Courtiers

The politics of Tacitus' *Annals* is the politics of the court, as senators, freedmen, and imperial relations scheme for the emperor's attention and approval. It is little wonder that admiration for Tacitus was at its height in the court cultures of early modern Europe. The intrigue of courtiers was more interesting to Tacitus than were foreign battles or imperial administration. Whereas in Livy's history, Rome's most dangerous enemies were Etruscans (Tarquin), Carthaginians (Hannibal), or Greeks (Philip V), the monsters of the *Annals* live in the imperial palace. The historian depicts a political world replete with conspiracy, informers, and paranoia as the decline of senatorial privilege is mirrored by the increased power of the extraordinary Julio-Claudian women, ambitious equestrians, scheming freedmen, and even eunuchs.

Court figures through the ages included the talented as well as the parasitic, yet when we use the term "courtier" we are not thinking primarily of Seneca, Thomas More, Shakespeare, Michelangelo, Raphael, Haydn, or Mozart—all men who survived at the court of a powerful and wealthy patron. If Tacitus and Machiavelli have most contributed to the negative image of the courtier, even they show virtuous men and women influenced court life. We have already examined at length the most "heroic" figure portrayed in the *Annals*, Tiberius' nephew and adopted son, Germanicus Caesar. This popular prince died in 19 C.E., a mere five years after the accession of Tiberius, and it is hardly accidental that Tacitus depicts him, with his chaste wife and six children, as the last example of traditional Roman virtue. At first glance he hardly seems to be a "courtier," insofar as he spent most of his last five years in Germany or the East, yet his influence at Rome became an obsession for the paranoid emperor. Germanicus was certainly the focal point of court politics—as we see in the "friends" who surrounded his deathbed—and that faction was later, and less prudently, led by his widow, Agrippina. He improbably becomes a political martyr who was, like his father, Drusus, believed to be a "sympathizer" with Republican values:

> The memory of Drusus among the Roman people was considerable, and it was believed that, if he had been in charge of affairs, he would have given them back their freedom. Hence goodwill toward Germanicus, and the same hope. (1, 33, 2)

The congeniality, clemency, and open good humor of this young aristocrat is repeatedly emphasized by Tacitus in contrast to the sinister gloom and obsessive suspicion of Tiberius. The dramatic contrast between their respective obituaries makes clear that, in Tacitus' eyes, one was loved and the other loathed.[4] And yet Tacitus gives his hero very few actual achievements. Though the reader is left with the overall impression of Germanicus' military success in Germany, scholars have shown that the bare facts in Tacitus instead record military disasters and

4. *Annals* 2, 73 (Germanicus); 6, 51 (Tiberius).

ignominious retreats.[5] But it is the impression that survives, and it stands out in a book filled with the evil denizens of the Julio-Claudian court.

Tiberius' praetorian prefect Aelius Sejanus is the evil courtier par excellence in the portrait rendered by Tacitus. He is ambitious, corrupt, murderous, and able to insinuate himself skillfully into the emperor's absolute trust. In fact, it is he who provides the model of a praetorian prefect (or head of the secret police) from the Roman Empire down to the twentieth century; such men, hired to protect their rulers, often amass the power to destroy them. Tacitus made this monster the dominant character of the second part of the reign of Tiberius—books 4–6—and it has all the elements of a classical tragedy, although the betrayal and death of the historian's most horrific creation, after Tiberius, occurred in the lost fifth book. In fact, almost sixteen centuries after Sejanus' execution, Ben Jonson presented his own play, *Sejanus, His Fall*, in 1603 at the Old Globe, relying on Suetonius and Cassius Dio to complete the missing parts of Tacitus' story. It is a drama of ambition and deceit, in which William Shakespeare played his last attested role as an actor, the emperor Tiberius.[6] Jonson's personally annotated copy of the play (now in the British Library) shows how much he drew on Tacitus for his picture of Tiberian court life.

From his formal introduction of Sejanus in 23 C.E. (when Tiberius was 64 years old), Tacitus makes clear that his contempt for this "small-town adulterer" (4, 3) is grounded in his outrage that an upstart equestrian from a small Italian city should exercise such authority over senators. As usual, Tacitus does not provide a physical description—such details were beneath him—but he allows the actions to define the man.

> Begotten at Vulsinii, his father being Seius Strabo (a Roman
> equestrian), in his early youth he was a regular follower of C.
> Caesar (grandson of Divine Augustus) and rumored to have

5. On fact versus impression, cf. Walker (1952); 82–137 on Germanicus, cf. 118–120.

6. Riggs (1989), 105.

offered the sale of illicit sex to the rich and prodigal Apicius; later, by various means, he shackled Tiberius to such an extent that the latter, dark as he was toward others, was rendered uniquely unguarded and unprotected in respect of Sejanus himself—not so much by artfulness (indeed it was by the same means that he was vanquished) as by the anger of the gods against the Roman cause, for whose extermination he alike thrived and fell. His body was enduring of toil, his mind daring. Always self-concealing, he was an accuser of others. Sycophancy coexisted with haughtiness. Outwardly he had a calm reserve, internally a lust for acquiring supremacy, and for that reason there was sometimes lavishing and luxoriousness, but more often industry and vigilance—no less harmful when they are molded toward the procurement of kingship. (4, 1, 2–3)

Here we get the typical qualities of the ambitious courtier: sexual immorality, sycophancy toward the powerful and arrogance toward his inferiors, and always calculating. Tacitus models Sejanus on the portrait of Catiline in Sallust's monograph. But his sudden emergence is contrived to fit Tacitus' narrative. The first three books of the Tiberian narrative focus on the virtuous Germanicus and his elimination, and the next three on the pernicious influence of Sejanus and his patronage not only of the soldiers but also of the army of flatterers who populated the Palatine.

But, as earlier brief allusions make clear, Sejanus hardly emerged overnight from obscurity. His father, Seius Strabo, had been praetorian prefect under Augustus, and the son held the position with his father at the accession of Tiberius in 14 C.E. He then held it alone when his father left in 15 C.E. to become prefect of Egypt. Seius himself had a noble Roman mother, and he married the sister of a consul, so his son had a considerably nobler genealogy than Tacitus himself. But Tacitus, himself a first-generation senator, had a particularly snobbish loathing for ambitious equestrians. Sejanus' deviousness first appears in 15 C.E., when he is said to have incited Tiberius' suspicions of Agrippina's ambitions:

These thoughts were kept burning and piled high by Sejanus, who, with his experience of Tiberius' behavior, sowed hatreds for the distant future, to be stored away and brought out when grown. (1, 69, 5)

Later, in 20 C.E., Tacitus alleges that Sejanus tricked Piso into believing that Tiberius would quash accusations that he had poisoned Germanicus if he did not produce incriminating instructions from the emperor (3, 16). Sejanus had long been ingratiating himself with Tiberius and, presumably, weaving the network of patronage for which he later became famous.

It was in 23 C.E. that Sejanus was said to have conspired with Livilla, the wife of Drusus, Tiberius' son and the heir to the throne, to poison him. It seems a remarkably dangerous maneuver for both of them, almost insane for Livilla, unless she was truly besotted with this dubious character, but we know that Sejanus was adept at seducing the wives of many distinguished senators to learn their secrets.[7] (Although Tacitus repeats the rumors that Tiberius was involved in the intrigue, he finds it unbelievable that the emperor would want to murder his son.) Despite Tacitus' portrait of him, we must assume that Sejanus had a considerable amount of charm with both women and men. He had already in 20 C.E. begun to consolidate his power by moving the praetorian cohorts to a camp on the outskirts of the city where they could be more effectively controlled. But there were also strange obstacles to his rise. When, after Drusus' death, Sejanus asked in a letter filled with oily flattery for permission to marry Livilla, seeming to equate himself with Agrippa, the second husband of Augustus' daughter, Tiberius in his own ingratiating letter promising greater rewards still seemed to discourage the marriage. Tacitus (4, 41) suggests that Sejanus felt a certain dread at some unspoken reluctance on the part of his imperial patron.

Like all successful opportunists, Sejanus had an amazing stroke of good fortune which is graphically recounted by Tacitus:

7. Cassius Dio 58, 3.

And by chance during those days Caesar was confronted with a double-edged danger which only increased the empty rumors—and presented the man himself with reasons why he should place more trust in the friendship and steadfastness of Sejanus. They were dining at a villa whose designation is Spelunca, between the Amyclan sea and the Fundanian mountains, in a natural cave. In an unexpected rock slide its mouth buried some servants. Hence dread among everyone and flight by those who were celebrating the party; but Sejanus, suspended over Caesar on his two knees and hands, placed himself in the way of a fall, and in such a posture was discovered by the soldiers who had come to their rescue. He was more influential after that, and, though his urgings had fatal consequences, he was listened to with trust as not being anxious for himself. (4, 59, 1–2)

Thereafter Tiberius trusted Sejanus absolutely. When the emperor decided to move to Capri in 27 for the last eleven years of his life, it was widely assumed to have been on the advice of Sejanus, who then served as consul, and led the persecution of Agrippina and her sons. Statues of Sejanus were set up around the city, eulogies were pronounced in his honor, and his birthday was publicly celebrated—by 29 C.E. he seemed poised to succeed Tiberius as emperor. It must have seemed to many senators that Sejanus, who controlled all access to the emperor, was the real ruler of the empire; Tiberius was merely master of Capri.[8]

The loss of book 5 of the *Annals* is especially unfortunate, since it undoubtedly traced the emotional and political duel in 29–31 C.E. between two masters of intrigue and paranoia, Tiberius and Sejanus. We are forced to rely on Cassius Dio for those years, but that later historian was less attuned to the politics and personalities of the early empire. Suetonius' *Life of Tiberius* (61) can be helpful, when he reports that the emperor in his autobiography blamed Sejanus for

8. Cassius Dio 58, 2–3.

persecuting Germanicus' children and plotting revolution. But since Tiberius put one of Germanicus' sons to death after Sejanus' downfall, that accusation is hardly credible. It seems more likely that Tiberius toyed with Sejanus, dangling rewards while punishing his allies, so that Sejanus was provoked into taking some action himself.[9] In any event, despite the opaqueness of palace conspiracies, the actual fall of Sejanus was extraordinarily public—perhaps the most spectacular coup de théâtre of Tiberius' reign. With the emperor still in Capri, on October 18, 31 C.E., the consul read in the Senate a letter from Tiberius accusing a stunned Sejanus of treason. The prefect's deputy, Macro, was prepared to take over the praetorians and to arrest Sejanus, who was soon executed. The rage of Tiberius is evident in the murders of some of Sejanus' clients and allies and his innocent young children.

Was there truly a plot? Did Sejanus fear that the popularity of Tiberius' new favorite, Gaius Caligula (the last son of Germanicus), would keep him from the throne? The deviousness of both protagonists make it likely that there were multiple plots, just as after the death of Stalin in 1953 the chief of the secret police, Lavrenti Beria (who boasted that he had killed Stalin), was arrested by army troops and murdered before his security forces could murder his political opponents. It has taken five decades, and the opening of Soviet archives, for historians to unravel the intrigues of that dark era. So, too, for Tacitus it took imagination and courage to understand the secret machinations of Tiberius and his courtiers. But, for the missing years, other sources such as the much later Cassius Dio did not have the political perspicacity of Tacitus; we are left with only a sketch of that terrifying time.

Sejanus is the most vividly portrayed of the dark agents of Julio-Claudian Rome, but Tacitus also provides sketches of numerous less important figures who served as informers and prosecutors in a world that is all too familiar in modern totalitarian

9. Cassius Dio 58, 6.

states. Recent books by Vasily Rudich and Steven Rutledge trace the suppression of political dissidence, not only by a governmental apparatus but by volunteers eager to gain political advantage by persecuting their senatorial colleagues.[10] Rudich left Soviet Russia as a political exile after having been imprisoned there as a dissident, so he brings a remarkable psychological insight into the dynamic of persecution. Rutledge catalogues and analyzes more than one hundred Delators who could, under the Roman legal system, bring independent prosecutions against those they perceived to be guilty (or vulnerable), and Tacitus uses the term *delatores* to describe a veritable army of accusers. Tony Woodman compares the situation to that of East Germany, where one in every 6.5 inhabitants was a Stasi informer and files were kept on a third of the population.[11] Tacitus mentions wives making secret reports on their husbands, a son publicly accusing his father, betrayals at dinner parties, and soldiers keeping detailed records of the visitors, correspondence, and conversations of Agrippina and her son. There were even agents provocateurs planted to trap them into treacherous actions:

> The soldiery assigned to them recorded, as though in annals, their messages, visits, disclosures, and secrets; and in addition persons were set up to warn them to flee to the armies in Germany or to embrace the like of Divine Augustus in the throne of the forum and to call upon people and senate for aid. (4, 67, 4)

If the friends and clients of Sejanus were feared during the prefect's lifetime, after his death they themselves became targets of ambitious *delatores*. Tacitus provides the brave, verging on insolent, defense of Marcus Terentius. When Terentius was accused of having been an ally of Sejanus, he pointed out that for sixteen years everyone thought the praetorian prefect was acting for the emperor, and so his own loyalty to Sejanus was no more than loyalty to the

10. Rudich (1993); Rudich (1997); Rutledge (2001).
11. Woodman (2004), xxvii–xxviii.

regime. So he was indeed delighted to be regarded as Sejanus' friend. He directly tells Tiberius that, if he was rewarding Sejanus with honors, why should mere senators doubt the prefect's integrity?

> "It is not ours to assess whom you exalt above the rest, and for what reasons: to you the gods have given the supreme judgment of affairs; to us is left the glory of compliance. Further, we look only at what is held in front of us, to whom you dispense wealth and honors, who is possessed of the greatest power for aiding and harming (which no one is likely to deny that Sejanus had); but to search out the hidden feelings of the princes, and his still more concealed intentions is unlawful, perilous." (6, 8, 4)

Terentius' argument showed the survival skills that the cleverest courtiers developed in the world of daily intrigue and mortal peril of Tiberian Rome. He succeeded brilliantly and was acquitted, and his accusers were punished with exile or death.

And yet, once again, there seems to be a significant gap between the facts that Tacitus provides and the overall impression of this dark time. During three years of what Tacitus calls *continua caedes* ("constant slaughter") there were only two executions and a handful of suicides. In fact, during the entire twenty-three years of Tiberius' reign, scholars can count only eighty-six accusations, with a smaller number of actual executions. However cruel the record, we must be careful with our analogies to twentieth-century political persecutions in which thousands or even millions were sent to death camps, gulags, political reeducation camps, or execution chambers. It is for Tacitus a particular horror, since the condemned were often senators and their families, but he has created an exaggerated vision of random murder. For Romans living outside the capital, the age of Tiberius was not much changed from that of Augustus: there was prosperity and an absence of civil conflict. The Tiberian terror was genuine: the emperor did create a culture of political paranoia, distrust, and fear. But it has been much amplified by Tacitus' lens.

3 | An Emperor on the Couch

The Greek and Roman analyses of the human psyche are less often contained in abstract theoretical treatises than embedded in poems, plays, or works of history. The modern view, of course, is that this process is "creative" rather than "analytical," yet Sigmund Freud relied on Sophocles for the characters from which he drew inspiration for his Oedipus and Electra complexes. More recently the psychiatrist and Vietnam War veteran Jonathan Shay has drawn on Homer's Achilles to deepen our understanding of the sources and consequences of post-traumatic stress syndrome among veterans.[12] The Greek poets had deep psychological understanding, even if their insights were expressed very differently than they would be in a contemporary medical diagnosis.

It is Tacitus who, in his portrayal of the emperor Tiberius, provides us with the most comprehensive psychological profile of any historical figure in classical antiquity. It is sufficiently detailed to enable a noted Spanish physician and psychologist, Gregorio Marañón, to examine the reign of the emperor in terms of his obsessive resentments.[13] In the imperial obituary, Tacitus devotes only a few sentences to Tiberius' youth to explain his introverted moodiness:

> His fortunes from earliest infancy were equivocal. Having followed his proscribed father into exile, on entering Augustus' household as his stepson he contended with numerous rivals while Marcellus and Agrippa, then subsequently, Gaius and Lucius Caesar, thrived; also his brother, Drusus, was held more favorable in the affection of the citizens. But his life was especially slippery after his taking of Julia in matrimony, enduring as he did his wife's immorality or evading it. Then, on his return from Rhodes, he remained in possession of the princeps's now vacant hearth for twelve years and

---

12. Shay (1994).
13. Marañón (1956).

subsequently of jurisdiction over Roman interests for almost three and twenty. (6, 51, 1–2)

After his father, also named Tiberius Claudius Nero, fought unsuccessfully against Octavian at Perugia in the civil war, he fled with his wife and infant son to join Mark Antony's faction. When young Tiberius was four, his father was pardoned, returned to Italy, and yielded his wife Livia (although pregnant) to Octavian; when his father died it was the nine-year-old Tiberius who delivered the funeral oration. Thus, Tiberius grew up in the house of the man who had defeated and humiliated his father and seduced his mother. Moreover, he doubtless heard unstinting praise of his charming younger brother, Drusus.

Young Tiberius was understandably introverted, but he found contentment with Vipsania, the daughter of Marcus Agrippa by his first marriage. But this was not to last. When Agrippa died in 12 B.C.E., leaving his second wife Julia and five young children, it was to protect his grandchildren that Augustus and Livia forced Tiberius out of his happy marriage to marry Julia—his ostensible stepsister. Julia's open promiscuity and contempt for her new husband was such that she sent a letter abusing him to Augustus which, Tacitus suggests, was actually written by one of her lovers (*Annals* 1, 53). This increased Tiberius' resentment to the point that he withdrew from Rome to the island of Rhodes; even after the disgrace and banishment of Julia, Augustus did not at first allow him to return. Finally, after seven years in quasi-voluntary exile, Tiberius was recalled to Rome; two years later the deaths of Augustus' grandsons Gaius and Lucius forced the emperor to swallow hard and anoint Tiberius as his successor. Tiberius knew full well that he was no better than Augustus' fifth choice as his successor. For twelve more years, he remained in the shadow of his stepfather and was bullied by his mother until finally, in 14 C.E., at the age of 53, he became emperor. Such a turbulent life gives ample material to psychologizing historians—from Tacitus to our own day.

Tiberius learned early to conceal his personal feelings; when he allowed his humiliation over Julia to get the better of his self-restraint, he paid the price with a lengthy exile. Thus he became a master dissembler who appears in the pages of Tacitus like a Roman Hamlet careful to confide only in himself. Even at the time of his initial appearance in the Senate after Augustus' death, Tiberius feigned hesitance to unmask any potential opposition:

> Afterward it was recognized that his hesitancy had been brought on to gain an insight into the attitudes of the aristocracy too: he stored away their language and looks, twisting them into an accusation. (1, 7, 7)

Tacitus suggests that what once might have been a mere tactic of duplicity had now become an integral part of Tiberius' personality. Thus he appears in the speech given on his accession:

> More in such a speech was impressive than credible; and Tiberius' words, even on matters which he was not for concealing, were—whether by nature or habit—always weighed and dark; but on that occasion, when he was striving to hide his feelings deep down, their extra complication led to uncertainty and ambiguity. But the fathers, whose one dread was that they seemed to understand, poured out complaints, tears, and vows. (1, 11, 2–3)

In contemporary Washington, D.C., it has been said that the only thing more dangerous than being caught lying on tape is being secretly taped while telling the truth. Likewise, for both Tiberius and the Senate, truth was especially frightening; it was more comfortable and convenient to pretend not to understand or simply to lie. Thus Tacitus shows Tiberius lying repeatedly—to Germanicus, to courtiers, and to the assembled Senate. The emperor became the model of deception, and senators, equestrians, and freedmen followed his example in a world of flattery and deceit. Yet, despite his intentional *misleading* of others, Tiberius could himself mistakenly *misread* their motivations, as he did with Agrippina and Sejanus.[14] Deception and self-deception are aspects of the same culture of secrecy.

14. On misreading in *The Annals*, cf. O'Gorman (2000), 13–14, 92–97, passim.

The Greek idea of character included both the personal traits and the ethics of an individual, so ancient psychology sought not merely to understand the motives behind an individual's actions but to pass moral judgment on them. So it was with Tacitus. When Francis Bacon ranked Tacitus above Plato or Aristotle as a moralist, he meant that he preferred the historian's vivid psychological sketches of Sejanus, Tiberius, and Nero to the philosophers' discussions of abstract ethical principles. Many ancient writers were very interested in the creation of personality types by which they could more easily characterize or stereotype individuals for the purposes of drama, history, or, especially, rhetoric. Aristotle's student and successor Theophrastus sketched thirty such types in his book, *Characters*, and provided an ethical analysis of each of them. Roman orators developed rhetorical pictures of the tyrant, the benevolent ruler, the hero, the villain, the political opportunist, the informer, the virtuous wife, and so on.[15] But even as Tacitus uses such rhetorical types in the *Annals*, he diverges significantly from these simplistic templates. Though Tiberius and Nero were tyrants sharing certain similarities, dependent on overbearing mothers and bloodthirsty praetorian prefects, they were remarkably different as human beings. Most simply, the ebullient golden boy Nero expected, even demanded, to be universally loved and sought to remain in the spotlight, whereas the moody outsider Tiberius suspected that he was widely disliked. Tacitus understood why Nero built his extravagant villa—the Golden House—in the very center of Rome and why Tiberius' favored retreat was his isolated Villa Jovis on the island of Capri. Despite his use of rhetorical stereotypes, Tacitus put an individual stamp on the participants in his story.

Discussions of moral character in our own times often resort to an argument between the primacy of "nature" or "nurture." Are serial killers or political monsters (e.g., Hitler, Stalin) born naturally evil as a result of heredity, or is their bad behavior the result of an environment of abuse, poverty, trauma, and so on? Most ancient thinkers saw character as innate, and many looked to astrology for explanations.

15. Walker (1952), 204–243.

(Shakespeare has the villain Cassius rebut this view when he gives him the line: "The fault, dear Brutus, is not in our stars, but in ourselves.")[16] Tacitus confirms the traditional view of the power of destiny or what later was known in Christian terms as "predestination":

> However, the majority of mortals cannot be parted from the thought that things to come are marked out from the first origin of each individual. (6, 22, 3)

Nonetheless, ancient philosophers believed in the possibility of moral improvement through education. This is most notable in Plato's dialogues, in which Socrates led his followers to an understanding of virtue so that they could act upon it. In his division of Tiberius' character into five stages, Tacitus vacillates over the question of whether all was predetermined.[17] There are contradictions between the virtuous early life and the dark evil of his later years:

> In his behavior too there were differing phrases: one exceptional in life and reputation as long as he was a private individual or in commands under Augustus, one secretive and guileful in its fabrication of virtues while Germanicus and Drusus survived: he was simultaneously a blend of good and evil during his mother's lifetime; infamous for his savagery, but with his lusts cloaked, inasmuch as he felt love or fear respectively for Sejanus; lastly he erupted into crimes and degradations alike when at last, with his shame and dread removed, he had only himself to rely on. (6, 51, 3)

The traditional view has been that Tacitus suggests that Tiberius' evil core was only gradually revealed, but Tony Woodman's definitive interpretation of this passage sees genuine change in Tiberius' personality over time.[18]

Tacitus certainly was biased against Tiberius, and he brought that contempt into his history. He was not alone in that view;

16. Julius Caesar I, ii, 140–141.
17. Gill (1983), 469–487.
18. Woodman (1989).

Suetonius' biography also recounts Tiberius' moral failings, and that image survived even three centuries later in the emperor Julian's satirical essay *The Caesars:*

> The third to hasten in was Tiberius, with countenance solemn and grim, and an expression at once sober and martial. But as he turned to sit down his back was seen to be covered with countless scars, burns, and sores, painful welts and bruises, while ulcers and abscesses were as though branded thereon, the result of his self-indulgent and cruel life. (309)[19]

But there is much in Tacitus to indicate that Tiberius had been an excellent general, a fine administrator, and in fact something of an intellectual with a considerable sense of humor—albeit a dark one. In the notable passage following the first appearance of Sejanus, Tacitus attributes to the emperor fairness in making appointments, restraint in overruling magistrates, and a remarkable sense of justice:

> His own affairs Caesar handed to those in his highest regard and to some unknowns on the basis of their reputation; and, once enlisted, they were held continuously without limit, since many grew old in the same activities. The plebs kept being exhausted by an admittedly acute food supply, but there was no blame on the princeps's part: in fact he confronted the problems of infertile lands and rough seas as much as he could by his expenditure and assiduousness; and he made provision that the provinces were not disrupted by new burdens and tolerated their old ones without greed or cruelty from magistrates: corporal beatings and deprivations of property were absent. Caesar's estates across Italy were scarce, his slaves restrained, his household limited to a few freedmen. And, if ever he was in dispute with private individuals, there was the forum and justice. (4, 6, 3–4)

19. Translated by W. C. Wright in volume II of the Loeb Classical Library, edition of Julian, Cambridge, Mass., 1913.

That remarkable paragraph is of course intended to make the appearance of Sejanus and his corruption of the emperor all the more tragic.

Did Tacitus believe, as Lord Acton did, that power corrupts and absolute power corrupts absolutely? There are certainly indications of this, as when he has a senator argue that Tiberius "had become unhinged and changed under the influence of being master" (6, 48). But even if power corrupted Tiberius or just revealed his hidden vices, it does not mean that his antisocial qualities—loneliness, gloom, paranoid suspicion—were the result of what the Romans called *ingenium*, innate traits acquired at birth. They were more likely the result of his youthful traumas, inflamed by the infidelity of his wife Julia, his overbearing mother, and the betrayal of Sejanus—the one adult friend he trusted for having saved his life. In the tragedy of *Annals* 1–6, the greatest victim is Tiberius.

The successors of Tiberius—Caligula, Claudius, and Nero—were descended from the family of Germanicus, and the authors writing under their reigns consistently blackened the image of Tiberius. When Tacitus disagrees with these sources, he seems to moderate them. In the words of Sir Ronald Syme, "Tacitus took that picture. He cleansed it of trivial accretions, heightened the colors, sharpened the outline, and converted it into a work of art."[20] Tacitus preferred to ignore the later histories in favor of contemporary documents, so a particular pleasure in his pages is catching echoes of the voice of Tiberius: his keen intelligence and his sarcastic wit. And there are times when a seeming wisecrack is actually a shrewd expression of policy or law. To an informer's frivolous accusation of perjury against a political enemy, Tiberius pithily responded (1, 74), *deorum iniurias dis curae* ("the gods' injuries will be the gods' concern"), which was in fact a principle of Roman law.[21]

The emperor had brains, aesthetic tastes, and a black sense of humor—a remarkable combination for any ruler.[22] Tacitus is not primarily interested in the personality of Tiberius, however, but

20. Syme (1958), 421.

21. *Annals* 1, 74. Cf. Sinclair (1992), 397–403.

22. Syme (1974), 496, compares Tiberius to Proust's Baron de Charlus.

rather in the moral judgment he should pass upon him. He examines his psychology to understand and explain the ethical failings of the emperor. Tacitus did not put Tiberius on a metaphorical couch to understand, much less justify, his pathology or even his actions, although at times he certainly did that. In the final analysis, Tiberius had to take responsibility for his own life. Tacitus concludes his treatment of Tiberius with a harsh but fair judgment, *suo ingenio tantum utebatur* ("he had only himself to rely upon"). The historian was most interested in explicating Tiberius as a moral example to others, in the writer's own time and in the future. Tacitus certainly achieved that goal.

·7·

Consorts of the Caesars

The women who appear in Roman historical sources are usually from the upper classes, and their importance comes from
their connection by marriage or blood to politically important
men. Even under the Republic, it was clear that upper-class Roman
women were more independent than women in ancient Greece: at
home, they were not only in charge of childrearing but also of man-
aging the household economy; outside the home, they attended
dinners, religious rituals, and performances, and even frequented
the baths. Although some aristocratic women exercised political influence through their husbands or sons, it was only under the
empire that the women of the imperial household wielded hitherto
undreamed-of power.

In the last decades of the Roman Republic, women such as
Clodia (the notorious lover of Catullus), Fulvia (Mark Antony's
third wife), and Cleopatra were pilloried by Cicero and others for
their sexual as well as their political activities, practices that were often
indistinguishable in these hostile sources. The civil wars between Antony and Octavian produced a propaganda campaign drawing on the
full repertory of sexual invective, and the deaths of Antony and
Cleopatra allowed Augustus to affirm the reestablishment of

"traditional Roman values." It was immorality, he said, that had imperiled the Republic, and uncontrolled sexual freedom—especially by women—that destroyed the family, society, and consequently masculinity itself; he passed his laws on adultery in 18 B.C.E. Few contemporaries would have forgotten that Augustus himself had, twenty years earlier, married the already pregnant Livia immediately after divorcing Scribonia, who also was pregnant—certainly Tacitus remembered it.

Augustus made "moral revival" an important part of his political program, and it is evident from the monuments of Augustan art how important his own family was in promoting themes of peace, harmony, and fecundity. On the Altar of Augustan Peace (*Ara Pacis*) Augustus and Livia lead their children and grandchildren in the grand procession that occurred at the dedication of the monument in 13 B.C.E. The family was an integral part of the Augustan ideology; his new legislation promoted fertility and criminalized adultery. Augustus became the Father of the country (*pater patriae*) as Livia was the Mother, and busts of the women of the imperial family appeared throughout the Mediterranean. As Augustus made the Roman state into a hereditary monarchy, family prestige was paramount, and women were essential to the succession. Already in the third paragraph of the *Annals*, Tacitus turns his attention to Augustus' family and issues of dynastic succession.

Despite their wealth and prestige, nNo Roman woman actually ruled the empire in her own name, as some foreign queens had done: Cleopatra over Egypt, Boudicca over the Britons, or, in a later era, Zenobia over Palmyra in Syria. Roman political power, from kings and magistrates to emperors, was exercised by men or in their name; women could exercise power only indirectly. Nevertheless, thanks to the *Annals*, there is recognition that women were among the most powerful and dynamic figures in the Julio-Claudian court. Their power and their court intrigues led Roman writers—and they were, of course, all male—to attack women's education, their political influence, their wealth, and their sexuality. In his innuendos Tacitus is not far from the contemporary satirists Martial and Juvenal. His *Annals* rarely gives these powerful women a voice, but he allows senators to attribute to them intentions and actions that add to the dark pall that he casts over the entire Julio-Claudian era. He records at length the vitriolic motion of Severus Caecina to prohibit the wives of governors from accompanying them to their provinces:

> In the company of women there were elements who prolonged peace by their luxuriousness, deferred war because of their alarm, and transformed a Roman column into something resembling a barbarian procession. The sex was not only weak and unequal to toil but—if the license were allowed them—savage, self-aggrandizing and greedy for power: they strode among the soldiers, had centurions to hand. (3, 33, 2–3)

Tacitus has often been labeled a misogynist, but that characterization is too simple, even anachronistic, depending as it does on each society's notion of the proper role of women.[1] A twenty-first-century critic might consider an emphasis on women's "weakness" misogynistic, but for millennia that was accepted as a biological and sociological given. Tacitus certainly regards some powerful women as worthy of admiration, and his own warm relations with his wife and mother-in-law are recorded in the autobiographical passages (44–45) of his *Agricola*. When he reports the arguments defending women against Caecina's motion (which the Senate rejected), that defense is paternalistic but hardly misogynist:

> "Husbands were often corrupted by the crookedness of their wives"; but surely not all the unmarried were therefore unsullied? . . . It was unreasonable that our own masculine failures should be expressed in other terms, for it was the man's fault if the female exceeded her limit. Moreover it was wrong that, on account of the weak will of one or two, husbands should be deprived of partnership in their prosperity and adversity. (3, 34, 3–5)

1. Barrett (1996), 205.

Tacitus does not hate women, but he hates the bad behavior of some—and there was much bad behavior at the Julio-Claudian court. But he frequently expresses the perennial Roman fear that a strong woman—*dux femina*—would usurp male power. We will see that the text of the *Annals* presents vivid examples of the Julio-Claudian women making just such attempts to receive ambassadors, speak to the troops, and participate in political and judicial decisions.

1 | Octavia and Julia

The first woman who formed part of Augustus' political intrigues was his dearly beloved elder sister, Octavia. Since she died a quarter-century before her brother, in 11 B.C.E., Tacitus mentions her only in passing when he comments that Augustus planned to use her son Marcellus as a bulwark of his succession (1, 3), and that he had also "enticed" Mark Antony into an alliance through his marriage to her (1, 10). Octavia was loyal both to her brother and her (second) husband, Antony—certainly longer than either of them deserved. Plutarch called her "a wonder of a woman" in his *Life of Antony* (31, 4), and, after the death of Antony and Cleopatra, she raised their children as her own. Her son Marcellus was married to Augustus' daughter, Julia, in 25 B.C.E., but died two years later. Octavia had financial independence and was a generous patron of a good portion of the "Augustan" building program. Despite her active political and diplomatic activities, ancient sources have little negative to say of her.

Octavia's younger daughter, Antonia, married Livia's son Drusus and was mother of Germanicus and Claudius. Antonia was particularly attached to the handsome and accomplished Germanicus, yet when funeral ceremonies were held for him, she did not participate. Although some attributed her absence to illness or uncontrollable grief, Tacitus voices his suspicions:

(I am inclined more easily to believe that Tiberius and Augusta, who made no attempt to come out of the house, restrained her, so it should appear that their sorrow was matching and that it was by the mother's example that the grandmother and uncle too were held back.) (3, 3, 3)

Antonia's finest moment was doubtless the unmasking of Sejanus' evil plots to her brother-in-law Tiberius, then isolated on Capri. It is unfortunate that that episode was described in the lost fifth book of the *Annals*, since it would be interesting to read Tacitus' account of the courageous intervention of a noble woman.

It was the only child of Augustus, his daughter Julia, who became the precursor of the image of sexually voracious Julio-Claudian women. Marcellus died two years after his marriage to the fourteen-year-old Julia, and the emperor, seeking an heir, married Julia, then sixteen, to a much older Agrippa, by whom she had five children (Gaius, Lucius, Postumus, Julia, and Agrippina). Tacitus reports that although Julia had been unfaithful to Agrippa, she did not become overtly promiscuous until after his death when she was rather heartlessly given to Tiberius. Julia was treated as a dynastic pawn, but Tacitus shows her little sympathy in his obituary, although he discreetly mentions only Gracchus as her lover, as opposed to the censorious philosopher Seneca, who mentions "scores" of infidelities.[2]

In the same year [14 C.E.] Julia passed her final day, who for her immorality had formerly been shut away by her father Augustus on the island of Pandateria, then subsequently in the town of the Regini who live near the Sicilian strait. She had been in a marriage to Tiberius while Gaius and Lucius Caesar flourished, and had spurned him as her inferior; and no other reason was so close to Tiberius' heart for his withdrawal to Rhodes. Once he acquired command, he ensured the annihilation of the outcast by deprivation and protracted atrophy, disgraced as she was and (after the killing of Postumus Agrippa) destitute of all hope, deeming that her execution would be obscured by the length of her exile. (1, 53, 1–2)

2. Seneca, *On Benefits* 6, 32.

Since all other ancient sources are equally scathing about Julia's conduct, Tacitus is here simply following the universal opinion. But there is also a tradition of her loving, bantering relationship with her father, which must have made the public scandal more hurtful and more embarrassing to the devoted, and ostensibly moralistic, Augustus.

2 | Livia

The first woman actually mentioned by name in the *Annals* is Livia, the wife of Caesar Augustus for fifty-one years. Near the beginning of his book, as the historian sets the stage for the death of Augustus and the accession of Tiberius, three rapid mentions of Livia prepare for the malign influence of women at the imperial court. He first suggested that Augustus' young grandsons died either by fate or "the guile of their stepmother Livia" (1, 3). The simple word "stepmother" (*noverca*)—freighted with hostile implications in Roman culture—alerts the reader to Livia's suspicious jealousy. (Livia was in fact the step-grandmother of the young men and became their "stepmother" only when Augustus adopted them.)[3] Later in the same sentence Tacitus continues that Tiberius was adopted and paraded through the assembled ranks of the army "not by his mother's secret intrigues, as formerly, but by her open instigation." As if these innuendos were not enough, Tacitus prepares us for the death of the ailing Augustus by echoing complaints of the majority of the crowd about their future under Tiberius:

> In addition, they said, there was his mother, with her womanly unruliness: his enslavement to the female would be compulsory . . . (1, 4, 5)

Tacitus then presents Livia as taking control of the succession, with a passing comment that, in connection with the emperor's death, "some suspected foul play on the part of his wife." She recalls

3. Barrett (2001), 171–175; Barrett (2002), 70; 241–242.

Tiberius from Illyricum to be present at the emperor's deathbed so that there could be a simultaneous announcement of Augustus' death and Tiberius' succession. Tacitus makes it seem that she instigated—with a "stepmother's hatred"—the murder of Agrippa Postumus, Augustus' last surviving grandson, who had been previously exiled for his violent temperament. (His daughter, Julia, and granddaughter Julia were also in exile for immorality.) She further persuaded her son, who was going to report this to the Senate, that such matters—"the mysteries of the household, the advice of friends and the services of soldiers"—should remain private. It is an early expression of what we today call executive privilege (1, 6).[4]

What are we to make of this? Other Roman sources depict Livia as a traditional Republican *matrona* of great beauty and impeccable sexual morality, who managed her household with great skill. She was devoted to Augustus and, like him, beautified the city with gifts of buildings and public gardens. She tried her best to manage the unruly imperial family, beset by occasional scandals and sudden deaths during the long reign of Augustus. (The marital and succession problems in the contemporary houses of Windsor and Grimaldi show that dynastic management remains difficult, if less bloody.) Suetonius preserves her letters to Augustus over the disabled young Claudius, and she had to deal with a promiscuous daughter-in-law and a moody, antisocial son. The most famous surviving statue of Augustus was commissioned by Livia for her villa at Prima Porta— her son Tiberius appears on the emperor's decorated breastplate. At Augustus' death she was his coheir with Tiberius and was adopted into the Julian family with her own honorific title, Augusta.

While the "historical" Livia is largely hidden from our sight, not least by her own discretion, it is clear that she had many friends and allies among the Roman elite. After her death Tiberius even complained about her friendships, presumably because she protected her favorites from him on more than one occasion. The Vestal Virgin Urgulania, "whom friendship with Augusta had elevated above the laws," arrogantly refused to appear in court, and Livia even

---

4. I follow here the interpretation of this passage in Woodman (1995).

persuaded the emperor to testify on her friend's behalf in a private lawsuit, thus hoping to intimidate her opponent (2, 34). Among her other dubious friends was Plancina, whose husband, Piso, committed suicide over the Germanicus affair. Livia shielded Plancina from any punishment—as is recorded both by Tacitus and in the inscriptional record of the trial, discussed in chapter 2. Her extraordinary authority created a second locus of power that made state administration much more complicated. This is not to say that Livia was any more corrupt than the leading politicians of the Roman Republic, who also viewed the courts as another forum in which to display personal and political loyalty. But she was a *woman* engaging in male behavior.

Tacitus, in fact, uses Livia to foreshadow the true female monster of his book, the younger Agrippina, who haunts the reigns of both Claudius and her son, Nero. He had reported that once, while Tiberius was sacrificing to Augustus, her mother Agrippina had claimed precedence, saying that "*she* was his real image, the offspring of his heavenly blood" (4, 52). Just as the Julio-Claudians themselves emphasize their dynastic connections, Tacitus likewise uses these links for allusion and innuendo. The historian's spiteful picture of Livia's friendships and palace plots could certainly be as easily applied to her husband or any other politician. When he says in her obituary (5, 1, 3) that she was "a good match for the qualities of her husband and the hypocrisy of her son," he virtually admits that a woman's "schemes" and "intrigues" can otherwise be called "diplomacy," "negotiation," or "dissimulation." Tacitus' hostility to Livia is in part rhetorical: she was the antecedent of the destructive empress who lived until his own boyhood. (The younger Agrippina was murdered in 59 C.E., when Tacitus was about four years old, and she must have repeatedly been held up as an ogre during his youth.) When, after Nero's accession, she had Junius Silanus murdered as "the first death of the new principate" (13, 1), Tacitus obviously recalled the murder of Agrippa Postumus in 14, which he had called "the first crime of the new principate" (1, 6). But the importance is in the foreshadowing; the more remote deeds of Livia are rhetorically arranged to demonstrate continuity with Agrippina. Suetonius never uses the term "stepmother" for Livia, and no other sources are as negative as Tacitus, with his repeated innuendos. It was Agrippina who poisoned Claudius, her husband, and who pushed her son to the throne ahead of her stepson. She was a supreme intriguer, as demonstrated by her seduction of, and marriage to, her uncle Claudius, her manipulation of the freedmen, and her open intrusion into state politics. Tacitus paints Livia with the same brush to prepare for the monster in the later act of his drama. The last mention of Livia in the *Annals* is at Claudius' funeral, where the historian tells us that Agrippina's magnificence now rivaled that of her great-grandmother (12, 69). Livia is repeatedly used by Tacitus as a mirror of her great-granddaughter.

Another telling parallel was between the mothers and their imperial sons. There is little question that Tiberius was respectful toward Livia and avoided any public confrontation. Even Tacitus suggests that in 23 C.E. there was still harmony, or at least the hostility was hidden. If he does not document such hostility, it is probably because he cannot. Perhaps the greatest tribute the unsympathetic historian pays to the first empress follows her obituary, when he acknowledges her role in keeping her son and his minions under control:

> Thenceforward it was sheer, oppressive despotism. With Augusta safe and sound, there had still been a refuge, because Tiberius' compliance toward his mother was deep-rooted and Sejanus would not dare to overrun her parental authority; but now, as if released from harness, they charged ahead. (5, 3, 1)

Her son did not even return from Capri to attend her funeral; she only received divine honors with the accession to power of her grandson Claudius.

Tacitus continually treats Livia very harshly. Even when he tells of her compassion for the younger Julia, he feels it necessary to append a sneer:

> There for twenty years she had endured exile, supported by the help of Augusta, who, though she had secretly

undermined her step-children while they flourished, openly displayed pity toward them when they were blighted. (4, 71, 4)

Yet the historian surprises us with a formal obituary at her death in 29 C.E. at the age of 89, in which he acknowledges Livia's decorum and nobility:

> Julia Augusta met her death in extreme old age, a woman of the most brilliant nobility through her Claudian family and by adoption into the Livii and Julii. Her first marriage and children were with Tiberius Nero, who, a refugee in the Perusine war, returned to the City on the pledging of peace between Sex. Pompeius and the triumvirs. Thereupon Caesar, in his desire for her good looks, removed her from her husband (her unwillingness being uncertain)—and so swiftly that he allowed not even an interval for childbirth, installing her at his own hearth while she was still heavily pregnant. She produced no progeny thereafter, but, being connected to the blood of Augustus through the union of Agrippina and Germanicus, had great-grandchildren in common with him. In the purity of her house she conformed to old-time convention but was affable beyond what females of antiquity approved. (5, 1, 1–3)

Despite the passing mention of her maternal imperiousness— Tacitus (4, 57) had already cited her bossiness and greed as a possible reason for Tiberius' move to Capri—this is a remarkably positive assessment. What aristocratic Roman *matrona* was not a bit imperious? As in his obituary of Tiberius, we seem to find the historian at his most measured. The puzzled reader might understandably wonder, "What did Tacitus *really* think?"

An even more sympathetic account might have reported that the tragedy of the Julio-Claudians derived from Livia and Augustus' inability to produce children of their own. (The single child was premature and stillborn.)[5] In a time of uncertain life expectancy,

5. Suetonius *Augustus* 63.

Livia's task was to ensure peaceful successions within an often rancorous blended family. Deaths and misfortunes were unfairly laid at the feet of a woman who embodied all of the virtues of a Roman *matrona*. Much worse would follow her.

3 | Agrippina the Elder

L ivia's most malign influence was upon the elder Agrippina, the proud widow of her grandson Germanicus. On several occasions Tacitus mentions Livia's hostility toward Agrippina, although on the first occasion it is clear that the family tensions had causes on both sides:

> In addition there were womanly affronts, with Livia's stepmotherly goadings of Agrippina, and Agrippina herself a little too volatile, except that, with her chastity and love for her husband, she turned her (albeit untamed) spirit to good effect. (1, 33, 3)

In the first three books of the *Annals*, Agrippina is depicted positively, despite her stubborn pride. Since that arrogance showed itself in support of her husband and in defense of her children, Tacitus finds her inner toughness quite admirable. When she resists being sent to safety during a mutiny, it is her husband who weeps:

> After much hesitation, during which his contemptuous wife attested that she was sprung from Divine Augustus and was by no means inferior in the face of dangers, finally, embracing her womb with much weeping, he drove her to leave. (1, 40, 3)

But it is against the German army led by Arminius that Agrippina asserted herself dramatically to prevent the Roman army from fleeing back across the Rhine:

> A female of mighty spirit assumed during those days the responsibilities of a leader and distributed clothing and

dressings to the soldiers according to each man's need or injuries. C. Plinius, the writer of the Germanic wars, said that she stood at the head of the bridge, extending praise and gratitude to the returning legions. That made an unusually deep penetration into Tiberius's mind: it was not the case that her concerns were straightforward, he reflected, nor was it with the aim of opposing foreigners that she was seeking the soldiers' affections. . . . Already Agrippina was more influential with the armies than legates, than leaders: the woman had suppressed a mutiny which the princeps's name had been unable to stop. (1, 69, 1–4)

If Tiberius recognized the danger in Agrippina's haughtiness as the only surviving grandchild of Augustus—and she would pay dearly for it—he was not alone. On his deathbed her husband Germanicus had urged her to rein in her headstrong nature and not to provoke Tiberius. He knew well that her behavior was acceptable as long as it was in support of her husband; without a husband such female aggression would endanger her entire family. So the tone of Tacitus changes when the widow Agrippina continues to pursue her ambitions and puts her children at risk. Faced with the increasing power of Sejanus, she foolishly laid herself open to his machinations. Since the children of Germanicus blocked his own dream of succeeding Tiberius, he used Agrippina's "arrogance" to arouse Livia's old suspicions and gradually persuaded the emperor to exile Agrippina and her sons—except Caligula.

For his account of Agrippina, Tacitus had an extraordinary source—the memoirs of her daughter. It is clear that the memoirs of Agrippina the Younger were understandably hostile to Tiberius and to Livia as well, even though she was the younger Agrippina's own great-grandmother. The younger Agrippina, like her mother, proudly insisted on her lineage from Augustus himself, so that Livia, Tiberius, and Claudius were styled as interlopers with no Julian blood. These memoirs and other sources provided stories, rumors, and angry tirades that allowed Tacitus to provide a selective picture of the female rivalries of the imperial family. But it was Tacitus himself who shaped the surviving story of the elder Agrippina, as her once admirable courage developed into self-destructive foolhardiness.

4 | Messalina

If Livia was the first empress to be mentioned in the *Annals*, she was already the dowager when Tacitus begins his story with the accession of Tiberius in 14 C.E. The next reigning imperial consort does not appear in Tacitus' text for more than three decades. Tiberius' wife Julia had long been imprisoned on an island, and she died (or was killed) soon after his accession. Thereafter a long gap in the transmitted text of the *Annals* effaces the entire reign of Caligula (37–41) and the first six years of Claudius (41–47). Two years before his accession, the forty-eight-year-old Claudius took his second cousin, Valeria Messalina, as his third wife. She was the great-granddaughter of Augustus' sister, Octavia. Her age is uncertain, but she was most likely fourteen.

Although the missing books had almost certainly provided an earlier hostile sketch of Messalina, the beginning of the preserved text introduces the empress as motivated by jealousy and avarice, with an entourage of henchmen to carry out her wishes.

> For she believed that Valerius Asiaticus, twice consul, had formerly been Poppaea's adulterer; and, at the same time gaping for the gardens begun by Lucullus and which was developing with distinctive magnificence, she sent Suillius to accuse them both. (11, 1, 1)

It seems that Messalina begrudged Asiaticus his liaison with Poppaea, the beautiful mother of Nero's second wife, Poppaea, because she had once been loved by the actor Mnester, with whom Messalina herself was for several years utterly besotted. If this seems convoluted, it was no more so than are the revelations of contemporary tabloids. The empress's chief motivation, however, was Asiaticus' elaborate Persian-style gardens on the Pincian hill—now the

Villa Borghese in northern Rome. Tacitus pictures her "gaping for the gardens" (*hortis inhians*), the same words he uses when the younger Agrippina lusts after the gardens of Statilius Taurus (12, 59), to indicate their intertwining of sex with their passion for real estate would feel at home in the evening soap operas of twenty-first-century television. Messalina skillfully had her minions cast Asiaticus as dangerous to the regime and, by playing on his fears, pushed the vacillating Claudius to have the praetorian prefect arrest him.

> He was given no chance of a hearing in the senate: he was heard in a bedroom, before Messalina, and with Suillius hurling at him imputations of corrupting the soldiers (who, he alleged, had been obligated by money, illicit sex, and every outrage), and then of adultery with Poppaea, and finally of physical softness. (11, 2, 1)

Here we are introduced to the senatorial stereotype of the bumbling Claudius oblivious to the machinations of his wives and freedmen. Messalina was even present at the trial *in camera*—a remarkable precedent! That negative image of the emperor has been challenged during the last century by scholars who found much in the sources—including contemporary inscriptions and papyri—to demonstrate that Claudius and his staff achieved some remarkable feats. Some of these will be detailed in the ninth chapter: the conquest of Britain, a new port at Ostia capable of welcoming larger grain ships, humane legislation concerning usury and slavery, as well as a thorough overhaul of government and the efficient collection of taxes. Claudius is hardly alone among rulers to see more clearly matters of policy than the psychology and personal flaws of his family and his entourage. If the emperor was unduly controlled by corrupt underlings, some of them must have had adequate competence to produce a budget surplus in an empire of sixty million subjects. We should not be as harsh as the senatorial historians have been on that unfortunate emperor.

Tacitus portrays Messalina as an instigator of violent cruelty through an excess of desire. Not only did her sexuality subject lovers of every class to her willfulness, but Claudius' deep attachment to her allowed her to use imperial power to gain her goals. Although scholars diverge on whether Messalina acted as a flighty, spoiled, and lascivious teenager or a calculating manipulator who actually had political aspirations, Tacitus in his surviving pages would most likely prefer the former view.[6] Actors and senators alike had to submit to Messalina's desires or be killed by an unwitting Claudius, who himself had been emasculated by the power of his wife. Juvenal's bitingly misogynistic sixth satire and Pliny the Elder's *Natural History* even portray Messalina plying the trade of a prostitute in a Roman brothel, but such lurid stories would be offensive to Tacitus. He prefers to condemn by innuendo and implication.

The most theatrical episode concerning Messalina—Tacitus calls it *fabulosus* (11, 27)—was her public passion for C. Silius, with its disastrous consequences for her, her lover, Claudius, and the empire itself. It was truly the turning point of the reign.

> She had become so inflamed for C. Silius, the finest of the Roman youth, that she evicted Junia Silana, a noble lady, from her marriage to him and took control of a now available adulterer. Nor was Silius unaware of the outrage or the danger; but—with extermination certain if he declined; with some hope of deception; and with rewards great at the same time—he found consolation in shutting out the future and enjoying the present. She for her part—not stealthily but with a sizable escort—frequented his home, clung to him when he emerged, and lavished wealth and honors upon him; finally, as if the transference of fortune were already complete, slaves, freedmen, the very trappings of the princeps were to be seen at the adulterer's house. (11, 12, 2–3)

What a remarkable scene—more worthy of a lurid gothic novel than a political history. The graphic image of imperial freedmen and furniture being delivered to the emperor's rival is perhaps more

6. Levick (1990), 66–67, argues for a political ploy; Joshel (1997), 221–254, prefers to emphasize motives of desire.

startling than the adultery itself. Mere adultery was already boringly familiar to this young woman—Messalina was still only about twenty-two and was eager for still new excesses. Silius was prepared to move from the bedroom to the throne room—a veritable coup d'etat. And Tacitus provides him with all the necessary rationalizations to appeal to the empress.

Tacitus assures his reader that Messalina's only scruples arose from her fear of being used, not any question of morality or loyalty. The bizarreness of the situation was not lost on the historian. Messalina is so sated by the ordinary vices that she desired marriage for "that magnitude of notoriety which is the ultimate pleasure for the prodigal" (11, 26, 3). In a world turned upside down, the legal status of *infamia*—normally bestowed on pimps, prostitutes, actors, and other morally dubious characters—is here sought through marriage. It almost seems that for Tacitus, Messalina is driven not by love or even lust, but rather by a need to flout all convention. Perhaps it is easier to understand her as a twenty-first-century Goth teenager with tattoos and body piercing than as something so ordinary as an imperial adulteress.

We have already seen how the headstrong girl and her suddenly dynamic paramour enact the Dionysian drama of a bigamous marriage while Claudius was in Ostia. Her disbelieving husband vacillates until his energetic freedmen force him to take action. Messalina walks across Rome from her precious Lucullan gardens to the Ostian gate to intercept Claudius' return, and she tries to use her children and a Vestal Virgin to plead her case, while Narcissus takes over investigation, trial, and execution of both conspirators and sympathizers.

> For, when Claudius had returned home and been soothed by a timely dinner, on growing warm with wine, he ordered someone to go and tell "the pitiable woman" (this is the expression they maintain he used) to be present on the next day to make her case. When Narcissus heard this, and anger started to wane and love return, the approaching night and the man's memory of his wife's bedroom became grounds for fear if there was any hesitation: so he burst out and told

the centurions and the tribune who were present to proceed with the slaughter. (11, 37, 2)

Her mother advised Messalina to die honorably; there was no other path open to her.

Sex is so often shorthand for female corruption in Roman writers that it is nearly impossible to sift through the sexual disinformation to find nuggets of truth.[7] Sexual behavior was an integral part of political invective, and it was a standard element in the arsenal of lawyers and classroom rhetoricians. Tacitus gives no direct speech to Messalina; her role is to provoke others through her behavior. The senators can talk, but they have yielded action to a woman. They, and her lover Silius, might yearn for power, but Messalina actually had it—even if she used it as a plaything to satisfy her whims, petulance, cruelty, greed, and seemingly prodigious lust. If Tacitus and his modern reader find her behavior inscrutable, it is because we expect power to be a goal rather than merely a means. Her successor Agrippina is more transparent.

5 | Agrippina the Younger

Tacitus depicts the younger Agrippina as the perfect monster: the homicidal wife of Claudius and the incestuous mother of Nero, as domineering and (temporarily) politically effective as any male member of the Julio-Claudian family. She combined a proud sense of family entitlement, steely determination, and sexual manipulation to impose her will on emperors, senators, philosophers, and freedmen. Tacitus chooses words from rhetorical invective to pass judgment on her: *atrox* (cruel), *servitium* (slavery), and *ferox* (fierce), which recalls his earlier description of her mother's *ferocia* and her own desire for *dominatio*. He clearly loathed the woman.

Modern scholars have discussed the source of this obvious hatred. A recent sympathetic biographer of Agrippina, Anthony

7. Joshel (1997), 226.

Barrett, suggests that Tacitus' hostility to Agrippina grows out of his evident bias against the entire imperial system of the Julio-Claudians, yet Tacitus does not merely accept scurrilous rumors but evaluates them.[8] Judith Ginsburg, who provides what she calls a "resisting reading" of the sources on Agrippina, points out that Tacitus has created a literary construct that is unlikely to be a reflection of the "real woman."[9] Other opinions have ranged from widespread criticism of Tacitus for misogyny to Sir Ronald Syme's praise of the historian's picture of Agrippina as "wholly authentic" and his depiction of Julio-Claudian women overall as "terrible and truthful."[10]

There are certainly reasons that a senatorial historian would be critical of Agrippina, not least the disastrous reign of her son, Nero. Tacitus was also offended by her "masculine" resolve to enter publicly the political and even military worlds. But most of all it is her image as the sexual transgressor that inspires innuendo and open hostility. Agrippina's sexual transgressions were not mere adultery but incest with her brother, uncle, and son. If she and her sisters were victims of their brother Caligula, she was the agent in choosing her future paramours. In Tacitus' view she seduced Claudius into marriage and slept with his freedman Pallas to ensure his support. Others who were sexually linked with Agrippina included the praetorian prefects Faenius Rufus and Tigellinus and even the philosopher Seneca. But these are small fry indeed, compared to her infamous seduction of her son, Nero. How much was true is less important than the effect these rumors had on the senatorial elite and historians like Cornelius Tacitus.

6 | Agrippina as Wife of Claudius

Aside from the mention of her marriage to Domitius Aheno-barbus in 28 C.E. (at the age of thirteen), Tacitus says nothing of Agrippina until she appears two decades later as Claudius'

8. Barrett (1996), 205.
9. Ginsburg (2006), 10.
10. On Roman misogyny, cf. Watson (1995), and Syme (1958), 535.

prospective bride (4, 75). For the ten years missing in the text (37–47), other sources provide the principal events in her life: the birth of Nero (37 C.E.); her seduction and banishment by her brother Caligula; and her return after his death (41 C.E.). (It is a bit surprising that, in his catalogue of Agrippina's perversions in *Annals* 14, 4, Tacitus makes no mention of any liaison with Caligula.) Even if the complete text of Tacitus had survived, Agrippina would have been a minor character through the years in which Messalina was still alive and ferocious toward any rivals. It was not until the mature age of 33 that the princess moves to the center of the stage.

If Tacitus was the most accomplished tragic dramatist of the Roman Empire, he shows his knack for comedy in the opening of Book 12. The "debate" over who should become the new empress of Rome is a parody of a meeting of the imperial *consilium*—an advisory privy council. It is unknown from any other sources and is probably a dramatized creation of Tacitus:

> As for Pallas, he praised especially in Agrippina the fact that with her she brought Germanicus' grandson, altogether worthy of a Commander's fortune: the princeps should espouse a noble stock such as the posterity of the Julian and Claudian families, lest a lady of proved fertility, her youth unimpaired, should take the brilliancy of the Caesars to another household.
>
> It was these points which prevailed, aided by Agrippina's allurements: by going to him very frequently under the guise of their relationship, she lured her uncle with the result that she was preferred to the others and, though not yet his wife, already enjoyed wifely power. (12, 2, 3–3, 1)

The historian provides a group of stereotypes from Roman comedy. Plautus provides many examples of the *senex stultus*—the somewhat dense old man who is manipulated by his wife and especially by slaves, pimps, and freedmen. Claudius is portrayed as being passive as well as open to his niece's sexual blandishments to decide the issue. The imperial freedmen assume the guise of the deceitful servant (*servus fallax*).[11] Here also we find the recurrent theme of the *saeva noverca*—the cruel stepmother who will resort to intrigue and poison was a popular stereotype. The same invocation of *novercalibus odiis* ("a stepmother's hatred") is applied to both Livia (1, 6) and Agrippina; and both empresses took charge after the deaths of Augustus and Claudius by barring the doors of the palace until the succession of their sons had been secured (1, 5; 12, 68). Tacitus uses the same phrase, *muliebris impotentia* "female lack of self-control"), to describe the unseemly political involvement of both Livia and Agrippina—another link between them.[12] Tacitus includes arguments of Pallas which deserve careful consideration. Amidst the allegations of seduction, there were excellent reasons to choose the daughter of the immensely popular Germanicus. After the embarrassment and execution of Messalina, Claudius needed to secure the loyalty of the troops. Agrippina would bring together the factions of the imperial family that had been at odds since the reign of Tiberius—the "Julians" and the "Claudians"—and it might be dangerous to allow her to marry an ambitious senator. So it was a more sensible decision at the time than Tacitus presents it—however badly it would turn out.

Tacitus would emphasize—early and often—the new empress' desire for control (*spes dominandi*) and, secure in her own power over Claudius, her willingness to do anything to ensure her son's succession (12, 8; 14, 2). After her death Tacitus reports her earlier determination, or perhaps it was maternal self-confidence, that she would always control her son:

> This was the end which Agrippina many years before had believed would be hers and had belittled: when she was consulting the Chaldaeans about Nero, they replied that he would achieve command and would slaughter his mother; and she for her part said, "Let him slaughter, provided he achieves command." (14, 9, 3)

11. On these comic stereotypes, cf. Ginsburg (2006), 23.
12. 1, 4; 12, 57. On women's paths to power, cf. Santoro L'hoir (2006), 111–157.

Tacitus exploits this image of the evil stepmother, in that she has Claudius, in a speech prepared for him by her lover Pallas, not only adopt Nero before the Senate but give him priority over his own son, Britannicus:

[In 50 C.E.,] adoption was being hurried up for Domitius [Nero] on the instigation of Pallas, who, bound to Agrippina as the arranger of her wedding and soon entangled with her in illicit sex, was goading Claudius to heed the interests of the state and to place a protective cordon of security around the boyhood of Britannicus: similarly in the house of Divine Augustus, although he had been supported by his grandsons, his stepsons had thrived; Tiberius, besides his own stock, had enlisted Germanicus: the princeps too should equip himself with the young man likely to take on a share of his cares. (12, 25, 1)

Taken at face value, the arguments are cogent: Augustus and Tiberius both lost several heirs, and keeping others in reserve is good policy for the family and the state. But in this passage the political reasoning takes second place to the sexual control exercised by Agrippina, the manipulation exercised by Pallas, and the weakness of Claudius. Poor Britannicus later appears in a toga, whereas Nero—only three years older!—wears the uniform of a triumphant general (12, 41). The stepmother has succeeded.

Not all of Agrippina's transgressions were those of a promiscuous woman or a stepmother; in other ways Tacitus portrays her as unwomanly in her arrogance. To show her influence over foreign peoples, she asked that the town of the Ubii on the Rhine (where she had been born) be renamed in her honor. In 50 C.E. it was given the name *Colonia Agrippinensis* and still retains that designation as Cologne (Köln), Germany. But she went still further in appearing in a military role to accept homage from the conquered British chieftain Caratacus and his brothers:

And on release from their chains they for their part venerated Agrippina too, conspicuous not far away on another dais, using the same praise and gratitude as they had for the princeps. (It was of course a novelty, quite unfamiliar to the customs of the ancients, for a female to preside over Roman standards; but she was presenting herself as partner in the command once won by her ancestors.) (12, 37, 4)

It was not only her ancestors Augustus, Agrippa, and Germanicus who had won triumphs, but also "a woman of great courage who took on the duties of a commander"—her mother, the elder Agrippina. We have already seen how angry that presumption had made Tiberius (1, 69), but now the docile Claudius says nothing.

Tacitus provides the dramatic arc as the power of Agrippina leads to its inevitable goal—the murder of Claudius. Other sources, like Suetonius, have doubts about how Claudius was poisoned, but Tacitus presents it as a long-planned plot of Agrippina. She waited until his most loyal freedman, Narcissus, had left Rome to recover from an illness:

> Everything soon became so well known that writers of those times transmitted that the poison had been poured into a delectable dish of mushrooms and that the power of the medicament had not been recognized at once, whether through Claudius' insensibility or his wine-bibbing; at the same time an opening of his bowels seemed to have come to his rescue. Agrippina was therefore terrified, and, since she feared the ultimate, she spurned the resentment of immediacy and called upon the complicity of Xenophon, the doctor. He is believed to have inserted into the man's throat, as though to aid his efforts at vomiting, a feather smeared with a quick-seizing poison, not unaware that the most critical crimes are begun with peril but performed with profit. (12, 67, 1–2)

Once again, as with Livia at the death of Augustus, the news was suppressed until Nero could be presented and acclaimed *imperator* by the praetorians. The Senate docilely followed; the claims of Britannicus were prudently forgotten.

7 | Agrippina as Mother of Nero

The opening of book 13 is intentionally ominous:

> The first death of the new principate was that of Junius
> Silanus, proconsul of Asia, contrived without Nero's knowl-
> edge through Agrippina's guile. (13, 1, 1)

The reference not only anticipates the official murders that will
follow, but looks back to the death of Agrippa Postumus that began
the reign of Tiberius. Agrippa was Augustus' grandson, and Silanus
was his great-great-grandson (as was Nero)—the main reason that
Tacitus offers for his death. Agrippina was responsible for a series of
dynastic murders to secure Nero's succession and her own dominance. This *ferocia* resulted in many deaths, including that of the able
freedman Narcissus. When Nero came to power, he gave the guards
the password, "Best of Mothers," but that was soon to change. Like
Tiberius, he tried to escape his mother's control and finally relied
on the praetorian prefect Burrus, his tutor Seneca, and a freedman
to provide buffers against her.

Agrippina's struggle for dominance continued through 54 and
55. Immediately after the young emperor's pious proclamation that
"the state and his household were separate (*discretam*)" (13, 4, 2),
Tacitus reports that the Senate sometimes met in the imperial palace where Agrippina could hear the deliberations separated (*discretam*) by a screen so that she was not seen (13, 5, 1). The repeated use
of the same word makes the irony clear. In the next paragraph Nero
is said to be "ruled" by a woman—the only time the word *regere* is
applied to a woman in all of Tacitus. More than any other woman
since Cleopatra—the lover of her great-grandfather Antony—
Agrippina is subject to scathing invective for her involvement in
politics, the military, and foreign affairs. This grasp for masculine
power is innately contradictory, since *virtus* in Roman life is
restricted to a man (*vir*).

As her struggle against her son's advisors intensified, Agrippina went too far. When Nero became infatuated with the freedwoman Acte, Agrippina lost control, calling her "[my] rival, the

freedwoman" and "[my] daughter-in-law, the maid" (13, 13). Tacitus regards such jealous acrimony as typical of women, and suggests that Agrippina would have been wiser to bide her time. She did not, and she increasingly strengthened Seneca's influence over her son. When Nero removed her detachment of guards, the enemies took it as a signal to strike, and an old rival, Junia Silana, arranged accusations of treason (and much else) against her. But Agrippina, in a powerful speech reported directly by Tacitus, successfully routed her opponents (13, 21). After a private audience with Nero, her accusers were indeed punished, but Agrippina then mysteriously disappears from the Tacitean narrative for three years. Her prudence was overdue.

It is far from clear—even in the text of Tacitus—why Nero decided to murder his mother after she had spent three years out of the public eye. As for the charge of incest, Tacitus believes it; he says that one earlier historian (Cluvius) attributed it to Agrippina, while Fabius Rufus blamed Nero for instigating it (14, 2). It is for Tacitus the ultimate example of Agrippina's use of sex for political advantage at court.

Although Tacitus suggests that Nero had "long contemplated" her elimination, he attributes the immediate impetus to the nagging of Nero's lover Poppaea, who threatened to return to her husband, Otho, unless Nero broke loose from his mother's control and married her.

> Therefore Nero avoided private encounters with her [Agrippina] and, on her withdrawal to her gardens or to her Tusculan or Antian estates, praised her pursuit of inactivity; finally, deeming her overburdensome wherever she was, he decided to kill her, debating only whether by poison or the sword or some other violence. (14, 3, 1)

Poison seemed too dangerous, since Agrippina herself was an expert and would be on the alert. So he invited her for a dinner at Baiae on the Bay of Naples and received her most warmly. The long and intimate conversations disarmed her, but her boat was booby-trapped to collapse on the return journey to her own villa.

Although the boat capsized, and Agrippina's maid in the water was mistaken for her mistress and killed, but the indomitable empress swam to safety.

Nero was terrified, and his advisors were little better. No soldiers would murder the daughter of Germanicus, so it was decided that the prefect of the fleet, Anicetus, who had failed to drown her, must finish the job. She was brave to the end and had no intention of yielding to suicide to solve Nero's problem. The story was put about that she had conspired to kill Nero, and Anicetus was sent to break into her villa.

> The assailants surrounded her bed, and initially the trierarch struck her head with his cudgel; and, as the centurion was already drawing his sword for death, she proffered her womb, crying out "Stab my belly!" and with many wounds she was dispatched.
>
> On these matters the tradition is in agreement; but, as to whether Nero gazed on his lifeless mother and praised the look of her body, there are those who have transmitted it and there are those who deny it. (14, 8, 5—9, 1)

Tacitus said that Nero continued to be haunted by dreams and visions of his mother; she obsessed him in death as in life.

The portrayal of Agrippina—in Tacitus and in other sources—is such a construct of rhetorical stereotypes that any historian must question the origins of the rumors. But however cautious we must be of these powerful negative stereotypes, most scholars accept Agrippina's use of her sexual attractions. It was for politics, not lust—and thus for some modern readers it was less threatening, for others more so.

Agrippina's energy and competence were evident; she was feared by all, including two emperors. And the times she most controlled Claudius and Nero seem to have been eras of effective administration. Tacitus and other senators loathed the bedroom conspiracies which allowed women like Agrippina to determine the succession to the imperial throne, and the numerous parallels between Agrippina and Livia are yet another rhetorical device.

Senators may have deplored the imperial matriarchs, but the empire as a whole found more peace under the Julio-Claudians than after that family, with its extraordinarily strong women, collapsed. The end of the dynasty in 68 allowed the armies to choose emperors in civil conflict that resulted in bringing no fewer than four emperors to the throne during the year 69.

8 | The Wives of Nero

As soon as Agrippina married Claudius, she fixed on his young daughter, Octavia—then about ten years old—as a suitable match for her twelve-year-old son, Nero. But Octavia had already been engaged to marry a brilliant young aristocrat, Lucius Silanus. Tacitus says, in dryly preparing us for another murder:

> When she was certain of her own marriage, she laid the foundations of something greater and engineered the wedding of Domitius [Nero], whom she had borne to Cn. Aenobarbus, and Octavia, Caesar's daughter—which could not be accomplished without crime. (12, 3, 2)

Silanus was driven to resign the praetorship and commit suicide, and, a few years later, Octavia and Nero were married. Tacitus repeatedly writes of the probity and virtue of Octavia, who, "though raw in years, had learned to hide pain, affection and every emotion" (13, 16, 4).

When Nero became besotted with the freedwoman Acte, Agrippina (correctly) saw it as a move by his courtiers to detach him from his mother's influence. After he had his stepbrother, Britannicus, murdered, Agrippina became desperate and allied herself with Octavia. The imperial palace became a complex ménage as Nero began an affair with the demanding Poppaea, kept up with Acte, and tried to keep his wife at a distance, while his mother made sexual overtures to him. His advisor, Seneca, tried to manage these entanglements for his now twenty-year-old ward, but his chief preoccupation was to detach Nero from his frantic mother.

After the murder of Agrippina, Nero could proceed to divorce Octavia and marry Poppaea.

Tacitus' account of the palace psychodrama is extraordinary—spies and informers, loyal servants resisting torture, diva-like outbursts by Poppaea that Octavia and her minions were persecuting and slandering *her*. Complaints about Octavia's infertility were followed by improbable accusations of an affair with an Egyptian flute-player. Octavia's servants responded bravely to these tortures:

> The majority persevered in defending the purity of their mistress—one of them replying to Tigellinus' hounding that Octavia's womanly parts were more chaste than his mouth.
> (14, 60, 3)

This is one of the crudest sexual allusions in the rather prim Tacitus—an almost certain indication that he found it in the sources or heard it bandied about after Nero's (and Tigellinus') deaths.

Divorce was not enough; Nero persuaded his ever compliant prefect Anicetus (who had killed Agrippina) to confess to adultery with Octavia. She was accused of treason and inciting an abortion. Tacitus mordantly points out that Nero seemed to have forgotten that he had recently accused her of barrenness. She was exiled to the island of Pandateria:

> No other exiled woman afflicted the eyes of beholders with greater pity. Some still remembered Agrippina's banishment by Tiberius, and confronting them was the more recent memory of Julia's by Claudius. Yet those two had the strength of years: they had seen some happy times and could alleviate their present savagery by the recollection of better fortune once. (14, 63, 2)

But Poppaea was not satisfied with Octavia's mere exile; she demanded the death of her twenty-year-old rival, and in a final horror her severed head was brought back to Rome for Poppaea to see. So died the descendant of Octavia, Livia, and the elder Agrippina, like them an example of virtuous Roman womanhood, loved by her servants and praised by Tacitus; her brutal slaughter was a final blot on the Julio-Claudian dynasty.

If Tacitus admired Octavia, it is clear that he shared the universal loathing of the ancient sources for Poppaea. When he first introduces her, after describing her as having great beauty, noble lineage, and affability—but no honesty—Tacitus continues:

> She never spared her reputation, making no distinction between husbands and adulterers; susceptible neither to her own or another's emotion, she would transfer her lust wherever advantage showed. (13, 45, 3)

She arranged for Nero to send his friend (and her husband) Otho to be governor of Spain, and then began her affair with the emperor.

Her manipulation of the immature Nero was brilliant as she drove a wedge between him and Agrippina:

> [Poppaea] censured the emperor with regular reproaches and sometimes by way of a witticism called him "the ward," susceptible to the orders of another and lacking not only command but even freedom. Why was her wedding being deferred? Evidently her looks were displeasing. (14, 1, 1–2)

We have already seen that her tantrums drove Nero to kill both his mother and Octavia; Poppaea seems to have been a match for his "artistic" temperament, and they were like two competing opera divas hogging the footlights.

In marriage, Poppaea was no less ambitious and no less cruel. She bore a daughter, Claudia, who died (and was deified) after a few months. Her own death in 64 C.E. was as violent and operatic as her life:

> After the end of the games Poppaea met her death owing to the chance rage of her husband, by whom she was struck, when pregnant, with a blow from his heel. (I am not inclined to believe it was poison, although certain writers so transmit, in hatred rather than from conviction:

for he was desirous of children and submissive to the love of his wife.) (16, 6, 1)

This was Nero's final act of violence against his own family.

Nero had a third wife, Statilia Messalina, but Tacitus' surviving text does not mention her. In their brief marriage before Nero's death, she could hardly rival the vivid pictures of Octavia and Poppaea. In fact, their images have survived in popular culture. The ancient play *Octavia*—once attributed to Seneca but probably written later—portrays her suffering, as does the great baroque opera *L'incoronazione di Poppea* by Claudio Monteverdi (1642). Although Poppaea appears elsewhere—she is strangled by Nero in the film *Quo Vadis* and was played by Claudette Colbert in *The Sign of the Cross*—it is in Monteverdi's masterpiece that her affair with Nero becomes a genuine love story with a magnificent final duet. The librettist is often on shaky historical ground, but the enforced suicide of Seneca and the piteous exile of Octavia both ring true to the spirit of Tacitus. Only in republican Venice could Tacitus have been used in the seventeenth century to depict a story as utterly immoral as the grand passion of Nero and Poppaea. Some, including the musicologist Wendy Heller, see *L'incoronazione di Poppea* as a cautionary tale about the fatal mixture of sexual passion and tyranny—despite the happy ending and the failure to punish evildoers.[13] The members of that Venetian audience would have known their Tacitus and would have been able to read between the lines of the ecstatic closing scenes. Nevertheless, it is certainly appropriate that Nero and Poppaea—both marvelously operatic characters in real life—should survive on the stage in such a form. For the Julio-Claudian women, opera best combines the wrenching drama, melodrama, and grisly Grand Guignol contained in the text of the *Annals*.

13. Cf. Heller (1999). A recent treatment of Monteverdi's *Poppea* by a classical scholar examines both the Platonic and the neo-Stoic elements in the libretto: cf. Ketterer (2009), 22–40.

Tacitus assuredly had an unfavorable impression of the women of the Julio-Claudian court. We should not forget that these were usually teenagers being married—more or less voluntarily—to much older men. In Rome it had long been common practice for girls just past puberty to marry husbands in their late twenties—twice their age. But under the Republic, those girls had access to their birth families for support; by contrast, the imperial palace was a claustrophobic environment suffused by power and fawning flattery. A modern parallel might be those teenagers who become pop culture icons and lose all sense of reality. The friction between the women ranged from dignified frostiness (Livia; the elder Agrippina) to diva-like catfights (Messalina; the younger Agrippina and Poppaea), and the weak men are portrayed as being out of their depth. Tiberius withdrew to Capri; Claudius was in denial; Nero becomes a matricide to satisfy his mistress.

We must always remember, too, how generally unfavorable in Tacitus is the picture of the *men* of the Julio-Claudian court. There are ample vices attributed to Tiberius, Sejanus, and Nero, but Tacitus does make universal vices such as *libido* ("lust"), *cupido* ("desire"), *fraus* ("deception"), and *superbia* ("arrogance") more sinister by describing them as *muliebris* ("feminine").[14] Tacitus is not a misogynist, but rather is a traditionalist who does not want to see women outside their family roles. In the words of A. A. Barrett, "Tacitus can surely be acquitted of misogyny, in the sense of a pathological hatred of women. He sees qualities in women, as well as faults, qualities like *constantia* ("perseverance") and *fides* ("trustworthiness"), and his women are at times capable of heroism."[15] The difficulty is that the most virtuous, and more courageous, women tend to be those on the margins: Octavia, and Nero's faithful mistress, the freedwoman Acte. But Tacitus knew that vice is more compelling than virtue, and he assuredly gave his readers what they craved.

14. Rutland (1978), 15–16.
15. Barrett (1996), 205.

· 8 ·

Courtiers on the Palatine: The *Familia* of the Caesars

In addition to evidencing borderline misogyny against powerful women, the text of the *Annals* is replete with Tacitus' other prejudices: his social snobbery toward lower orders, and especially his hostility to Greeks and other easterners, whom he thought of as "talkers" who would flatter, lie, and sophistically justify their lies. These suspicions were clearly evident in his presentation of the equestrians, freedmen, sponging intellectuals, and assorted disreputable rascals who populated the household (called *familia*) of the Julio-Claudians. Senators (among them, Tacitus) were particularly outraged that they were shut out of the court intrigues that determined the fate of the empire. In fact, the most important political decisions of the time were taking place in the antechambers and bedrooms of the Palatine.

I | Freedmen

For centuries the Romans had treated their freed slaves with far more generosity than had other ancient societies: freedmen (*liberti*) received Roman citizenship and bore the family name of their last owner. Of course, such emancipation or manumission—when a slave escapes the *manus* (control) of the owner—was given only to urban or household slaves whose loyalty and skill had been especially valued by the master; the vast armies of agricultural or industrial slaves could never expect such treatment. Thus we first read of slaves from southern Italy and Greece who served as tutors, administrators, and resident intellectuals in the homes of prominent Romans during the Republic. For their accomplishments and devotion, some notable slaves were granted freedom.

The owner remained the *patronus* of the freedman; he was due political and personal loyalty for life from the *libertus*, who often continued to serve in the former master's entourage. The first surviving author in Latin, Livius Andronicus, was brought to Rome in the third century B.C.E. as a slave of the Livii, and the great comic poet Terence was later brought as a slave from Carthage in North Africa.

This desire for decorative tutors, philosophers, and poets soon gave way to the more practical needs of powerful senators. In the absence of any state bureaucracy, the Roman political elite administered their provinces, armies, and other official duties through their household slaves and freedmen. Pompey was so fond of his Greek freedman Demetrius that he rebuilt Demetrius' home city of Gadara in Judaea, which had been destroyed, and the wealthy Demetrius in turn contributed to the building of the Theater of Pompey in Rome. Cicero's loyal secretary, Tiro, invented a system of shorthand to record his master's speeches, first as a slave and then as Cicero's freedman. Julius Caesar's freedman Licinus progressed from being a slave captured in the Gallic campaign to a successful administrator sent by Augustus to serve as procurator in Gaul some four decades later. His ill-gotten wealth was so enormous that he completed the Basilica Julia in the Roman Forum to honor his old master and thank his new one for acquitting him of corruption charges. As these freedmen acquired great wealth, they also adopted the proud arrogance of their masters.

During Augustus' severe illness in 23 B.C.E., his life was saved by his freedman, an Egyptian doctor, Antonius Musa, who had earlier served Mark Antony and received freedom from him. A statue was erected in his honor. An even greater honor was given to the freedman Menas, who betrayed his master Sextus Pompey and transferred to Octavian the islands of Sardinia and Corsica, three legions, and sixty ships. Octavian granted him the gold ring of a freeborn man and enrolled him in the equestrian order. Suetonius tells us that Augustus even had his freedmen help him in writing his will, which contained "the names of his slaves and freedmen from whom the financial details might be demanded" (*Augustus* 1). A freedman named Polybius read the will aloud in the Senate.

With that background, we might expect Tacitus to focus more on the excesses of freedmen in the time of Tiberius. But the emperor at first relied for political advice on experienced senators, such as Piso, or his heirs, Germanicus and Drusus; later, with his own military experience leading armies along the Rhine and Danube, the soldiers Sejanus and Macro became his closest confidants. If Tacitus finds few outrages to report, the Jewish writer Josephus shows that freedmen were indeed an important presence at court. Herod Agrippa, the grandson of Herod the Great, who spent most of his life as an exile in Rome, spent an enormous fortune giving bribes to Tiberius' freedmen. To ingratiate himself with the young Caligula, he borrowed one million *sesterces* from a Samaritan freedman of Tiberius'. After Tiberius' death Caligula made Agrippa king of Judaea.[1] Yet Tacitus does report that, in the last years of Tiberius, an aged senator included in his will "many frightful things against Macro and the principal freedmen of Caesar" (6, 38, 2). With his typical desire to keep everyone nervous, Tiberius ordered that the will be read aloud in the Senate.

It was in the reign of Claudius that freedmen became richer, more powerful, and easier targets for senatorial resentment. Tacitus depicts Claudius as the weak tool of his freedmen and wives, and there is certainly considerable truth in that picture. Since Claudius was crippled from childhood polio and suffered from a stutter, the imperial family tried to keep him out of the public eye. While his

1. Josephus *Jewish Antiquities* 18, 6, 1; 18, 6, 4. Cf. Millar (1992), 73.

brother Germanicus commanded armies, Claudius devoted his attention to antiquarian studies and the writing of history, and he held no important political posts under his uncle Tiberius. Suddenly catapulted to the throne with no administrative experience, he relied on trusted freedmen for advice and support, since men of senatorial standing were not trained for the financial and clerical tasks of running an empire. In the words of Tacitus, he raised the freedmen "up to the same level as both himself and the laws" (12, 60, 4). He even on occasion used them as his intermediary with the troops and as advisors on how to select and remove his wives.

Though the freedmen might be arrogant and greedy opportunists, they were usually deeply loyal to the emperor and were trusted by him. The empire was administered from the imperial residence on the Palatine, and that is where the freedmen resided with the emperor's family. Senators saw Claudius at formal meetings, banquets, or games, but the leading freedmen had confidential private access to him. While senatorial obsequiousness tended to be contained in official pronouncements at public meetings, freedmen had more effect, with their private and very personal flattery. Senators resented these outsiders who controlled access, just as elected members of Congress and Parliament today are deeply offended by staff members who control the schedule and appointments of presidents and prime ministers.

Claudius' freedmen managed to amass such vast personal fortunes through bribes and business dealings that Pliny the Elder compared their circumstances to the phenomenal wealth of the triumvir Crassus, who had property worth 200 million sesterces:

> We have seen many men freed from slavery who were richer, and not long ago three simultaneously in the reign of Claudius, namely Callistus, Pallas and Narcissus. (*Natural History* 33, 47)

These men also seem to have been remarkable administrators, who helped the inexperienced emperor conduct a successful foreign policy, pass humane legislation, and leave the treasury with a surplus. But Tacitus was less interested in administrative effectiveness than in making Claudius appear weak and passive. The historian portrays the emperor dithering over the flagrant adultery of Messalina, until his freedmen forced him to confront it and sign a death warrant.

Tiberius Claudius Narcissus was an exceptional freedman whose loyalty to Claudius never wavered. His formal position was *ab epistulis* (secretary for correspondence), but he was involved in every aspect of the regime, like a modern "chief of staff." Perhaps the greatest crisis was when the empress Messalina celebrated a public marriage with her lover Silanus while the emperor was a few miles away in Ostia. The chief freedmen were terrified both of doing nothing in the face of a possible *coup d'état* and of unsuccessfully trying to separate Claudius from the wife he adored.

> [The freedmen] discussed whether they should deflect Messalina from her lust for Silius by secret threats, dissembling everything else. But later, dreading that they themselves might be dragged to ruin, they desisted—Pallas through cowardice, Callistus with his experience both of the previous court too and that one's power is more safely kept by careful than by drastic counsel; but Narcissus persisted, his only charge being that in no conversation at all would he forewarn her of charge and accuser. Attentive for any opportunity, during Caesar's long delay at Ostia Narcissus used lavishness and promises, as well as the prospect of increased power on the overthrowing of the wife, to compel the denouncement to be undertaken by the two concubines with whose bodies the man was most familiar. (11, 29, 1–3)

When Claudius overcame his panic—he ran around asking, "Am I emperor or is Silius?"—he realized that he could not even trust his praetorian prefect.

> Narcissus therefore, having enlisted the services of men whose dread was the same as his own, affirmed that there was no hope of Caesar's preservation unless he transferred jurisdiction of the soldiers to one of the freedmen for that

single day, and he offered himself as the one to undertake it. And, lest Claudius on his journey to the city should have his mind changed to regret by L. Vitellius and Largus Caecina, Narcissus demanded a seat in the same conveyance and was taken along. (11, 33)

After Claudius had safely returned to the city and secured his position, he ate, drank, and grew sentimental about giving Messalina another chance to plead her case. It was Narcissus who was adamant; he summoned the centurions, and the empress realized that suicide was her only recourse. While others feared Messalina's power and Claudius' well-known indecision, Narcissus alone among the freedmen courageously protected his master. He was rewarded with the insignia of a quaestor (11, 37–38).

By nature uxorious, Claudius soon called his freedmen together in a parody of an imperial *consilium* (cabinet meeting) to find a new wife:

> On the slaughter of Messalina the princeps' household was wrenched apart, competition having arisen among the freedmen as to who would choose a wife for Claudius, intolerant as he was of celibate life and submissive to spouses' commands. No less was the self-aggrandizement with which the ladies burned: each brought into contention her nobility, good looks, and wealth and paraded herself as worthy of so great a marriage. . . . Claudius himself, sometimes tending in one direction and sometimes in another (depending on which of the recommendations he had heard), called the quarrelers to a council and ordered them to tender opinions and adduce reasons. (12, 1, 1–2)

The three freedmen each favored a different candidate and, while Tacitus portrays the scene as sordid bargaining, it is little different from the pragmatic evaluation of candidates for royal weddings down the ages. In fact, for centuries a Roman paterfamilias would have met with his family council to discuss the pros and cons of various alliances; the scandal for Tacitus is that freedmen were the key figures in the process. Yet it is little wonder that Claudius, the family outcast, should turn to those whom he regarded as his only friends. On paper, his marriage to Agrippina looked sensible, as it would unite the house of Livia (Claudius) with the house of Augustus (Agrippina and her son, Nero).

Agrippina never forgot that it was Narcissus who had opposed her selection as empress, and she watched for opportunities to undermine his position. Early in his reign Claudius had begun the enormous public works project first envisioned by Julius Caesar to build a three-mile tunnel to drain the Fucine lake. Thirty thousand men worked on it for eleven years, and Tacitus describes the festive opening ceremonies in 52 C.E., when the assembled courtiers watched gladiators imitate an infantry battle. But the water surging through the tunnel almost swept away Claudius, Agrippina, and the other celebrants, and Tacitus used it as an opportunity to highlight the emperor's timidity, his wife's opportunism, and Narcissus' temerity:

> At the same time, Agrippina took advantage of the princeps' trepidation to accuse Narcissus, the agent for the work, of cupidity and embezzlement; nor did he stay silent for his part, criticizing her womanly unruliness and excessive hopes. (12, 57, 2)

Later Roman authors praised Narcissus for this great engineering achievement, but Agrippina saw it only as a tool to use in her struggle to ensure her domination in the palace.

> Amid such a storm of concerns Narcissus was seized with adverse health and proceeded to Sinuessa to restore his vigor by the softness of the climate and salubriousness of the waters. It was then that Agrippina—long determined on her crime, quick with the opportunity offered, and not short of servants—debated about the type of poison. (12, 66, 1)

Without Narcissus around to protect Claudius, Agrippina suborned the palace cooks, eunuchs, and doctor to ensure that the emperor would succumb to poisoned mushrooms. After Agrippina's scheme had succeeded, Narcissus loyally burned Claudius' private correspondence to prevent it being used by Nero, and he was executed within weeks of the change of regime.

Tacitus regarded Marcus Antonius Pallas as a far more unscrupulous freedman; he first appears in history as a secret agent carrying messages from his mistress, Antonia, to her brother-in-law, Tiberius. After Pallas passed into the household of her son Claudius, he served as the financial secretary (*a rationibus*) and later as a stalwart and successful supporter of Agrippina. Tacitus is especially disgusted at their sexual relationship; while emperors commonly had freedwomen as mistresses, the notion of a respectable Roman matron taking an ex-slave as a lover would have seemed outrageous. So Narcissus put it to his friends:

> Though not even immorality was now lacking, with Pallas as her adulterer, lest anyone be in any uncertainty that she held esteem, shame, her body, everything, cheaper than the kingdom. (12, 65, 2)

Pallas pompously pretended to trace his ancestry back a millennium (!) to a king of Arcadia, for his name echoed the name of the son of the mythical king Evander, who was allied with Aeneas. Tacitus reports that, when Claudius had credited Pallas with formulating a law about liaisons between free women and slaves, a senator sycophantically proposed that the freedman be rewarded with the decorations of the praetorship and fifteen million sesterces. The historian continues, with considerable irony:

> Scipio Cornelius added that gratitude should be expressed publicly because an offspring of Arcadia's kings was subordinating his very old nobility to the public good and allowing himself to be regarded as one of the princeps' servants. Claudius asserted that Pallas was content with the honor only and would stay within the limits of his former poverty. And fixed in official bronze was a senate's decision whereby a freedman possessing three hundred million sesterces was heaped with phrases for his old-fashioned frugality. (12, 53, 2–3)

We might think it a Tacitean exaggeration, but his friend Pliny the Younger had also written two lengthy letters about this very incident, after he found a monument honoring Pallas on the road to Tivoli.

> You should have heard from my last letter (7, 29) that I had recently seen a monument to Pallas with this inscription: "To him the Senate decreed in return to his loyal services to his patrons, the insignia of a praetor and the sum of fifteen million sesterces, but he thought fit to accept the distinction only." I took the trouble afterwards to look up the actual decree of the Senate, and found it so verbose and fulsome in tone that the insolence of this inscription seemed modest and positively humble by comparison. . . .
>
> To such lengths did the Emperor, the Senate, and Pallas himself push their—I can't think of a word to express their conduct—as if they intended to set up a record in the sight of all, Pallas of his insolence, the emperor of his complaisance, the Senate of its degradation. (*Letters* 8, 6, trans. B. Radice)

When we read Pliny's furious pages, the account of Tacitus appears one of restrained irony.

The historian also attributes to Pallas, "at the instigation of Agrippina," the pressure on Claudius to adopt Nero "for the interests of the state." The emperor delivered "before the senate a speech along the same lines as those which he had been given by his freedman" (12, 25, 2). It would have been thought shameful to a rhetorician like Tacitus to see a Roman aristocrat mouthing the words written by another. A few years later, when Nero delivered an entire speech written by Seneca at Claudius' funeral, Tacitus feels the need to praise the fluency of his predecessors Caesar and Augustus (13, 3).

Pallas' actions also had an impact on Judaea and the rise of the Christian religion. He had installed his brother Felix as governor in 52 and he remained until 60 C.E., and, immediately after the story of Pallas' "refusal" of the Senate's reward, Tacitus sarcastically says that Felix was the less "moderate" of the two:

But his brother, with the nomenclature Felix, did not act with similar moderation. Installed now for a long time over Judaea, he deemed that such powerful backing would guarantee him impunity for all his misdeeds. (12, 54, 1)

Felix was corrupt and ruthless, and disorder increased throughout his province. He used the *sicarii* (assassins) to murder the high priest Jonathan in an attempt to undermine the faction of the zealots, and his actions greatly contributed to the unrest which led to the great Jewish revolt. Although Felix was recalled to Rome for trial, his brother's influence protected him. On his return to Judaea, Paul of Tarsus was brought to him at Caesarea. According to Christian sources, he kept Paul out of the hands of his Jewish opponents in the hope of a substantial bribe.[2] It is a small glimpse from the local perspective of how corruption and nepotism in the imperial palace affected the destinies of both Jews and Christians.

As Nero turned against his mother, Agrippina, he became suspicious of her entourage and removed Pallas from control of finances.

(In fact Pallas had struck a bargain that he should not be questioned for any action in the past and that his accounts with the state should be held as balanced.) (13, 14, 1)

Tacitus, who had already told of Pallas' sexual intrigues, his false modesty, his vast wealth, and his nepotism, here points out his skillful mastery of the age-old bureaucratic strategy of protecting one's posterior. Yet it was perhaps his avarice that was his downfall. Nero was not satisfied with excluding him from power; he had him poisoned, because the emperor grew impatient for his inheritance: "He was tying up inordinate money by the length of his old age" (14, 65, 1). Tacitus barely conceals his pleasure at seeing this arrogant freedman become a victim of his own greed.

If Nero dispensed with Claudius' favorite freedmen, he had his own to do his dirty work, most notably the fleet commander

2. Acts 24:26.

Anicetus, who booby-trapped Agrippina's boat. When she survived, the praetorian prefect told the terrified Nero that the soldiers would not murder the daughter of the beloved Germanicus, and he turned again to his trusty Anicetus:

> And he for his part actually demanded the climax of the crime. In response to these words, Nero professed that that was the day on which command was being given to him, and the author of so great a gift was a freedman. (14, 7, 5)

Tacitus later perceptively observes that such favors cause resentment, since rulers look on their agents as a standing reproach to them. Having dispensed with the mother, the freedman was then assigned to get rid of Nero's inconvenient wife:

> There was no need of brawn or weapon; he should merely confess adultery with Octavia.—Nero promised rewards, concealed for the moment but large, and an attractive retirement; or, if he refused, he brandished the prospect of execution. (14, 62, 3–4)

Anicetus eagerly complied and finished his days in comfortable retirement in Sardinia.

The theme of freedmen and their abuses recurs throughout the *Annals*, as when legislation is proposed in the Senate in 56 C.E. to reduce criminal freedmen back into servitude. As Roman politics moved into the imperial palace, the emperor's entourage increasingly displaced the senators, to their fury. Tacitus enjoys stories of the Roman Rasputins who played on the fears of their masters, but it is also likely that the great majority of freedmen were competent administrators who kept an enormous empire together while senators played at politics. Even Tacitus, who usually equates morality with social standing, admires the remarkable loyalty and courage of the freedwoman Epicharis, who refused to betray the Pisonian conspiracy against Nero, despite two days of savage torture that led to her death:

> But in her case neither beatings nor fires nor the torturers' anger (all the fiercer, lest they be spurned by a female)

prevailed over her denials of their imputations . . . a woman and a freedwoman defending, by her more brilliant example in such an extremity, others whom she scarcely knew, when the freeborn—men and Roman equestrians and senators, all untouched by torture—were each betraying the dearest of those to whom they were bound (15, 57, 1–2)

If the Roman Empire was well administered in the century after the Battle of Actium, much of the credit must be given to freedmen. They oversaw finances, organized all correspondence and record-keeping, and collected the data on which emperors made decisions. If Claudius decided to build an enormous new port at Ostia to receive grain ships from Alexandria, it was the imperial freedmen who developed the plans to remedy the shortages. They brought the business abilities of the eastern Mediterranean into the service of the empire.

Yet, where there is power there is also greed and corruption—especially when emperors like Claudius and Nero were themselves weak or preoccupied. The spectacularly corrupt freedmen at the apex of political power provided ammunition for senatorial critics like Tacitus, who loathed them for reasons of snobbery, racism, and jealousy. Tacitean anger toward a handful of famous, or infamous, freedmen should not blind his readers to a larger administrative picture in which most did their jobs well.

2 | Eunuchs

Perhaps the most despised of the Julio-Claudian courtiers were the eunuchs—men who were castrated as boys. The Greeks first encountered them at the Persian court, where the eunuchs were especially loyal to their royal masters, and later sacred eunuchs of the goddess Cybele came to Rome, though Romans regarded the practice of castration with disgust. When eunuchs were brought to Rome as a result of the conquests of Egypt and Parthia, they were of course valued by emperors for their abject loyalty.

Even Sejanus owned eunuchs, and Pliny reports that one Paezon was sold for a record price of 50 million sesterces.[3] When Tacitus refers to secret emissaries who came to Tiberius from Parthia, he mentions

> Abdus, who had been deprived of his manhood; (among barbarians that is not despised but actually confers power). (6, 31, 2)

His contempt for eunuchs is obvious, as when he tells of Nero's eunuch Pelago acting like the agent of an eastern tyrant when he murdered the distinguished and wealthy senator Plautius Lateranus.

> In this state the centurion butchered him in the presence of Pelago, an eunuch, whom Nero had placed in charge of the centurion and his maniple like a royal servant over satellites. (14, 59, 2)

So the court eunuchs, such as Halotus the taster (and poisoner) of Claudius, were for Tacitus a despicable sign of the baseness and servility of Julio-Claudian court culture.

3 | Poisoners

A new element in Roman politics was the use of poison, and Tacitus delights in recounting its popularity as another indication of feminine (or emasculated) corruption.[4] During the Republic, when violence entered political life, it usually took the form of gang warfare (the brothers Gracchi) or simple assassination (Julius Caesar). Although poisoning had long been regarded by Romans as a cowardly crime deployed only by women or barbarians, there was an eruption of poisoning in the domestic conspiracies of Julio-Claudian Rome. Tacitus alerts us to the recurring theme when he repeats a rumor that Pansa, the consul of 43 B.C.E., may have had

3. Pliny, *Natural History* 7, 129.
4. On the adulteress-poisoner, now see Santoro L'hoir (2006), 158–195.

poison poured into a battlefield wound to allow Octavian to take power (1, 10). While this and some subsequent accusations of poison seem unlikely, Tacitus' insistent repetition fixes the image of ubiquitous poisoners in the reader's mind.

This image first reappears in the illness of the headstrong imperial prince Germanicus. While traveling in the eastern Roman provinces and being shadowed by Tiberius' legate Piso, Germanicus fell ill in Syria.

> The savage violence of the disease was increased by his conviction that he had been given poison by Piso; and in fact there were discovered, unearthed from the ground and walls, remains of human bodies, spells and curses and the name "Germanicus" etched on lead tablets, half-burned ashes smeared with putrid matter, and other malefic devices by which it is believed that souls are consecrated to the infernal divinities. (2, 69, 3)

Tacitus later comments that a certain notorious poisoner, Martina, who was a close friend of Piso's wife, was arrested and dispatched back to Rome, but she herself died suddenly after arriving in the port of Brundisium in southern Italy with poison concealed in her hair. But Tacitus leaves the deaths of both Germanicus and Martina under a cloud of uncertainty.

Not so the death by poison of Tiberius' son and heir, Drusus, although Tacitus reports different versions. Both accounts agree that the praetorian prefect, Sejanus, had seduced Drusus' wife, Livilla, and that the eunuch Lygdus helped in the conspiracy to administer a slow-acting poison. Tiberius seemed genuinely distraught as he reported Drusus' death to the Senate. But Tacitus cannot resist reporting another version implicating the emperor himself:

> In transmitting Drusus' death I have recorded what has been recalled by most authors and those of the greatest credibility; but I am not inclined to neglect from those same times a rumor so effective that it has not yet abated. . . . Then, when the place and time of the poisoning had been agreed

between the accomplices, Sejanus had advanced to such a pitch of daring that he changed things and by means of anonymous information ensured that Drusus was accused of aiming to poison his father and that Tiberius was warned to avoid the first drink to be offered to him when banqueting at the house of his son. Taken in by the deception, the old man on entering the party had handed Drusus the cup he received; and he for his part had unknowingly drained it (as a young man would), increasing the suspicion that through dread and shame he was inflicting upon himself the death he had set up for his father. (4, 10, 1–3)

It is typical of Tacitus to record at greater length a more negative account which he innocently proclaims ought to be ignored. Thus the historian continues to weave a tapestry of deviousness around the entire court and envelop the emperor in suspicion. Decades earlier Cicero had mastered the courtroom tactic of claiming to "pass over in silence" libelous material which he was in fact calling to the jurors' attention. Such rhetorical devices are common in the pages of Tacitus' *Annals*.

If Tiberius was innocent of the poisoning of Germanicus and Drusus, which seems likely, Tacitus continues to include similar allegations made against the emperor. The tortuous story of Sejanus' plots against Agrippina and her three sons—Nero, Drusus, and Gaius Caligula—recurs through books 4, 5, and 6 of the *Annals*. Since the widow and children of Germanicus still were enormously popular with the troops, who had given the boy Gaius the nickname of Caligula ("booties") after his miniature military boots, any move against them would have to be surreptitious. Tacitus reports labyrinthine intrigues, as Sejanus maneuvers Agrippina into offending Tiberius, so that the emperor might take decisive action:

But Sejanus struck more deeply at the sorrowing and misguided woman, sending in people to warn her, in a display of friendship, that poison had been prepared for her and that she should shun a banquet of her father-in-law's. She for her part was innocent of all pretense and, when she reclined at his side, changing neither her look or conversation, touched none of the food, until Tiberius noticed—by chance or because he had been told. To test the matter more minutely, he praised some fruit as it lay on the table, presenting it to his daughter-in-law with his own hand. Agrippina's suspicion was thereby increased, and she passed it over, untouched by her lips, to the slaves. Still no utterance came from Tiberius in her presence but, turning to his mother, he said it was no wonder if he had decided to be more strict with one by whom he was being incriminated for poisoning. (4, 54, 1–2)

Sejanus' plan was to eliminate all possible Julio-Claudian heirs and to leave himself as Tiberius' successor. In a bizarre irony that Tacitus surely understood, however cruel the elimination of Germanicus' children would have been, it would have spared Rome the tyrannical rule of his son Caligula and grandson Nero.

We have already seen the most notorious case of poisoning when Agrippina the Younger dispensed with her husband, the emperor Claudius, to allow her son, Nero, to take the imperial throne. This was an elaborate plot with at least three other conspirators named: Locusta, the specialist in poisons; Halotus, a eunuch who served and tasted the emperor's food; and the suborned doctor Xenophon, who inserted a poisoned feather into the emperor's throat on the pretext of helping him to vomit. Suetonius gives much the same story, but provides minor variants, such as the suggestion that Agrippina may have administered the poison herself (*Claudius* 47).

Agrippina and Nero continued to make use of the valuable Locusta during the next two decades. On the accession of Nero, the first crime of the new regime was the poisoning of Junius Silanus, proconsul of Asia and great-great-grandson of Augustus. In this case Tacitus suggests that Agrippina carried out the crime without Nero's knowledge, but by the next year the young emperor himself used Locusta to prepare a poison for his step-brother and coheir, Britannicus. Agrippina had become annoyed with her increasingly independent son for developing his own circle of cronies, taking a freedwoman as mistress, and generally neglecting his mother, so she haughtily suggested that she had created Nero and could as easily have the troops replace him with Britannicus. Thus she doomed her stepson:

> With Britannicus dining there, and because a chosen servant sampled his food and drink by tasting, the following trick was devised to avoid abandoning the routine or betraying the crime by the death of both of them. Britannicus was handed a drink, still harmless, very hot, and sipped at the tasting; then, after it was spurned for being scalding, the poison was added in cold water, and it so pervaded his whole frame that his voice and breathing suffered a simultaneous seizure. A shudder came from those sitting around, the misguided scattered; but those of a deeper understanding remained transfixed and gazing at Nero. (13, 16, 1–3)

Agrippina understood fatalistically that she had fashioned her son in her own likeness and that her own life would always be at risk.

Nero's instigation of the poisoning of Britannicus made it easy for courtiers, and hence for the historians who report the intense paranoia of the court, to assume that poison might be used against the emperor's nearest and dearest: mother, mentor, teacher, and wife. First was Nero's desire to relieve himself of his overbearing mother, who had withdrawn from the court to her country villas. He thought first of poison, but then realized how difficult it would be to deceive a specialist in poison; who can poison a poisoner?

> The favorite at first was poison; but, if it were administered during a banquet of the princeps, it could not be referred to chance, such having already been the means of Britannicus' extermination; and it seems a steep risk to manipulate the servants of a woman alerted against subterfuge by her own experience in crime; and in fact she had personally fortified her body by taking prophylactic remedies. (14, 3, 2)

Tacitus then reports, with an element of dark farce, Nero's attempt to drown Agrippina by sabotaging her boat, until he finally resorted to direct assassination.

The death of Nero's praetorian prefect and close advisor, Afranius Burrus, was more likely from poison than natural causes. Once
again, as with Claudius, the poison is disguised as a medicine:

> Burrus departed from life, whether through ill health or
> poison being uncertain. Ill health was inferred from the fact
> that, when he stopped breathing, his gullet had been gradu-
> ally extending inward, and his passageway was blocked; but
> the majority asserted that on Nero's, as if some remedy was
> being applied, his palate had been smeared with a noxious
> medicament and that Burrus, realizing the crime and avert-
> ing his gaze when the princeps came to visit him, had given
> no other reply to his persistent queries than "*I* am well."
> (14, 51, 1)

But, according to Tacitus, neither Nero's tutor, Seneca, nor his wife,
Poppaea, actually were killed by poison, although Nero considered
it in both cases. Seneca was warned by a loyal freedman, and then
was careful to live on a diet of wild fruits and fresh water from a
running stream on his estate. (15, 45) Later, under direct orders from
the emperor, he committed suicide with a sword (15, 63), after talk-
ing (like Socrates and Cato before him) with his friends. As for
Poppaea, we have already seen that Tacitus ironically exonerates
Nero from devising her murder by poison: he loved her too much
for poison; he merely kicked her to death in a rage (16, 6).

4 | Scholars and Philosophers

Ever since the banqueting Homeric chieftains were entertained
by bards, there was a long tradition in antiquity of kings surrounding themselves with poets, astrologers, physicians, and philosophers. Aristotle was summoned to the Macedonian court to tutor
young Alexander and, after Alexander's conquest of the East, his
successors built libraries and research institutes and gave patronage
to scientists, intellectuals, and artists. As Roman magistrates began
to imitate Hellenistic monarchs, they included such men in their

entourages. Augustus' patronage of, and friendship with, the poets Vergil and Horace is much better known than his sponsorship of the small army of doctors and astrologers, poets and historians, grammarians and philosophers who converged from East and West upon the most affluent court in the Mediterranean.

Tacitus was continually suspicious when intellectual pursuits— especially involving foreigners—distracted the emperors from their political and military duties. When Tiberius removed himself to Capri for the last eleven years of his reign, the historian is obviously aghast at the implication that the emperor values his entertainment more than the government:

> His departure was made with only a restricted company: one senator who was a former consul, Cocceius Nerva, with his expertise in the law: a Roman equestrian (apart from Sejanus) from their illustrious ranks, Curtius Atticus; the rest were endowed with liberal studies, mostly Greeks, in whose conversations he might find alleviation. (4, 58, 1)

Perhaps in the lost fifth book of the *Annals* Tacitus provided more specifics about these conversations on Capri, but we get an idea from Suetonius, who writes about Tiberius' own compositions, as well as topics for discussion like "What song did the sirens usually sing?" (*Tiberius* 70).

Suetonius reports that during an earlier period of self-imposed exile, in Rhodes (6 B.C.E.–2 C.E.), Tiberius attended lectures on Greek literature (*Tiberius* 32), and Tacitus himself tells of his intense involvement with the Alexandrian astrologer and philosopher Thrasyllus. Tiberius was in the habit of taking astrologers to the Rhodian cliffs, and, if he decided they were frauds, he had them tossed into the sea. So it began with Thrasyllus:

> Thus it was that Thrasyllus was led over the same crags, and, after he had impressed his questioner by a skillful disclosure of the man's command and future circumstances, was asked whether he had also discovered his own natal hour: what year and what kind of day was he currently experiencing?

Having measured the positions and distances of the planets, he hesitated at first, and then began to panic, and, trembling more and more in amazement and dread as his insight increased, he finally exclaimed that an ambiguous and almost final crisis was descending upon him. Then with an embrace Tiberius congratulated him on the grounds that he was prescient of his perils and would be safe and sound. And, taking what he had said as an oracle, he kept him among the most intimate of his friends. (6, 21, 2–3)

Thrasyllus then became so close to Tiberius during his Rhodian exile that the prince himself learned to cast horoscopes and gave his teacher Roman citizenship as Tiberius Claudius Thrasyllus. The astrologer remained close to the imperial family, even living on Capri with Tiberius.

The ancients regarded astrology as an aspect of the science of astronomy, and in the early empire the Roman elite were quite devoted to it. The emperors both believed in astrology and feared that astrological forecasts could destabilize the state by encouraging assassination or rebellion. Although Tacitus himself uses portents and omens as dramatic devices—a comet, a storm, clouds across the moon, or the bolt of lightning that broke Nero's table—in the *Annals* he was skeptical of the "science" of astrology. When he describes the plot against a young aristocrat, Libo Drusus, Tacitus calls him a naive young man who was taken in by astrologers' promises, rites of magicians, and interpreters of dreams (2, 27, 2). Other courtiers used Libo's gullibility and self-regard to ingratiate themselves with Tiberius by denouncing the young man for plotting rebellion. Tacitus acknowledges that he is "uncertain whether it is by fate and immutable necessity that the affairs of mortals evolve or by chance" (6, 22, 1). He seems to avoid the notion of destiny in favor of a doctrine that requires personal choice and responsibility:

> Contrariwise others think that fate does indeed correspond
> to affairs, though not as a result of roving stars but depend-
> ing on first principles and the links of natural causes; they

nevertheless leave us a choice in life, but, when you have chosen it, there is a fixed order of inevitable events. (6, 22, 2)

The most brilliant courtier of the age of Nero was the philosopher and dramatist L. Annaeus Seneca. Tacitus makes of the last fifteen years of Seneca's life the sort of minidrama in which he was such an expert. Born in Cordoba in Spain to an Italian family, Seneca was brought to Rome as a child, although we know little about his early life. At the instigation of Messalina, the newly enthroned Claudius had exiled Seneca to Corsica for adultery with one of Caligula's sisters, but recalled him eight years later as a result of the influence of Agrippina—another sister—so that, at the age of about fifty, Seneca could become tutor to the twelve-year-old Nero. Agrippina also arranged a praetorship for the Stoic philosopher, since she thought

> it would be publicly welcome owing to the brilliancy of his studies; also so that Nero's boyhood might develop under such a master and they might likewise use his counsel for their hope of domination, because it was believed that Seneca would be loyal to Agrippina owing to the memory of her good deed, and ferocious toward Claudius owing to indignation at pain of his wrong. (12, 8, 2)

And indeed Seneca was devoted to Agrippina—at least until his student came to the throne in 54. Then, allied with the praetorian prefect Burrus, Seneca tried to restrain the murderous tendencies of Agrippina and her influence over her son.

> These mentors of the Commander's youth were mutually harmonious (a rarity in an alliance of power) and equally forceful by different means, Burrus in military concerns and the severity of his behavior, Seneca in his precepts for eloquence and an honorable affability, each helping the other so that they might more easily retain their hold on the slipperiness of the princeps' age by permitting him pleasures if he spurned virtue. They both had the same struggle against the defiance of Agrippina. (13, 2, 1–2)

Seneca took over the intellectual aspect of the regime: the recruitment of loyal staff, the distribution of patronage, and control of propaganda (art, coins, literature) that every great empire requires, including speechwriting. So when Nero first spoke at the funeral of Claudius, he evoked memories of the "good old days":

> The elders—whose inactivity consists in comparing past and present—noted that, of those who had been in charge of affairs, Nero was the first to have needed someone else's fluency. (13, 3, 2)

Nero may have been the best performer to sit on the imperial throne, but he needed someone else to provide his material: poets for his songs and a philosopher for his policy addresses. Tacitus knew Seneca was showing off—whether his ideas or his rhetoric—when he has Nero

> pledging clemency in frequent speeches which Seneca, to testify to the honorableness of his precepts (or for vaunting his talent), publicized in the voice of the princeps. (13, 11, 2)

Seneca becomes one of Tacitus' favorite character types, the "collaborator."[5] He is a courtier who does whatever the regime requires and is usually richly rewarded for his loyal services. Tacitus rarely attributes evil motivations to Seneca; the philosopher's goal is to ensure rational government in a state trapped in the dangerous circumstance of having an impressionable young emperor with a psychopathic mother intent on exercising control. Tacitus certainly approves when a prudent advisor on the scene prevents the headstrong Agrippina from creating a scandal:

> And furthermore, when legates from the Armenians were pleading their case before Nero, she was preparing to mount the Commander's dais to preside next to him, had not Seneca, with everyone else transfixed in panic, warned him to go to meet his advancing mother. The disgrace was headed off by a display of devotion. (13, 5, 2)

5. Walker (1952), 220–225.

As Agrippina flew further out of control when Nero fell in love with his freedwoman Acte, Seneca and Burrus used the opportunity to remove Pallas from the massive authority he had acquired as Agrippina's lover. It was a direct assault on her power, and her response was a furious tantrum launched at her son, openly bewailing all she had done for him (including the use of poison) and threatening to confront Seneca and Burrus before the praetorians:

> Let them listen to Germanicus' daughter on the one hand and to the cripple Burrus and the exile Seneca on the other, claiming—naturally with maimed hand and professorial tongue—control of the human race. (13, 14, 3)

Tacitus shows Nero's mother totally out of control, revealing her own crimes against Claudius and others, threatening to support her stepson, Britannicus (whom she had cheated out of his own succession), and venomously insulting Burrus and Seneca, the "cripple" and the pedant, who had actually kept order in the state. This rant has the ring of truth—a mother who feels she sacrificed all for her son only to be pushed aside. It sealed her fate with Nero's loyal courtiers, but it took still more for Nero to face his mother's perfidy. When Agrippina pressed her incestuous kisses and caresses on her half-drunken son,

> Seneca sought from a female some defense against these womanly allurements and sent in the freedwoman Acte, who, tense though she was at the danger to herself and at Nero's infamy alike, was to tell him that their incest had been publicized by his mother's boasting and that the soldiers would not tolerate the command of a perverted princeps. (14, 2, 1)

Although Nero ordered his mother's murder, after her death Seneca bore the opprobrium for writing Nero's speech justifying it and accusing his mother of an attempt on his life:

> Therefore it was no longer Nero, whose monstrousness outstripped the complaints of all, but Seneca who was the

subject of adverse rumor, because in such a speech he had inscribed a confession. (14, 11, 3)

Within the harsh ethos of *raison d'état*, Seneca was the ideal courtier.[6]

If Seneca has often been portrayed in later times as a greedy, lecherous hypocrite posing as an austere, sanctimonious philosopher, that is likely attributable to a passage in which an elderly senator, Suillius, charged with having illegally argued law cases for a fee, turned on his old enemy Seneca:

> At the same time, he said, Seneca was accustomed to aimless studies and the inexperience of youth, and was green with envy at those who employed a lively and incorruptible eloquence to protect citizens. While he himself had been Germanicus' quaestor, Seneca was an adulterer in his household, or was it to be reckoned a more serious matter to acquire a prize for honest effort at the wish of a litigant than to corrupt the bedrooms of the principes' ladies? By what wisdom, by which precepts of philosophy had he procured three hundred million sesterces within a four-year period of royal friendship? (13, 42, 3–4)

Tacitus presents Suillius as a corrupt courtier in the early days of Claudius when Seneca had been in exile, and yet his accusations of Seneca's enormous wealth seem to have hit the target. A few years later, after Burrus died, Seneca's own power was fading as Nero's new confidants, including his wife, Poppaea, told him that he no longer needed to defer to his old tutor. Seneca prudently tried to withdraw from society and give his wealth to Nero. He knew well that others had been executed for no reason other than imperial avarice. He suggests that he had wealth only because he could not refuse Nero's generous gifts.

6. The concept of *raison d'état* ("reason of state") first appears in the Jesuit theorist Giovanno Botero's 1589 book on the subject, *Ragione di Stato*. Meinecke (1957) shows that Botero was engaging with Tacitus and Machiavelli. "Reason of state" refers to action in support of a state's own self-interest, although it may violate normal legal or moral standards. Cf. Burke (1995) for a brief discussion of this topic.

"Order my estate to be administered by your procurators and accepted as part of your fortune. Not that I shall drag myself down into poverty, but, having handed over the things that dazzle me by their flash, I shall reclaim for my mind the time which is set aside for the care of my gardens and villas." (14, 54, 2–3)

Tacitus moves to the last act of the tragedy. Nero's hostility to Seneca is mentioned several times, as is a failed attempt at poisoning the old man. But it was with the discovery of the Pisonian conspiracy in 65 C.E., which did include Seneca's nephew Lucan, that an extended death scene is granted to Seneca. Tacitus, who did not like the ostentatious self-righteousness of other Stoic "martyrs," is here sympathetic, as Seneca becomes yet another victim of Julio-Claudian tyranny. Since Tacitus loved to use moral exempla in his histories, he understood that Seneca also used *exempla* to teach and that the Stoic philosopher's own life and death were his most enduring example.[7]

The latter, unafraid, demanded the tablets of his will and testament; and, on the centurion's refusal, he turned to his friends, and testified that, since he was prevented from rendering thanks for their services, he was leaving them the image of his life, which was the only thing—but still the finest thing—he had; if they were mindful of it, men so steadfast in friendship would carry with them the reputation for good qualities. At the same time, partly in conversation and partly in the more intense role of reprimander, he recalled them from their tears to fortitude, asking repeatedly where were the precepts of his wisdom? Where, after contemplating it for so many years, was that reasoning in the face of looming adversity? For who had not known of the savagery of Nero? Nothing else remained, after the killing of his mother and brother, except that he should add the execution of his teacher and preceptor. (15, 62, 1–2)

7. On Seneca's concern with his exemplum, cf. Turpin (2008), 392.

Seneca has come full circle. Tacitus knew, although he does not mention it, that Seneca was the leading Roman philosopher of his time, and his *Moral Epistles* and dialogues on anger, clemency, and other topics were filled with Greek wisdom carefully adapted and modernized for Roman social and political life. His nine plays, drawing on Greek mythological themes (*Phaedra*, *Agamemnon*, etc.) remain the only corpus of tragic writing to survive from Rome. When Tacitus mentions Seneca's wit, he was perhaps thinking of the satirical *Apocolocyntosis*, in which the dead Claudius is not transformed into a god by apotheosis but is put on trial and led into Hades to meet his victims. Tacitus, of course, did not know the effect that Seneca's moral essays would have on such later great minds as Erasmus, Montaigne, and Francis Bacon, that his drama would have on Corneille and Racine, and that his Latin style would have in transforming the "plain style" of English away from Ciceronian excess.

Tacitus was always eager to pounce on the toadies of the imperial court—and Seneca was one of them. But our historian also recognized that Seneca, like his own beloved father-in-law, Agricola, tried to do what a good man could under an evil system. While other Stoics in Tacitus cursed the system and accepted the proud death of a martyr, Seneca and Burrus for five years moderated the fury and arrogance of Agrippina by exerting their own control over the impressionable Nero. Those years are probably the period praised by the later emperor Trajan as the *quinquennium Neronis*—a golden age. If the boy became uncontrollable and turned into Nero, we can hardly blame his teacher for the results. Even the severe Tacitus seems to recognize that Seneca did as well as one could.

Even more than Seneca, the senator and novelist C. Petronius, the courtier par excellence, redeemed the dissolution of his life with a remarkable death. To modern readers Petronius is best known for his fragmentary novel the *Satyricon*, a bawdy romp that combines prose and poetry, pornography and social criticism. That extraordinary book has given later centuries the exaggerated view of Roman orgies recounted in numerous modern novels and films. While Tacitus presents Petronius as a connoisseur of pleasure, the archpriest of good taste, he recognizes his efficiency as an administrator.

> Then, recoiling into vice, or by imitations of vice, he was enlisted by Nero among a few of his establishment as the arbiter of elegance, inasmuch as he thought that nothing was attractive or had the soft feeling of affluence except what Petronius had approved for him. Hence the resentment of Tigellinus, as if against a rival and a superior expert in pleasures. (16, 18, 2–3)

When the Pisonian conspiracy was uncovered, Nero's prefect Tigellinus used the opportunity to rid the court of any whom he regarded as competitors. So Petronius was arrested, and his fate was clear. But even the serious Tacitus cannot resist the spectacular joke with which Petronius concludes his life.

> He bore no further delay in his fear or hope, yet neither did he expel his life precipitately, but, having slit his veins and bound them up at whim, he opened them again and addressed his friends, though not in grave terms or such as would bring him the glory of steadfastness. And he listened to them speaking, not about the immortality of the soul and the tenets of the wise, but light poems and easy verses. Of his slaves, he treated some to his lavishness, others to beatings. He embarked on a banquet, indulged in sleep, so that his death, though forced, might resemble the natural. Not even in his codicils (like many of those perishing) was he sycophantic to Nero and Tigellinus or any other of the powerful, but he listed the princeps' outrages (under the names of the pathics and females) and the novelty of each sexual crime, and dispatched the signed contents to Nero. He also broke his ring, lest it should later prove useful for the manufacturing of danger. (16, 19, 1–3)

Petronius certainly parodies the long tradition of philosophical suicide: Socrates, in his turn imitated by Cato the Younger, and then Seneca. He too plans to die with dignity, surrounded by his friends, but with his tongue firmly in his cheek: a few jolly songs instead of lugubrious philosophy. With his final display of wit, Petronius tells Nero that his "secret" vices are well known, but there is no way the undoubtedly furious emperor could strike back. The final act of a consummate courtier is to thumb his nose at the regime—not with sanctimonious philosophy but with a display of self-confident verve. We are left after two millennia in awe at the stagecraft of his departure. Nero must have been a bit jealous as well.

· 9 ·

Performances at the Court: The
Reigns of Claudius and Nero

Tacitus has been regarded as the greatest dramatist to write under the Roman Empire, and many of his characters—Germanicus, Sejanus, Agrippina, Octavia, Seneca, and Nero—reappeared in operas and plays of the seventeenth and eighteenth centuries. But the historian did not invent political theatricality—rather, he shaped it into dramatic form. For centuries Roman public and political life was dominated by men, and the occasional woman, for whom performance was an essential function of their success as statesmen. Their legends included dramatic tales of Romulus, Lucretia, Horatius, Virginia, Brutus, Coriolanus, and Cincinnatus. Later, in historical times, their descendants spoke in public assemblies from the rostrum or in the Senate house, they sponsored games and festivals, they erected public buildings from "their own" funds (usually the spoils of war), and they carried death masks of their ancestors at family funerals. A successful Roman general was sometimes granted a "triumph" in which he marched with his troops and elaborate floats (depicting his successful battles) in a triumphal procession that culminated with the general—perhaps with a painted face—and his chariot drawn up in front of the Capitoline temple so that he could there dedicate his gold wreath to Jupiter. So Roman leaders, in performance and even personal adornment (as when Pompey imitated the hairstyle of Alexander the Great), had long been using public display in the service of politics.

Some Roman officials dramatized their duties to a degree that we might regard as egotistical self-aggrandizement. In 196 B.C.E., at the Isthmian Games in Corinth, T. Quinctius Flamininus announced to tens of thousands of roaring spectators that the Greeks were now "free." There were wild celebrations, and some cities even worshipped Flamininus as a god, before the Greeks learned that the Roman idea of freedom was somewhat different from their own. When Popilius Laenas was sent in 168 B.C.E. to warn King Antiochus of Syria to withdraw from the lands of Rome's ally Egypt, he drew a circle in the sand around the reluctant king and told him to decide before he left the circle. Likewise the elder Cato, not content with ending every senatorial speech with a thunderous "and Carthage must be destroyed," and wishing to bring home to his fellow senators the dangerous proximity of the enemy, brought succulent figs in his cloak to a meeting of the Senate and noted that they had been picked in Carthage only three days earlier. Such stories were repeated with admiration by later Romans. On his deathbed Augustus was said to have asked whether he had played his part well in the comedy of life (*mimus vitae*), and, if so, he asked for approval as a Roman comic actor asked for applause at the end of a play (Suetonius *Augustus* 99). Theatricality was an essential component of a successful political career.

So it is hardly surprising that the political leaders of the Roman Empire would seek to continue these practices, even if there were no longer meetings of the assembly or public election campaigns. Scholars have examined the ways in which the rulers and the ruled interact on public occasions, most notably gladiatorial contests or races in the circus where the emperor appeared as the sponsor and patron of the occasion.[1] On some occasions the will

---

1. For discussions of the relations between emperors and the audiences, cf. Cameron (1976), Hopkins (1983), and Bartsch (1994).

of the crowd was even "allowed" to sway the emperor to spare or condemn a gladiator. We can see the seriousness with which some rulers viewed the importance of such occasions when Suetonius tells us that Augustus wrote to Livia about her disabled grandson, Claudius:

> The question is whether he has full command of all his senses. . . . Should he be deemed physically or mentally deficient, the public (which always like to scoff and mock at such things) must not be given a chance of laughing at him and us. . . . I am against his watching the Games in the Circus from the imperial box, where the eyes of the whole audience would be on him. (*Claudius* 4)

The emperor was concerned with keeping a *bella figura* lest the imperial family lose popular support. Politics was performative, and public relations is hardly a modern invention.

The first six books of Tacitus' *Annals* display relatively few imperial performances, since Tiberius was himself rather shy and agoraphobic. He had enjoyed the company of soldiers when on campaign for most of thirteen years (20–7 B.C.E.) in the East and along the Rhine and Danube, but he found the political atmosphere of Rome treacherous and oppressive. He twice withdrew from Rome into voluntary exile: for seven years under Augustus to Rhodes and for the last eleven years of his own reign to Capri. While in Rome, he is portrayed as continually uncomfortable among senators and at public events, and Tacitus depicts him as having to repress or disguise his feelings (*Annals* 1, 11). In fact it was the fawning senators and sycophantic courtiers who could have won dramatic prizes. The most notable melodramatic scenes are dominated by the young power couple of his regime: Germanicus and his wife, Agrippina. We have seen them performing in the German camps, in Antioch, and even on Agrippina's return to Rome with the prince's ashes. It is not totally surprising that the most histrionic of emperors would be their son Caligula and their grandson, Nero.

1 | Caligula

Modern scholars often lament the lost books of antiquity—for example, hundreds of Greek tragedies or nearly a hundred volumes of the Roman historian Livy—which did not survive the millennium between the fall of Rome and the Renaissance. Every scholar has his favorite desideratum. I would especially like to have books 7–10 of Tacitus' *Annals*, which covered the years between 37 and 47 C.E.—the entire reign of Caligula and the first six years of Claudius'. The text picks up in the middle of a sentence in book 11.[2] We have certainly been deprived of much entertainment. Suetonius and Cassius Dio record Caligula's incest with each of his three sisters, his self-deification, his bridge of boats across the Bay of Naples (imitating Xerxes' Bosporus bridge), his bizarre army maneuvers on the beaches of the English Channel, his wild profligacy and ruthless greed, his intention of making his horse Incitatus senator and consul, and the melodramatic assassination. Suetonius attributes his behavior to illness and madness, but Tacitus would have certainly found deeper political and psychological elements in Caligula's performances. Unless a papyrus appears in Egypt, however, or a manuscript is discovered misfiled in a European monastery, we will never read Tacitus on Caligula.

2 | Claudius

Claudius' performances had begun long before his accession to the throne. He was cursed from an early age—perhaps by a bout of polio—with a limp and a stutter, along with twitches and drooling, which led even his closest relatives to doubt his mental capacities. His mother called him "a monster: a man whom nature had not finished

---

2. In actuality, a single ninth-century manuscript (First Medicean) contains books 1–6 of *The Annals;* an eleventh-century manuscript (Second Medicean) contains books 11–16. There are many other manuscripts of this second block, though they all derive from the Second Medicean.

but had merely begun" (Suetonius *Claudius* 3). He himself claimed, as Suetonius recounts, that his "stupidity" was just a mask he assumed to protect him from the cruelty and suspicion of Caligula (*Claudius* 38)—a conception richly developed by Robert Graves in his influential novel *I, Claudius*. It was better to be regarded as a fool and a dullard than to be killed by his uncle Tiberius or his nephew Caligula. He had developed the defenses of an adolescent outsider: a peculiar nervous laugh and a knack for invisibility. Acting obviously ran in the family, since his brother Germanicus roamed through his troop encampment in disguise. Even Claudius' vocation as a historian and his desire to learn Etruscan must have placed him in an "ivory tower" safely removed from imperial politics. He always seemed more interested in the past than in the politics of his own time. These antiquarian avocations, along with his physical weaknesses and reported mental limitations, became protections in a dangerous age.

None of these details are contained in Tacitus; even if we had the missing books, the stiff-necked historian is unlikely to have provided much information on physical disabilities. But Tacitus would be invaluable as an addition to the various ancient versions of Claudius' accession. Suetonius and Cassius Dio tell the story of the terrified Claudius discovered hiding in the palace by the praetorians, who, fearing the senatorial abolition of the regime and their own privileges, whisked him to the Praetorian Camp for acclamation as emperor.[3] The Jewish historian Josephus provides two versions, both giving an important role to Claudius' boyhood friend King Herod Agrippa. In the *Jewish War* he is depicted as an ambassador between Claudius and the reluctant Senate; in the later, more nationalistic *Jewish Antiquities* Herod is the instigator who persuades the terrified Claudius to accept the imperial crown from the praetorians.[4] Here Tacitus' political acuity might have cut through the dramatic, but not wholly convincing, narrative of the fraught days following the death of Caligula. Later Romans regarded those days as the last opportunity to restore the Republic—or at least the last

3. Suetonius *Life Of Claudius* 10; Cassius Dio *Roman History* 60, 1.
4. Josephus *Jewish War* 2, 204–213; Josephus *Jewish Antiquities* 19, 212–267.

occasion on which the matter was seriously debated. But the surviving sources hardly provide a plausible political context for those events; the absence of Tacitus' analysis will forever leave the accession of Claudius murky.

Tacitus generally accepted the negative senatorial tradition in believing that Claudius was nothing more than a bad joke that Fate had played on the Roman people. After the death of Germanicus, a senator made a motion to thank members of the imperial family for "avenging" him, but he neglected to mention Germanicus' brother Claudius. When he reports the episode Tacitus adds his ironic philosophical musing:

> But as for me, the more I reconsider recent or past events, the more am I confronted by the mockeries made of mortal affairs in every activity: for in terms of reputation, hope, and veneration, everyone was marked out for command rather than the future princeps whom fortune was keeping in hiding (3, 18, 4)

And yet there is a very serious contradiction. Claudius seems, in Tacitus and in the other sources, considerably more energetic and engaged in state business than were Tiberius, Caligula, or Nero. Tiberius had been an effective general and provincial administrator *before* he came to the throne, but he gradually withdraws from public appearances. Claudius, on the other hand, moved from virtual invisibility to hyperactivity.

Despite Tacitus' general contempt for Claudius, he is positive about the emperor's conduct of foreign affairs. One of Tacitus' grievances toward Tiberius is that he followed the injunction of Augustus to retain the old frontiers of the empire (1, 11). Tacitus scorns that inertia and yearns for the more aggressive imperialism of the Republic, whereas Tiberius—although once a successful general—was more concerned with effective administration than with additional conquest. Yet Claudius embarked on the conquest of Britain in 43 C.E.—an island invaded and then abandoned by Julius Caesar almost a century earlier—and thus expanded the boundaries of the empire. This decisive expedition to enlarge the empire took place only two years after Claudius' unexpected accession to the throne; he dispatched four legions and personally led the troops across the Thames. The new emperor had earlier only held one suffect (replacement) consulship and had no military experience. He was obviously seeking to avoid the fate of Caligula by linking himself with the military exploits of his father, Drusus, and brother Germanicus from the very beginning of his reign. He slowly returned to Rome in a stately progress through Gaul—he had been born in Lugdunum (Lyons) while his father was serving there—to allow the provincials to acclaim their successful emperor. He celebrated his grand triumph on his return to Rome the following year.

While Tacitus' account of the initial invasion and triumph is in the lost books, he does record a second triumph in 51, when the defeated British king Caractacus was paraded through the city in chains. The historian called it a *clara victoria*—a notable victory—and, in praising the reputation and skill of Caractacus, contributed to Claudius' own reputation. The speech Tacitus writes for Caractacus becomes part of the performance of the emperor's acclaim and magnanimity:

> "But my present lot, disfiguring as it is for me, is magnificent for you. I had horses, men, arms and wealth: what wonder if I was unwilling to lose them? If you wish to command everyone, does it really follow that everything should accept your slavery? Now if I were being handed over as one who had surrounded immediately, neither my fortune or your glory would have achieved brilliance. It is also true that in my case any reprisal will be followed by oblivion. On the other hand, if you preserve me safe and sound, I am an eternal example of your clemency." (12, 37, 2–3)

Caractacus and his family were spared in a performance of Claudius' *clementia*—one of the central imperial virtues on which Seneca had written a famous essay. Tacitus himself was impressed by the clemency, although he was scornful of the grandiloquent speeches delivered by servile senators in praise of the emperor. The historian is more sympathetic toward Claudius' conduct of foreign affairs than toward that of any other of the Julio-Claudians. That in itself is remarkable.

Not only did Claudius perform the role of conquering general in the provinces and in the triumphal procession that took him to the Capitoline Hill, the *Annals* also shows other ways in which he competently managed imperial policy in the provinces. Although aggressive in Britain, he enforced a cautious policy of containment along the Danube and on the German frontier, where (to his general Corbulo's annoyance) he withdrew the legions to the near side of the Rhine. He had more peaceful policies toward the provinces, and he greatly increased grants of citizenship. These new citizens and the recipients of land in new colonies became loyal clients of the emperor.

Despite Tacitus' senatorial condescension toward Claudius' domestic policies, he includes examples of Claudius' acts of benevolence as he tried to win over the people. He often presided over the courts, and he once brokered what seems to be a reasonable compromise in a dispute in the Senate. In response to a particularly greedy lawyer who took four hundred thousand sesterces and then betrayed his client, some senators demanded the enforcement of an ancient law that forbade any lawyer to take pay for his services. Others responded that it was all very well for wealthy senators, but many men had devoted their lives to study in the hopes of making a living from the practice of law.

> The princeps, deeming these words (if less becoming) not without point, decided on amounts up to 10,000 sesterces as the limit of money to be accepted, transgressions of which would be liable to a charge of extortion. (11, 7, 4)

Tacitus reports other Claudian initiatives—an increase of the water supply and legislation prohibiting the lending of money to young men in expectation of their fathers' death—which were performances of imperial benevolence. But he devotes much more attention to Claudius' quirky addition of three new letters to the Latin alphabet. Tacitus' almost gleeful comment that they "were consigned to oblivion" after Claudius' death demonstrates his desire to highlight the emperor's futile pedantry.

Despite his unpromising beginning, there is ample evidence that Claudius, although he stuttered in private conversation, was at least acceptable as a public speaker. He had been trained as a historian by Livy himself and had undergone rigorous rhetorical instruction. Even his step-grandfather Augustus acknowledged his skill in a letter to Livia:

> Confound me, dear Livia, if I am not surprised that your grandson *Claudius* could please me with his declaiming. How in the world anyone who is so unclear in his conversation can speak with clarity and propriety when he declaims, is more than I can see. (Suetonius *Claudius* 4)

Tacitus also made this distinction between Claudius' conversation and speechmaking:

> Nor in Claudius' case, whenever he held forth on prepared material, would you have wanted for elegance. (13, 3, 2)

Tacitus leaves his reader in little doubt that Claudius was willing and even eager to deliver public orations. In addition to his famous speech in favor of the admission of Gallic nobles to the Senate (11, 23–24), Tacitus records summaries of several other speeches. In addition, scholars have attributed Tacitean digressions on the alphabet, priestly divination, and the *pomerium* (sacred boundary) of the city of Rome to speeches of Claudius.[5] There are also other antiquarian discussions which the historian most likely found in Claudian speeches contained in the *acta senatus*, since Tacitus delighted in demonstrating the fussiness of the emperor. But the most fascinating remains Claudius' speech concerning the Gauls, since an inscription from the emperor's birthplace of Lyons preserves a portion of the text as it was actually delivered.[6]

5. Syme (1958), 703–708 (in an appendix titled "Some Claudian Orations"), and Griffin (1982), 404–418, discuss material surviving in Tacitus from Claudian speeches.

6. *Inscriptiones Latinae Selectae* 212; translation in Braund (1985), 199–201 (#570). Cf. Woodman (2004), xvi–xvii, for a discussion of the differences between the inscription and Tacitus' text.

This is one of the very rare instances in which an ancient historian's report of a speech can be compared with the speech as officially recorded on a contemporary inscription. While every Greek and Roman historian from Herodotus and Thucydides to Tacitus believed he should present the core of an oration—as far as he knew it—for dramatic purposes, none felt any responsibility to preserve the words or even the specific arguments. Here we can see the personality of Claudius—humane, pedantic, unfocused, complacent—evident in the long, if fragmentary, inscription. Since the emperor's own *consilium* (privy council) had opposed his proposal, his speech begins with reference to those objections:

> I deplore the first thought of all men, which, I foresee, will stand in my path first and foremost, lest you shy away, as if from some revolutionary innovation: rather think instead how many changes have occurred in this state and through how many forms and constitutions our state has been taken, from the very foundation of the city.

The emperor continues with nearly a page of an erudite and somewhat irrelevant survey of the early kings of Rome from Romulus to the Etruscan Tarquins. He asks a series of four rhetorical questions, each beginning, "Why should I remind you now . . ." which might have tried his listeners' patience, until he dismisses the irrelevance with "But let me rather leave that aside." Suetonius criticized Claudius for his feeble jokes and we see one very much in evidence when the emperor addresses himself:

> It is now time, Tiberius Caesar Germanicus [Claudius], to reveal to the senators where your speech is leading.

We can almost hear the senators reply, "At last." The proposal of Claudius was unquestionably an important one: a century after Julius Caesar had conquered Gallia Comata (literally "long-haired Gaul") referring to the less civilized areas of Gaul, it was high time for the local Gallic elites to become Roman senators as had citizens from older provinces like Spain and Gallia Narbonensis (modern Provence). The text confirms that the supposedly malleable Claudius had come to the Senate to speak *against* the advice of his privy council. He was hardly as weak as the senatorial sources often depict him.

Tacitus creates a very different sort of speech. He begins by presenting the arguments advanced in the emperor's council that Italy could adequately provide members of the Senate. The rambling pedantry of Claudius' long historical beginning is replaced by a much better argument: Claudius' own Sabine ancestor Clausus gained admission to the Senate, as did the Julian family, and so Rome should continue to profit from new blood. The speech is much condensed, although there are several points of argument in common. The expansionist ideology would have perhaps become more familiar by the time Tacitus wrote in the early second century than when Claudius actually gave the speech in 48 C.E. The mention of the Balbi from Spain would carry more weight in the reign of the Spanish emperor Trajan. Likewise, Tacitus compared the self-defeating chauvinism of classical Greek cities unfavorably to the Roman generosity toward conquered peoples. Although Tacitus obviously had seen a copy of the original speech, there are no verbal echoes, and in every way he has given the emperor a better speech than he actually delivered. There are even some elegant turns of phrase, with a very stirring peroration:

"Everything, conscript fathers, which is now believed most olden was new: plebeian magistrates came after patrician, Latin after plebeian, those of other peoples of Italy after the Latin. This too will grow old, and what today we defend by examples will be among the examples." (11, 24, 7)

Tacitus' briefer speech is considerably more persuasive, and it is more dignified than Claudius' self-conscious jokes and pedantic digressions. The historian has given the much-scorned emperor a speech that would have been more enjoyable and more effective, but less genuinely Claudian. And there is no reason to believe that Tacitus would have cared at all about such a divergence. And he does retain the fact that Claudius uncharacteristically had the fortitude to oppose his own council. The two versions of the emperor's speech allows us to hear the voice and performance of Claudius, as well as assess what Tacitus thought of it.

3 | Nero

Nero was the ultimate player-king among Roman emperors; he performed for all fourteen years of his reign, in public and in private, on stage and off. Theatricality was, of course, in his blood. His great-great grandfather Mark Antony reveled in the streets of Alexandria dressed as Dionysos, and Tacitus shows his maternal grandparents, Germanicus and Agrippina, as notable actors in the imperial melodramas. Tacitus himself was born about the time of Nero's accession, and he must have heard much about Nero's performances during his impressionable boyhood. Young Nero began his reign with what Tacitus calls an "imitation of sorrow," when he delivered the funeral oration for Claudius, his adoptive father:

> Even the recollection of his liberal arts, and that nothing grim had befallen the state at the hands of foreigners during his rule, was listened to with favorable attention. But after he turned to the man's foresight and wisdom, no one restrained their laughter, although the speech, composed as it was by Seneca, presented considerable refinement, given that the latter's was an attractive talent and one well adapted to contemporary ears. (13, 3, 1)

If that speech was taken as comedy, there was little laughter the following year when Nero brazenly feigned unconcern when his stepbrother Britannicus took sick at a banquet. The young prince had been poisoned and would soon be dead, but Nero was prepared to put on an act and forced his mother and stepsister to do so as well:

> He for his part, reclining and apparently unwitting, said that this was usual, owing to the epileptic illness with which Britannicus had been afflicted since early boyhood, and that his

vision and feeling would return gradually. But in Agrippina's case, such panic, such mental shock flashed out, despite her attempt to suppress them in her look, that it was agreed that she had been as unaware as Octavia, Britannicus's sister. (13, 16, 3–4)

It was hardly enough for the emperor merely to pretend insouciance at his brother's murder; he soon began to adopt more daring roles.

With Q. Volusius and P. Scipio as consuls [56 C.E.], there was inactivity abroad but at home a foul recklessness, with Nero wandering through the streets of the City and its love-lairs and distractions in servile apparel, accoutered to dissemble his identity and accompanied by men who would seize things displayed for sale and inflict wounds on passers-by. (13, 25, 1)

There was a long tradition of masters and slaves pretending to reverse social roles at the celebration of the *Saturnalia*, but Nero's carousing more resembled Mark Antony's in Alexandria. It was self-indulgence more than any ritual—and of course it became extremely dangerous. Once it was known that the disguised emperor and his cronies could rob and beat without any penalty, other young aristocrats would do the same, hoping to be taken for Nero's thugs.

Later—when it had become known that it was Caesar who was on the prowl, and injuries against distinguished men and women were increasing and some people, now that license was permitted, went unpunished under cover of Nero's name, as they carried on the same behavior with their own personal groups—nighttime was passed as if in a state of captivity. (13, 25, 2)

Nero had not yet learned, if he ever did, that imperial performances had consequences in real life.

As Nero became more besotted with his mistress Poppaea, she saw his overbearing mother as an impediment to their marriage.

Tacitus tells us how she taunted him with still being the "ward" of his mother:

> Why was her wedding being deferred? Evidently her looks were displeasing, and her triumphal grandfathers; or was it her fertility or her true heart? (14, 1, 2)

As Poppaea raged, she impelled Nero to think about freeing himself from his mother, and Agrippina in turn began to maneuver to secure her own position. During the year 59 C.E. there was much imperial soap opera: tears, kisses, reconciliation, and, if we believe Tacitus' sources, even incest—although he is uncertain whether mother or son initiated it. These were actors caught up in their own performances, pushing themselves out of control. At first Nero seemed content when his mother withdrew to her country estates, but soon he was plotting to have her murdered on a boat on the bay of Naples. This was staged as (another) reconciliation:

> There he lured his mother, insisting that the rages of parents should be borne and tempers calmed—all so he might produce a rumor of reconciliation which Agrippina might accept, the credulity of females being responsive to joyful news. (14, 4, 1)

Tacitus delights in recounting the banquet at Nero's seaside villa at Baiae, where Agrippina's son put on a performance of extraordinary warmth and affection:

> He had dragged out the party for a long time by numerous conversations, at one moment in youthful intimacy and at another as of communicating something serious, Nero escorted her upon her departure. (14, 4, 4)

She was to be taken across the bay in what she saw as an ornate ship outfitted in her honor; it was of course a trap, designed to collapse at sea. As another element of the theatrical, Dio (62, 12) reports, this ship was modeled on a "ship" seen in the theater that had come apart, disgorged animals, and reassembled. And we have seen that, when the ship sank, she played her role by feigning ignorance until the end. Her last words were in keeping with her family's dramatic flair. "Stab my belly!" she cried to the approaching centurion, while pointing to her womb, which had produced the monster Nero.

Of course scholars have had great fun analyzing what one has called a "sensational novelette."[7] The murder plot seems comically inept—why not just kill Agrippina on the boat to make certain she died?—and the chronology of the many events that night seems impossible. Did Tacitus confuse, or intentionally conflate, stories of the "fatal charades" in which Nero liked to execute criminals in reenactments of mythological stories?[8] Many of the events reported necessarily took place in private and were reported only through rumor or gossip—the *Acts of the Senate* may have recorded Nero's speech, but they hardly contained the last words of Agrippina. So it is not surprising that Tacitus would weave together the public and the private, facts and rumors, into what he saw as a compelling, moralizing narrative. And so it is—one of the most appalling, and amusing, sections of his entire history. It is worse than futile to deconstruct this episode to attempt to re-create the "real" story; that would be to lose a masterpiece by the greatest dramatist of his age.

It is perhaps unsurprising that Nero should have engaged in some pretense of devotion toward his onetime tutor and counselor Seneca; students routinely feign such interest and enthusiasm, especially when a grade or letter of recommendation is outstanding. But Nero continued that pretense long after his affection for Seneca had waned. By 62 C.E., when both Agrippina and Burrus had died—the former certainly and the latter possibly at Nero's order—the philosopher Seneca was the last surviving advisor who had helped the young emperor in his early years on the throne. Other courtiers undermined him for "arrogating praise for eloquence to himself

7. There are many discussions of the theatricality of the murder of Agrippina; cf. especially Dawson (1969), 253–267.

8. For the best treatment of these reenactments, cf. Coleman (1990).

exclusively" (14, 52), since he had written Nero's speeches, and he was accused of mocking the emperor's skill as a singer and a charioteer. As Seneca became aware of these accusations and sensed Nero's increasing distance, he requested a private meeting at which he offered Nero his considerable estates and asked, fawningly, for a quiet retirement.

In a long speech that Nero said he owed to Seneca's own tutelage in rhetoric, the emperor rebuffed the old man's requests. He said in part:

> "It will be neither your moderation, should you return the money, nor your rest, should you abandon your princeps, but my greed and the dread of my cruelty which will be on the lips of all." (14, 56, 2)

Nero's speech is in fact cogent, since a twenty-four-year-old emperor could well use his most experienced advisor. But Tacitus ensures that the speech is not taken at face value, but merely as a bit of imperial theater:

> To these words he added an embrace and kisses, being constituted by nature and trained by habit to screen his hatred with treacherous blandishments. Seneca (such being the end of all conversations with one's master) expressed his gratitude; but he reversed the routines of his previous powerfulness: he stopped the throngs of well-wishers, avoided companions and was rarely in the City, as if detained at home by adverse health or the study of wisdom. (14, 56, 3)

Three years later it was Seneca's turn in the theatrical spotlight. After the discovery of the conspiracy of Piso, the emperor sent word that the old philosopher would have to die. Seneca said to his friends and his wife, Paulina, that they had all considered adversity for many years and that their wisdom should have prepared them for a philosophical death. When he had slit his wrists, the blood flowed so slowly that he demanded of his doctor poison—"by which those condemned by the Athenians' public court had their lives extinguished" (15, 64). Thus he assumed the role of Socrates and, like several others at the court of Nero, was able to write the script of the final act of his life.[9]

Perhaps the most lasting image of Nero is as a singer—notably the rumor reported by Tacitus that the emperor sang of the destruction of Troy while Rome itself burned. He had long craved to perform on the stage and as a charioteer in the circus, but he was restrained until his mother had passed from the scene. Tacitus portrays Burrus and Seneca trying to protect the dignity of the imperial office, but Nero countered that kings once drove chariots at festivals and that Apollo himself was the patron of singers. When his advisors finally relented, the emperor first rode in a chariot race in a remote area near the Vatican hill, but he soon felt that the public should not be deprived of the pleasure of seeing him. Tacitus (14, 14) is especially outraged that Nero enticed and even bribed aristocrats to accompany him on the stage. Of course the image of Charles I of England performing in court masques or Louis XIV dancing in Lully's ballets dulls our shock at such behavior, but in Rome, where actors, acrobats, and athletes were widely regarded as deeply immoral creatures, Tacitus is merely expressing a traditional Roman repugnance.[10] Although Nero was still deterred from giving vocal performances publicly in Rome, as opposed to private recitals in the palace, he was eager to appear before his planned grand tour of the Greek festivals. Tacitus reports his debut in 64 C.E. in the "Greek city" of Naples with an audience packed with soldiers and visiting sailors from Alexandria. We read in Suetonius (*Nero* 20) that Nero so loved the rhythmic applause of the sailors that he had Roman knights and youths learn how to imitate it and paid them handsomely to "perform" when he performed.

In the following year, Tacitus (16, 4) tells of Nero's song recital in the capital. The Senate cravenly offered a victory crown, but the emperor

9. For a recent comprehensive examination of the literary and visual representations of Seneca's death from Roman times until the twentieth century, cf. Ker (2009).

10. Edwards (2002), 98–100.

wished to rely on the fairness of the judges and waited for their decision on one knee in "feigned anxiety." The plebs greeted his performance, and the performance of humility within the theatrical show, with the same organized rhythmic applause he had experienced in Naples. The provincial and morally self-righteous Tacitus reminds us that there were still those who found this behavior shameful:

> But those from remote municipalities and an Italy still austere and retentive of ancient custom, and those who had arrived on official legations of some private errand, unused to recklessness in their distant provinces, neither tolerated the sight of it all nor were competent for the dishonorable task, since with their untrained hands they soon grew weary, they disrupted the experts, and often they were beaten by soldiers, who stood between the blocks in case a single moment of time should pass in inadequate shouting or sluggish silence. (16, 5, 1)

The names of the absent and unenthusiastic were recorded for later punishment; even the dozing general Vespasian was saved only by the intercession of friends. The text of the *Annals* ends before the Greek tour of 66 C.E.; it was only after that tour that Nero actually appeared in dramatic roles in tragedies. For anecdotes of his performances and repertoire choices, we must rely on Suetonius. Just as the biographer includes more titillating reports of the sexual peccadilloes of the emperors, so he is more interested in the details of these appalling public performances than the more severe historian, who cares little for roles and more for the continued evidence of moral degradation.

Nero's most bizarre performance in the *Annals* was in an elaborately staged orgy arranged by his praetorian prefect Tigellinus. The courtier constructed an artificial island in the pool near the public Baths of Agrippa in the Campus Martius. There, in the middle of Rome, was an extraordinary seascape:

> The ships were picked out in gold and ivory, and their pathic rowers arranged by age and expertise at lust. He had

sought birds and wild beasts from far-flung lands, and sea animals all the way from Ocean. On the dykes of the pool stood love-lairs filled with illustrious ladies, and, opposite, whores could be seen with naked bodies. (15, 37, 2–3)

This hardly seems real; Tony Woodman rightly sees it as Tacitus' *fabula* in which he can override literal truth to evoke another sort of truth—as Herodotus once did.[11] The misuse of a public pond that could in no way have been large enough for such boats; the importation of sea monsters; all that should be most secret and intimate put on public display. This fantastical scene evokes the city of Canopus, at the mouth of the Nile, where the wealthy notoriously lounged alongside canals; Hadrian replicated it at his Villa near Tivoli, and the satirist Juvenal refers to the place as an icon of immorality.[12] Therefore Tacitus turned to Egypt, pretending to peer into the emperor's mind, to report that, for the emperor, "the provinces of the East, especially Egypt, were stirring his private visualizings (*secretis imaginationibus*)" (15, 36, 1). From Nero's ancestor Mark Antony to his uncle Caligula, who had ordered pornography from Egypt to titillate his own great-uncle Tiberius, the Romans imagined Egypt as a source of illicit sexual pleasures. Tacitus would have Nero ready to re-site Rome on the banks of the Nile.

The historian implies that this was only one of many outrages; he reports it "as an example, to avoid the obligation of narrating too often the same prodigality" (15, 37, 1). So he spares his reader Nero's elaborate marriage to his beloved eunuch Sporus, reported by Suetonius (*Nero* 28). But it is difficult to imagine anything Tacitus would see as equal in squalor to his dramatic pièce de résistance— the emperor's wedding to his freedman Pythagoras, in which Nero played the role of the not-so-blushing *bride*.

He took one of that herd of perverts (his name was Pythagoras) in the fashion of a solemn espousal to be his husband: there was placed on the Commander a bridal veil, the

11. Woodman (1992), 176–177.
12. Juvenal *Satires* 6, 84.

officials were admitted, there was a dowry, a marriage-bed, and wedding torches. Everything, in short was observed which even in the case of a female is covered by night. (15, 37, 4)

Here Tacitus culminates his theatrical play with boundary crossings: ships and wild beasts in the center of the city; night turned into day; bedroom secrets made public; and finally the extraordinary phrase "the commander wearing a bridal veil"—*inditum imperatori flammeum*. The immediate juxtaposition of the military title and the bridal veil would disgust any respectable Roman, as Tacitus intended.[13]

Nero was not alone in inspiring his courtiers to play roles. Even his most determined opponents consciously or unconsciously took on parts in the grand spectacle of the Pisonian conspiracy. There is something in assassination plots that encourages melodrama: Julius Caesar's *et tu, Brute*; Caligula's murderers' use of the password *Libertas;* and John Wilkes Booth's triumphant shout of the motto of the Commonwealth of Virginia, *sic semper tyrannis* ("thus always to tyrants"). Marcus Junius Brutus was inspired to act against his erstwhile patron Caesar by the heroism of his ancestor, Lucius Junius Brutus, who expelled the Tarquin kings from Rome five centuries earlier. John Wilkes Booth, whose actor father was (incredibly enough) named Junius Brutus Booth, actually played the part of Mark Antony in 1864 in Shakespeare's *Julius Caesar*, along with his brothers Edwin (Brutus) and Junius Brutus Booth, Jr. (Cassius). It was difficult for men like Brutus and Booth to separate theater from reality.

The so-called Pisonian conspiracy is the longest episode in the *Annals*, and Tony Woodman has shown that Tacitus has given to the conspiracy "a coherence and unity it did not possess in real life."[14] The conspirators were taking part in "amateur dramatics" in which

13. Champlin (2003), in his intriguingly sympathetic biography, 167, suggests that the "marriage" may have been a parody of a religious initiation.

14. Woodman (1993), 104.

Scaevinus even uses the theatrical term in demanding that he be given the "leading role" (*primas partes*) in the drama (15, 53). Tacitus recounts that he melodramatically finds his dagger too blunt and orders his freedman to sharpen it, as Ajax did in Sophocles' play, offers a lavish banquet, then gives his favored slaves their freedom before falling into a melancholic funk (15, 54). It is all playacting of the sort that Stoic "martyrs" indulge in elsewhere in Tacitus. After the freedman Milichus treacherously brings the dagger to Nero to report the conspiracy, the craven Scaevinus portrays himself as a victim and spins an elaborate justification that the dagger was merely a family relic, thus turning it into a convincing denunciation of the freedman. Tacitus compliments his "conviction of delivery and demeanor" (15, 55), which almost carried the day with Nero—a good review for his performance—until the conspirator Natalis confessed, and the plot collapses. Tacitus then displays the conspirators rushing to implicate one another; the poet Lucan, angry at Nero for trying to rival his poems (15, 49), actually bore witness against his own mother before committing suicide (15, 56–58).

Only a few cases of nobility emerged among the plotters. Seneca, Lucan's uncle, who had no part in the conspiracy, shows nobility, albeit theatrical, in his suicide. But Tacitus was most impressed by the praetorian tribune Flavus, who confessed directly to the emperor, Nero being genuinely puzzled at why he might be so hated.

> Asked by Nero what reasons had led him to forget his oath, he said: "I hated you, and yet none of your soldiers was more loyal to you as long as you deserved affection. I began to hate you only after you turned out to be the parricide of your mother and your wife, a charioteer and an actor and an arsonist." (I have recorded his actual words, because they were not, as were Seneca's, publicized, and it was no less fitting for the military man's feelings to become known. The rough and vigorous sentiments of a soldier ought to be no less known, unadorned and yet effective as they were.) It was agreed that nothing in that conspiracy weighed more heavily on the ears of Nero, who, though ready for the commission

of crimes, was unaccustomed to hear of what he was committing. (15, 67, 2–3)

Note that, in the mind of Flavus (and of Tacitus, who makes a rare point of quoting him), Nero's public performances as actor and charioteer are ranked equally with matricide and arson as horrific crimes.

All through the *Annals* Tacitus presents public life as a performance. His role as historian and moralist is to unmask the hypocrites—be they emperors or courtiers. The theatrical metaphor becomes literal in the applause-crazed world of Nero. The dramatic fictions spread from the emperor to the senators and freedmen, imperial wives and philosophers. In confronting Nero's fantasies, the conspirators construct their own imaginary world in which they allude to Greek tragedy and the assassination of Julius Caesar. Of course, we will never know how much of their public performances was intentional, just as the overly emotional lives of contemporary actors spill over into their "real lives," as detailed in supermarket tabloids and television exposés. Tacitus hardly invents the theatricality of Nero's court, but he certainly gives the performances a dramatic structure and a moral force that these pathetic acts would never have otherwise had.

Roman emperors were often deified at their death, so as to continue their presence in the Roman pantheon. Temples of deified emperors abounded in the capital and throughout the empire. But Nero alone was believed by many to have somehow survived. In the *Histories*, Tacitus tells of "Nero's" reappearance the year after his death:

At the same time Greece and Asia were frightened by a false story that Nero was returning. There were different rumors about his death, so many people imagined and believed that he was alive. I will report about the adventures and the challenges of other pretenders in the course of this book, but this man was a slave from Pontus or, as others tell it, a freedman from Italy. He was skilled at both the lute and singing from which—added to a facial similarity—belief in his imposture was easier. (*Histories* 2, 8)

How extraordinary that so many awaited the return of an arsonist and mass murderer of Christians, a matricide and charioteer, an outlandish performer of drama and spectacle who married both women (as a man) and men (as both a woman and a man). Why did his charisma last so long? We can only attribute it to the intense theatricality of his persona—his myth was rivaled in antiquity only by that of Alexander the Great, who also was thought to have returned after death in *The Alexander Romance*. When Oscar Wilde had his hair curled in the manner of Nero's bust in the Louvre, he honored his forebear by wishing to make his life into a work of art.[15] Tacitus, as much as anyone else, contributed to that desire.

15. On Wilde, cf. Champlin (2003), 236, 333.

·10·

The Importance of Tacitus' *Annals*

Although we consider Tacitus to be the greatest Roman historian, he had relatively little impact on the Romans themselves. His contemporaries Pliny and Suetonius knew his work, but for more than a millennium there were only sporadic references to it. Few followed his practice. Succeeding Latin historical writers preferred to write biographies or historical abridgments, which made fewer intellectual demands on their readers, and Christian writers scorned Tacitus because of his supposed bias against them and the Jews. Only a fourth-century Greek from Syria, Ammianus Marcellinus, who continued Tacitus' history in Latin from 96 down to his own time, captured something of his master's psychological perceptiveness and rhetorical skill.

It was not until the Renaissance, when European rulers and thinkers wished to examine and emulate the political and legal institutions of the Romans, that Tacitus became enormously important. Since the theory and practice of Roman politics are best found in the historical narratives of Livy and Tacitus, their work moved to the forefront of intellectual life between the Renaissance and the Age of Revolutions. Tacitus exerted an enormous influence on philosophers and poets, princes and popes, painters and political theorists. Although his other books had intermittent significance—especially the *Germania* in Germany and the *Agricola* in England—it was the *Annals* that inspired and horrified scholars and leaders across the continent.

Tacitus' influence shaped, among noteworthy historical works, Thomas More's depiction of Richard III, Guicciardini's political history of Italy, Paolo Sarpi's probing analysis of the Council of Trent, and Edward Gibbon's account of the late Roman and Byzantine court. But he had an even greater influence beyond historical writing. In the eyes of early modern European and even American writers, he was not merely a historian, but a moralist who ranked with Plato and Aristotle, a political thinker whose influence vied with Machiavelli's, a dramatist whose tragic vignettes rivaled those of Seneca, and a stylist whose penetrating, aphoristic prose came to be preferred to the more discursive periods of Cicero. Since his histories lent themselves to conflicting political interpretations, republicans and royalists alike learned from him; courtiers looked to his characters for models of behavior; German humanists and English Puritans used him to forward their own agendas; French and American revolutionaries drew inspiration from him. Tacitus was present at the origin and evolution of modern political thought.

1 | Tacitus in the Italian Renaissance

The first reappearance of Tacitus in Italy was in an eleventh-century manuscript from Germany that appeared in the monastery of Monte Cassino. That manuscript, now in the Laurentian library in Florence as Mediceus II, contained the *Histories* and books 11 to 16 of the *Annals*.[1] Giovanni Boccaccio (1313–1375), a decade after completing his ribald *Decameron,* had turned to the investigation of ancient Latin texts and the compilation of a mythological encyclopedia and biographical compendia. About 1362 he found

1. Schellhase (1976), 5–7.

the manuscript of Tacitus in the dilapidated monastery library and probably purloined it, as humanist scholars were accustomed to do. He first used it in his series of 104 brief biographies of ancient women, *Famous Women* (*De mulieribus claris*)—the first such collection in Western literature.[2] His depictions of the lives of Agrippina the Younger, Poppaea, Paulina (the wife of Seneca), and Epicharis all show clear borrowings from the *Annals*.[3]

The first edition of Tacitus, once again lacking *Annals* 1–6, was printed in Venice in 1470. The Florentine humanist and statesman Niccolò Machiavelli (1469–1527) made some use of that edition as he worked on *The Prince* after his exile in 1513.[4] In this work, dedicated to the arrogant Lorenzo de' Medici in an effort to regain ducal favor after the fall of the Republic, Machiavelli advises on how to promote stable rule, but his cynicism led to later criticism that *The Prince* was amoral and even atheistic. The book overturned much of humanist political morality (derived from Cicero) in advising the ruler that it is better to be feared than loved (xvii). Secrecy is indispensable to the ruler who may have to violate truth and even morality to maintain his government (xviii). Although Machiavelli's prince resembles Tacitus' Tiberius, he makes specific reference only to the second half of the *Annals,* since the first edition of *Annals* 1–6 was not published until 1515, after the completion of *The Prince*. Despite their close links in the minds of later Renaissance thinkers, Machiavelli was less influenced by Tacitus' ideas than he was attracted by the antimonarchical aphorisms, which would buttress his own arguments in his later, overtly republican *Discourses on the First Ten Books of Livy*.[5] This lack of concern about the actual context of the Tacitean material would establish a

2. For a recent bilingual edition, cf. Boccaccio, *Famous Women,* edited and translated by V. Brown (Cambridge, Mass., 2001), which contains a very useful introduction by Brown.

3. Nolhac (1892) prints the texts of Tacitus and Boccaccio in parallel columns.

4. Von Stackelberg (1960), 64–66.

5. Schellhase (1976), 69–70 and 197 n. 12, shows the importance of Tacitus in the *Discourses*; also cf. Syme (1960), 4–6. The parallels are collected in von Stackelberg (1960), 70–73.

pattern followed by later writers. Machiavelli's basic link with Tacitus was his essential pragmatism; both men were realists who attempted to describe real rulers rather than the ideal. In other ways their ideas were quite different, but Machiavelli understood the necessary evasions and ambiguity of life under despotism that Tacitus knew so well, and he quotes one memorable passage in the *Annals* in which Agrippina mistakenly thought she could still control her son, Nero.

The Prince

> I conclude then by saying that no prince is secure without his own troops, on the contrary he is entirely dependent on fortune, having no trustworthy means of defense in time of trouble. It has always been held and proclaimed by wise men *quod nihil sit tam infirmum aut instabile quam fama potentiae non sua vi nixae* ("that nothing is so weak or unstable as the fame attached to power not based on its own strength").[6]

When Machiavelli's works were placed on the *Index of Forbidden Books* by the Catholic Church in 1559, it was to Tacitus that Italian political theorists eventually turned for similar inspiration and authority. In the words of the great Italian philosopher Benedetto Croce, they attempted "to hide Machiavelli under the mask of Tacitus, and his prince under the figure of Tiberius."[7]

It was only in the sixteenth century, after the invasion of Charles VIII (1495) and the brutal sack of Rome in 1527 by German mercenaries had shattered confidence in the Republican values of Livy and Cicero, that Tacitus truly burst upon European intellectual and political life. The political trauma of invasion and the reestablishment

---

6. Chapter xiii. Translated by Luigi Ricci (1903). The quotation by Machiavelli is not precise. *Annals* 13, 19: *nihil rerum mortalium tam instabile ac fluxum est quam fama potentiae non sua vi nixae* ("of all human things nothing is so unstable or transitory as the fame attached to power not based on its own strength"). Though Tacitus refers to Agrippina's lack of supporters at court, Machiavelli applies the sentiment to the question of mercenary troops.

7. *Storia della età barocca in Italia* (Bari, 1946), 82.

of absolutist monarchies turned Italy of the sixteenth century toward Tacitus' cynical political ideas. As the movement, later called "Tacitism," spread, contemporary scholars published collections of aphorisms—books that were virtual mosaics of Tacitus' words. They also produced detailed political commentaries on Tacitus—as Machiavelli had on Livy. They thought that, since the *Annals* described the duplicity of princes and their courts, Tacitus could provide guidance for those who lived under them. The Florentine Francesco Guicciardini, like Tacitus himself, turned from politics to history, and his masterly *History of Italy* (1561) is Tacitean in its probing analysis of politics, personalities, and events. He learned discretion from Tacitus, but he also warned that history can be a two-edged sword:

> Tacitus teaches well the mode of life under tyrants and how to govern oneself prudently, just as he teaches tyrants how to establish tyranny.[8]

Here the Republican Tacitus and the monarchical Tacitus are juxtaposed in the same aphorism. Tacitus found particular favor with the Italian urban elite who identified themselves with the Roman Senate. During the Middle Ages, philosophers argued that the paternal king dispensed justice to all, but Renaissance thinkers were more interested in the nature of arbitrary rule and the character of rulers. These discourses and commentaries are the origins of modern political science.

2 | Tacitus in Reformation Germany

German humanists saw in Tacitus' *Germania* an ideal text with which to assert German national identity.[9] After the text was published in 1470, it was used to fan the fires of German nationalism, and Tacitus provided the basic elements of the myth of

8. Guicciardini, *Ricordi*, chap. 18. Cf. La Penna (1976).

9. On the reception of Tacitus in Germany, cf. Schellhase (1976), 31–49; Borchardt (1971); Kelley (1993).

"Germanism": the high standard of German morality and the simplicity of their customs, their racial purity, and the native freedom of German tribes as opposed to the immorality and servility of imperial Romans. The Reformation was only decades away.

Since they had no surviving historians of their own, patriotic German humanists saw in "our Tacitus" a Roman who had shown such love for Germany that his text could be used to praise their ancestors. After the 1515 publication of *Annals* 1–6, the ancient German general Arminius became the focus of German nationalism and German hostility to Rome. A few years later, the extreme nationalist Ulrich von Hutten wrote his Latin dialogue *Arminius*.[10] There the god Mercury summons Tacitus to the pagan underworld to appear before the judge Minos to bear witness that Arminius had surpassed Scipio, Hannibal, and Alexander the Great in his military achievements.

Arminius

> Minos: This, gentlemen, is the former leader of the Germans, Arminius, who once fought for freedom against the Romans and defeated them. When he heard that you had contended about your standing as generals and that I had made a decision on the matter, he claimed that he had been unfairly excluded. He thinks he has some evidence that will show that no one deserves the prize more than he does.
>
> Alexander: Then let him speak.
>
> Scipio: Absolutely.
>
> Hannibal: I am not opposed.
>
> Minos: Speak, Arminius.
>
> Arminius: First I would like a certain Tacitus, from Italy, to appear here so that he may say what he wrote about me in his history.
>
> Minos: Call him as well, Mercury.

10. On von Hutten, cf. Holborn (1937), 76–77.

> Mercury: Here, Tacitus, here, come here to me, so that you
>   might speak at last! And here he is.
> Arminius: I ask a service, Italian: that you repeat here the
>   eulogy of me that is in your history.
> Tacitus: The passage where I also write about your death?
> Arminius: Exactly.[11]

Yet the *Germania* continued to dominate discourse in newly resurgent Protestant Germany. Tacitus' comments that the ancient Germans were indigenous and racially uncorrupted were much cited; his censure of their drunkenness was generally forgotten. His reports on Germanic practices became the basic truths of German historiography, and more than twenty editions of the *Germania* appeared in Germany alone between 1500 and 1650.[12] Pastors and princes alike took pride in what they saw as their heroic ancestors. From the *Germania* German humanists created a potent political myth that has endured into our own times.

3 | Tacitism in the Counter-Reformation

While the Germans used Tacitus to project their national identity into the past, elsewhere in Europe the establishment was hardly likely to welcome the recurrent Tacitean injunction to examine the motives of princes. Tacitus had been tarred with the brush of "Machiavellianism," and the prevailing Catholic view was that Tacitus wrote biased, anti-Christian history in terrible Latin.

In the bloody world of the Reformation and Counter-Reformation, while opposing camps of Christians contested their beliefs on the battlefield, in the pulpit, and on the printed page, Tacitean pessimism became popular. Like the baroque age, with its anxious preoccupation with death, the Flavian Rome of Tacitus was

---

11. Mellor (1995), 13–23, includes the first translation of *Arminius* into English.
12. Burke (1966), 141; Schellhase (1976), 47.

a time of dark intrigues through which even the elite had to struggle to make peace with the status quo to survive.

A turning point in the modern appreciation of Tacitus was indeed bizarre. A brilliant young French humanist Marc-Antoine Muret, once the tutor of Montaigne, fled France in 1554 after conviction for heresy and sodomy and took the chair of Ciceronian rhetoric at Padua, where he showed himself to be the best writer in Latin of his time.[13] When he came to Rome a decade later, he supported a leaner and drier style and promoted Tacitus as a writer whom princes and even popes would profit from reading. A combination of the crisis of Ciceronian style and the interdiction on the use of Machiavelli resulted in the widespread acceptance of Tacitism. In this, Muret was hardly a dissident; his patrons were the Cardinal d'Este and even reforming popes who were attempting to create a new literary movement. For thirty years Muret was at the center of Roman ecclesiastical humanism.[14] In 1567 the young Justus Lipsius attended his Roman lectures on Tacitus. Muret's brilliant 1580 oration on Tacitus, only recently translated into English, defends Tacitus against religious, historical, and especially stylistic criticism. Muret and Lipsius became the leading advocates of the *genus humile* of Seneca and Tacitus—the so-called "plain style," which had an enormous effect as Europe moved increasingly from Latin to the vernaculars through the seventeenth century.[15]

Oration on Tacitus (XIV)

There remain two charges of those that I said were usually made against Tacitus by the uninformed: that he is rather obscure and harsh in his writing, and that he writes bad Latin. Really, when I hear these fellows complaining about the obscurity of Tacitus, I think how readily men transfer

13. On the influence of Muret on style, cf. the classic 1924 essay by Croll (1966), "Muret and the History of 'Attic Prose'", 103–165, which first showed Muret's central role; also cf. Salmon (1980), 322.

14. Fumaroli (1980), 162ff.

15. Croll (1966), 51–101 and 181–188; Martin (1981) 240.

their own fault to others, and how much more easily they blame everything but themselves. At the same time there comes to my mind the story of a certain old man, about whom Seneca wittily relates that, since because of the defect of old age he saw less well, he used to remark, of whatever chamber he entered, that it was badly lit, and that the windows ought to be larger.[16]

The greatest Tacitean of the time was the immensely learned Dutch philologist Justus Lipsius (1547–1606), who produced excellent editions of Tacitus. Although he lectured and wrote on the political and moral ideas of the historian, Lipsius admired Tacitus' pithy prose style and his pragmatism more than any political ideology: "a sharp and shrewd writer—the most useful for men of our time."[17] Thus Lipsius brought Tacitus to the center of political discourse. Although born a Catholic, as a Lutheran in Germany he forcefully used the *Annals* to compare Tiberius with the Spanish Catholic duke of Alba. Lipsius was hardly a man of fixed principle—he returned to the Catholic Church at his death—although he claimed to have found detachment and peace in a Christian Stoicism.[18]

This turning to Tacitus became a virtual obsession in the seventeenth century, with the spread of absolutist rule. With the growth of the Inquisition, Italy, Spain, and France increasingly resembled Julio-Claudian Rome of the *Annals,* and Tacitus replaced Livy as the most popular and relevant Roman historian. In fact the first half of the seventeenth century saw more editions of Tacitus than of any other Greek or Roman historian, and commentaries on Tacitus, who was thought to be best at explaining the causes of events, became an important genre of political discourse.[19] Scholars and politicians of all ideological stripes regarded the *Annals* as a central literary, moral, and political text for their own times.

16. Translated by A. R. Scott in Mellor (1995), 33 and 37–38.
17. "Dedication to Emperor Maximilian II."
18. Croll (1966), 43–44.
19. Burke (1969), 154, 162.

One fascinating republican, Traiano Boccalini, in his satiric dialogue *News from Parnassus* (1612–1613), used hundreds of Tacitean citations to comment on the princes and courtiers of his own time.[20] Boccalini regarded Tacitus as one who brought the art and science of politics to the people as well as to the princes: he portrays Apollo praising Tacitus for warning people about tyranny and giving them "certain Spectacles" with which to see into "the very essence and quality of Princes souls."

Boccalini's virulent hostility to the Spanish domination of the papal court forced him to flee Rome for Venice.[21] A few years later, also in the safety of Venice, Paolo Sarpi used Tacitus as the model for one of the great masterpieces of European historiography, *History of the Council of Trent*.[22] Sarpi, who was also the object of a Vatican assassination plot, saw Trent as the repudiation of any real reform. He uses the Tacitean tactic of juxtaposing public speech and private intrigues, and thus penetrates beneath the masks of public theater to the underlying reality: religious "reform" is merely a disguise for secular ambition. Sarpi's *History* was widely translated and was inevitably placed on the Catholic Church's *Index of Forbidden Books*. Tacitean cynicism with a Tacitean plot also appears in Giovanni Busenello's libretto for Monteverdi's *L'incoronazione di Poppea*, performed in Venice in 1643, which closes happily with Nero and Poppaea's ecstatic love duet. Nowhere in Christian Europe but in Venice would Sarpi's history and Busenello's libretto have been tolerated.

As knowledge of Tacitus grew, criticism of his ideas also increased. Early in the seventeenth century the Jesuits, the shock troops of the papacy, assailed Tacitus as a disloyal subject who undermined government by revealing its secrets. They regarded the Tacitean spirit of inquiry as a threat to the status quo; it might endanger papal orthodoxy and Spanish rule. For the Jesuits, a historian should be a panegyrist of established virtue. Livy was the ideal; Tacitus was

20. Meinecke (1957), 71–89.
21. Schellhase (1976), 146.
22. Bouwsma (1968), 556–623.

nothing more than a revolutionary, a bad historian, and an irreligious and evil man. This is the "Red Tacitus."[23]

But there was also a "Black" Tacitus who provided advice to tyrants and models for sycophantic courtiers. Clerical and secular princes alike regarded him as a "master of prudence" in an age when dissimulation was ranked with the highest princely accomplishments, as in the aphorism *Qui nescit dissimulare, nescit regnare* ("He who cannot pretend, cannot rule"). Philip II of Spain, known as the Prudent, revealed more than a few Tiberian characteristics in his bloody suppression of the revolt in the Netherlands, which perhaps partly explains the growing Dutch interest in Tacitus. When Philip's learned courtier, Antonio Perez, fled to England, he described himself to Queen Elizabeth with some pride as "the Sejanus who got away."[24] In an age of intrigue, the *Annals* provided a convenient point of reference.

4 | Tacitus in Tudor-Stuart England

English scholars did not show an early interest in the style or politics of Tacitus, since the Livian approach to history remained dominant. Thomas More used the *Annals* to display the aura of hypocrisy in his *History of Richard III*.[25] The Tiberius-like Richard III passed from More (via Holinshed's chronicle) to Shakespeare's play, which is also Tacitean in tone. Although early Tudor English historians adapted the *Agricola* as a source for their national history, the humanist tradition of the Tudors came to full flower during the reign of Elizabeth, when the queen and many of her ministers were

23. The terms "Tacito Rosso" and "Tacito Nero" come from Toffanin (1921).

24. Syme (1960), 7–10.

25. *The History of King Richard III*, Vol. 2 of *The Complete Works of St. Thomas More* (New Haven, Conn., 1963), includes More's English and Latin versions. The editor, Richard Sylvester, details the use of Tacitus for Richard's deceitful character. There are also verbal parallels; e.g., *structis in principem insidiis* (p. 23, lines 3–4) recalls *structas principi insidias* (*Annals* 4, 28).

trained in the classical languages and literatures.[26] Leading courtiers themselves became patrons of learning in the 1580s when a group at Oxford became devoted to Tacitus. On the Continent Lipsius (who dedicated a book to Sir Philip Sidney) had recently shown in his *Politics* (1589) how Tacitus could expose political corruption and the secret workings of the factions at court—issues dear to the heart of Elizabethan intellectuals.[27]

This literary circle included Sidney, Henry Savile, Fulke Greville, Francis Bacon, and John Hayward, and was led by the queen's favorite, the Earl of Essex.[28] All were involved in the use and propagation of Tacitus, whose pungent political epigrams and moral maxims were collected into popular anthologies.[29] When he was warden of Merton College, Oxford, and Latin secretary to the queen, Henry Savile completed the first English translation of Tacitus' *Histories,* adding his own reconstruction of the missing section of the *Annals* dealing with the death of Nero and accession of Galba. It is hardly surprising in a circle which showed considerable interest in Machiavelli that Savile's reconstruction of the year 68 emphasized political maneuvering and Nero's political bungling, rather than a more properly Tacitean moral analysis. He attributed the horrors of civil war not only to the evil of rebellion but to the weak monarchy of Nero.[30] The Earl of Essex said in the preface to the second edition (1598), "There is no historie . . . so well worth reading as Tacitus."[31]

On the occasion of Savile's being knighted for his scholarly achievements, his friend Ben Jonson paid him tribute in a long epigram that praises both the translation and the completion of "the breach I grieved before"—the missing section of the *Annals*. The poem presents Savile as a reincarnated Tacitus—the "doctrine of Pythagoras"—and is a paean to the courage of historians.

26. Smuts (1994), 24.
27. Grafton (1987) has emphasized the practical use of Lipsius.
28. Levy (1967), 251.
29. Maxims: Burke (1966), 149, and (1969), 167–168.
30. Womersley (1991), 316; Smuts (1994), 26.
31. Reprinted in Mellor (1995), 83.

To Sir Henry Savile

> If, my religion safe, I durst embrace
> > That stranger doctrine of Pythagoras
> I should believe the soul of Tacitus
> > In thee, most weighty Savile, lived to us:
> So hast thou rendered him in all his bounds
> > And all his numbers, both of sense and sounds.
> But when I read that special piece restored,
> > Where Nero falls and Galba is adored,
> To thine own proper I ascribe then more,
> > and gratulate the breach I grieved before.

Another prominent member of the circle of Essex, Sir Francis Bacon, called attention to the idea espoused by both Tacitus and Machiavelli that all men wear masks. His love of the concise style inspired many later writers to imitate Tacitus. In the tense atmosphere following the execution of Essex, Sir John Hayward's *Henry IV*, with its frank Tacitean account of Richard II's deposition, so offended the Privy Council by its contemporary parallels to Essex that Hayward landed in the Tower and was almost executed.[32] Bacon defended his friend to the queen in a backhanded way: he was not guilty of treason but only of stealing "sentences and conceits out of Cornelius Tacitus."[33]

King James I of England included many Tacitean allusions in a new edition of his *Precepts on the Art of Governing* in his year of accession (1603). As king of Scotland, James had had a reputation as a devoted Tacitean, although once in England he became aware that Tacitus was also used by opponents of Stuart rule.[34] Even the royal princes Henry and Charles read the *Agricola,* and Henry was said to have heard "Tacitus represented by everyone as a writer of admirable sagacity."[35]

32. Smuts (1994), 22; Levy (1967), 252.

33. "Apophthegms New and Old," in Bacon's *Works*, Vol. 7, ed. J. Spedding et al., (Boston, 1859), 133.

34. Bradford (1983), 138–139, used Edmund Bolton's *Hypercritica* for evidence for James' suspicion of Taciteans.

35. Smuts (1994), 34, who cites T. Birch's 1760 biography of Prince Henry.

The seventeenth century was an age of witty repartee and pithy moral judgments. Bacon, who rated Tacitus above Plato and Aristotle as a moral thinker, was one of the first to turn from the amplitude of Cicero to the mordant Tacitean epigram, which became characteristic of the English prose of the age. Bacon frequently used Tacitean examples in his essays, as when he discussed intentional political obscurity in *Of Simulation and Dissimulation*. The notorious difficulty of Tacitus, known as the Prince of Obscurity, appealed to the erudite Jacobeans. Bacon did much to bring Tacitus to the attention of politicians, and in this era the historian became, in the words of the contemporary poet and Tacitean sermonizer John Donne, the "Oracle of Statesmen."[36]

An even more devoted Tacitean, Ben Jonson, wrote his *Sejanus* (1603) for the King's Men at the Globe Theater; Shakespeare acted in it, and he well may have played the role of Tiberius.[37] Jonson saw Tacitus as a guide to the political dissimulation and corruption of his day, and annotated the quarto edition of *Sejanus* with hundreds of allusions to the *Annals*. Jonson even urged in Epigram 92 that statesmen carry a pocket text of Tacitus with them as a guide to the secrets of political power.

The recurring theme in *Sejanus* is excessive desire—whether for money, sensual pleasure, or power—in the ambitious society of Jacobean London, and in this play Jonson focuses on a world in which the lust for power has become the norm and family ties are sacrificed to political advancement. There was more than a passing similarity between the intrigue and factional politics of the court of Tiberius and the Whitehall of James I, and Jonson's carefully annotated text of Lipsius' *Politics* shows the source of his political theory.[38] As Sejanus says, "Ambition makes more trusty slaves than need" (1, 366). Tiberius' corrupt courtiers here promote the state's interest to forward their own ambitions, as when the

36. For Donne as a Senecan and a Tacitean, cf. Williamson (1951), 243–245.

37. Barish (1965), I. Riggs (1989), 105, notes that it is Shakespeare's last appearance in a cast list.

38. Evans (1992), 24–27, 111–130.

sycophantic Macro justifies his actions in a classic statement of *raison d'état:*

> Macro: I will not ask why Caesar bids do this,   3, 714
>   But joy that he bids me. It is the bliss
>   Of courts to be employed, no matter how.
>   A prince's power makes all his actions virtue.
>   We, whom he works by, are dumb instruments,
>   To do, but not enquire. His great intents
>   Are to be served, not searched.   720

Though the play failed, its themes were topical enough: the twilight world of spies and informers was well known to the Roman Catholic Jonson, who had already served time in prison, and the ambitious courtier Sejanus might well represent the recently fallen Essex.[39] For whatever reason, Jonson was charged before the Privy Council with treason, although the case seems not to have come to trial.

When in 1627 the poet and courtier Fulke Greville (Lord Brooke) founded the first chair in history at Cambridge, he selected a Dutchman, Isaac Dorislaus, as incumbent.[40] A friend of Bacon's, Greville set Tacitus as the topic for his lectures. Dorislaus chose to explicate the first words of the *Annals*: "The City of Rome from its inception was held by kings." Complaints were made that Dorislaus spoke "too much for the defense of the Liberties of the People," and he was soon silenced. The obsequious letter by Matthew Wren, master of Peterhouse, to Bishop Laud of London denouncing Dorislaus survives as a model of academic and political slander; he concludes with the request that his name not be used lest he be called an informer—which is what he was!

Wren enclosed Latin excerpts from the lectures, which is all that survives of them, and they show that Dorislaus addressed such sensitive subjects as the people's rights over kings, the differences

---

39. Riggs (1989), 100; Barish (1965), 16–19.

40. Mullinger (1911), 81–89. See Mellor (2004) for a complete discussion of the Dorislaus affair.

between absolute monarchy and a monarch subject to law, and the people's ultimate authority. Although Dorislaus seems to have successfully fought against the ban, and his family continued to live in college accommodations, he never lectured again. The very anglicized Dorislaus became involved in Puritan politics and later helped to draw up the charges against King Charles; he was in turn assassinated by English royalists in The Hague in 1649, not long after the king's execution. Academic politics here led to regicide and murder.

Tacitus remained a favored preserve of English republicans and revolutionaries. In 1626 the Puritan Sir John Eliot moved in the House of Commons to impeach the king's chief minister the Duke of Buckingham, quoting Tacitus (in Latin) on Sejanus. King Charles responded, "He must intend me for Tiberius."[41] Eliot was arrested the next day and sent to the Tower. (He was the last member to be imprisoned for words spoken in Parliament.) In prison he wrote the *Monarchy of Man,* which relies heavily on Tacitus to make the case for a constitutional monarchy constrained by the laws.

Although some Stuart partisans thought that Tacitus should be suppressed as seditious, other royalists, like some Continental supporters of absolutism, could support their case with Tacitean aphorisms. They particularly savored Tacitus' comment on the ancient Britons, "As long as they fought separately, they were conquered together" (*Agricola* 12), which was quoted repeatedly to urge unquestioning loyalty to the Crown and to suppress dissenting religious publications. Even such a figure of royalist orthodoxy as Archbishop Laud, writing before his execution, quoted Tacitean phrases, although taken out of their historical context. We see an example of this dishonest style of argument when the poet and political radical John Milton, Latin secretary to the commonwealth, rebutted the French royalist Salmasius, who had quoted Tacitus out of context in support of absolute monarchy. (Milton gave his Satan in *Paradise Lost* clear characteristics of the Caesars,

41. Tenney (1941), 160.

especially Tacitus' Tiberius.)[42] Milton was a brilliant polemicist who was not about to permit Tacitus to be misused by what he regarded as royalist hacks.

5 | Tacitus under the Ancien Régime

In France of the ancien régime, after the wars of religion, Tacitus was less a part of the rough and tumble of political life than he was in England—since the absolutist state allowed no such political divisions. His histories became sources rather for moral guidance and character examination. Michel de Montaigne (1533–1592) relied heavily upon Tacitus.[43] As the first great master of the intimately personal essay, Montaigne used his *Essais* as "tests" of his own thoughts. As such the form had enormous effect on later French and English literature.

Montaigne initially focused on Tacitus' style, and he displayed a preoccupation with Stoic humanism. Later in life, he turned to a human-based morality and regarded Tacitus as a moral and political model. Unlike Christian polemicists, the tolerant Montaigne saw no problem with Tacitus' paganism: "That was his misfortune, not his fault." His essay on freedom of conscience attacks book burning carried out in the name of religion and points out that Tacitus' few offensive sentences on the Christians caused his books to be so savagely treated in earlier generations that they almost perished completely.[44] At just the time that the Jesuits were making Tacitus politically unacceptable, Montaigne used him as the model of an honest man.

It was not Tacitus' history but his judgments that fascinated the French moralist. Montaigne was particularly attracted to the introspective approach to historical motivations: emperors may act for

42. Davies (1981), 385–398.

43. On Montaigne, cf. von Stackelberg (1960), 159–186; Schellhase (1976), 128–134.

44. Montaigne, *Essays* 2, 19.

reasons of state, but they also act from hatred, resentment, lust and foolish pride. He responded profoundly to Tacitus' deep psychological insight into political malignity. When Montaigne states that "the very laws of justice cannot subsist without some mixture of injustice,"[45] he goes on to cite Plato and Tacitus' *Annals* 14, 44: "Every exemplary punishment has in it some injustice against individuals, which is compensated by public utility." Montaigne does not seek a cynical precedent for the idea that the ends justify the means, but rather a realism free of political cant and religious hypocrisy.

Essays III 8: "Of the Art of Discussion"

> I have just run through Tacitus' History at one reading (which rarely happens to me; it has been twenty years since I put one whole hour at a time on a book) . . .
>
> This form of history is by far the most useful. Public movements depend more upon the guidance of fortune, private ones on our own. This is rather a judgment of history than a recital of it; there are more precepts than stories. It is not a book to read, it is a book to study and learn; it is so full of maxims that you find every sort, both right and wrong; it is a nursery of ethical and political reflections for the provision and adornment of those who hold a place in the management of the world.[46]

Montaigne was soon translated into English and used by Bacon and Shakespeare. Like Tacitus, he has been interpreted and reinterpreted to suit later tastes.

During the seventeenth century the greatest French playwrights brought the pages of Tacitus to the Parisian stage. Pierre Corneille (1606–1684) looked to Tacitus in the darker mood of his old age for material for a drama of despair, as in *Othon* and *Attila*.[47] But it was

45. Ibid., 2, 20.
46. *The Complete Essays of Montaigne*, translated by D. Frame (Stanford, Calif., 1958), 718–721.
47. Allott (1980).

his rival Jean Racine (1639–1699) who became the greatest exponent of French classical tragedy, which usually treated topics from Greek and Roman history and mythology. Racine was educated in austere Jansenist schools that left him with both a pervasive sense of evil and a better knowledge of Greek than any other literary figure of his day.[48]

In *Britannicus* (1669), he drew both characters and politics from the *Annals*, and he shared with Tacitus a high moral tone and a fixation on evil. In his preface to the second edition of the play, Racine explains his devotion to Tacitus.

Second Preface to **Britannicus** (1676)

> In truth I have worked on models which have given great support to the picture I wished to paint of the court of Agrippina and Nero. I have copied my characters from the greatest painter of antiquity—I mean Tacitus. And I was so full of my reading of that excellent historian that there was hardly one striking effect in my tragedy for which he had not given me the idea.[49]

He follows the historian in showing the political conflict that lay behind the passions of the Neronian court: the political ambitions of Nero and his jealous mother propel the drama. Although the playwright shares Tacitus' grudging admiration for Agrippina's courage, he has only contempt for the corrupt and corrupting relations between weak rulers and their parasitic courtiers. Racine drew his characters from Tacitus, but the core of the drama lay in the seventeenth-century preoccupation with the political justification for immoral action. Racine was nothing if not a supporter of absolute monarchy, and the contemporary controversy over *raison d'état* lies at the heart of the play.

Tacitus still inspired those who were looking beyond questions of historical accuracy to more general issues of natural law and

---

48. For a sketch of Racine's life and education, cf. Butler (1959), 11–17.
49. Racine, *Théâtre Complet*, edited by J-P Collinet (Paris, 1982), 305–308.

political morality. Trained in the law, Baron Charles de Montesquieu's (1689–1755) interests ranged across history, political philosophy, economics, geography, and what today we call anthropology. In his *Considerations on the Causes of the Greatness of the Romans and Their Decline* (1734) Montesquieu sketched a philosophical history of the Roman people. He followed Tacitus (and inspired Gibbon) in seeking moral causes for social and political change.

Later, in his search for the principles of natural law, Montesquieu explored political theory itself in that vast tapestry that is his *The Spirit of the Laws* (1748), which cited Tacitus more than any other author. He said that Tacitus "summarized everything because he saw everything" (30.2). Here Montesquieu analyzed the forms of government (republic, based on virtue; monarchy, based on honor; tyranny, based on fear) and developed his theory of the separation of powers which had so much influence on the U.S. Constitution. The book became the central philosophical work of the French Enlightenment and was placed on the Catholic Church's *Index of Forbidden Books.* Montesquieu is always concerned to distinguish monarchy from despotism, and he cites the *Annals* for the judgment that "monarchy is corrupted when important men are stripped of respect and made into vile instruments of arbitrary power" (8.7). Rather, it is best that the government seem benevolent, even gentle: "The prince must encourage and the laws must menace" (12.25). Even in Tacitus, Montesquieu was able to find evidence for his concept of the separation of powers.

6 | Tacitus in Eighteenth-Century England

If Tacitus had begun to move away from the center of the political stage in seventeenth-century England, the aftermath of the Glorious Revolution of 1688 found both the Whigs and the Tories invoking Tacitus in their struggle to overcome the legacies of Cromwell and the Stuarts and to find the correct constitutional balance between the Crown, the lords, and the commons.[50] One manifestation of the struggle was the competing translations of the *Annals* by both political factions. The Whigs themselves were particularly attracted to Tacitus as an enemy of tyranny whom they might justly study and admire: "a penetrating genius," in the words of the Scots historian and philosopher David Hume.[51] Thomas Gordon produced a Whig version of Tacitus (1728), a translation that long remained popular in the American colonies for its sharp criticism of monarchy.[52] In that Whig reading, Tacitus becomes more overtly hostile to Augustus, since Whig theorists maintained that the arts could flourish only in a free society.[53] Later editions included Gordon's essays on a range of Tacitean problems; they show his devotion to Tacitus' style as well as his hyperbolic interpretation of the historian as a proto-Whig in his criticism of autocratic rule.

Discourse II. Upon Tacitus and His Writings

[Tacitus was] a mighty genius, for which no conception or design was too vast; a powerful Orator, who abounds in great sentiments and descriptions; Yet a man of consummate integrity, who, though he frequently agitates the passions, never misleads them: A masterly Historian, who draws events from their first sources; and explains them with a redundancy of images, and a frugality of words: A profound Politician who takes off every disguise, and penetrates every artifice: An upright patriot, zealous for public Liberty and the welfare of his Country, and a declared enemy to Tyrants and to the instruments of Tyranny.[54]

The Tories more often simply attacked Tacitus for his style, his wicked hostility to religion, his "meanness," the abusiveness of his wit, and his political stance.

50. Weinbrot (1993), 169.

51. Gay (1974), 25.

52. Benario (1976), 107–114.

53. Weinbrot (1978), 70.

54. Gordon, *The Works of Tacitus with Political Discourses upon that Author,* 3rd ed. (London, 1753). Spelling has been modernized.

Whig writers had found in the *Germania* indications that the Saxon "witan" was a prototype of Parliament and thus gave additional ancient authority for a restricted monarchy. The British liked to oppose this northern political freedom to the tyranny of Bourbon France, papal Italy, or ancient Rome. The London theater saw an *Arminius* and a *Boadicea* use the words Tacitus originally gave to the heroic Briton Calgacus in the *Agricola,* where he delivered a splendid indictment of imperialism and tyranny.[55] Such speeches cast no aspersions, of course, on Britain's own empire; Tacitus had been domesticated as an Englishman, and a Whig at that.

The greatest historian of the eighteenth century was a Whig and a devoted Tacitean. Though Edward Gibbon's stylistic influences lay elsewhere, his role model as a philosophical historian was Tacitus, and both pondered the moral corruption that led to political decay. Gibbon took much else from Tacitus: a view of history as theatrical performance; a focus on the personalities of the court; and, most of all, an ironic stance. Despite the great difference in sentence structure between Tacitus' harsh brevity and Gibbon's elegant periods, the same ironic polarities appear, and Gibbon's mordant wit owes much to his Roman soul mate; his pithy maxims and his recurrent irony give his history a Tacitean tone.[56] These historians of decline were both determined to strip away the pretenses of the powerful, whether in Tacitus' attacks on tyrants and sycophants or in Gibbon's attacks on the same, as well as on the Christian Church. He acknowledges his admiration for Tacitus' determination to explain the moral reality beneath superficial appearances.[57]

The Decline and Fall of the Roman Empire

(Chapter ix) In their primitive state of simplicity and independence, the Germans were surveyed by the discerning eye

55. Weinbrot (1993), 181.
56. Clive (1977), 183–191.
57. Brownley (1977), 651–666.

and delineated by the masterly pencil, of Tacitus, the first of historians who applied the science of philosophy to the study of facts. The expressive conciseness of his descriptions has deserved to exercise the diligence of innumerable anti-quarians, and to excite the genius and penetration of the philosophic historians of our own times. (I 213)[58]

Later in life Gibbon regretted having begun his history in the happy times of the second century; he thought he could have exposed the evils of empire more easily if he had begun, as Tacitus did, with the tyranny of Tiberius or the civil wars.[59] Although Gib-bon had a philosophical detachment, which might seem far from the burning anger Tacitus brought to his exposure of Tiberius, the English historian also drew scathing portraits of the theatrical per-sonalities of the late imperial and Byzantine courts.

7 | Tacitus in the Age of Revolutions

France

Tacitus thought that history should become the conscience of mankind, and the revolutionary climate of late-eighteenth-century France increased his influence. The great figures of the Enlightenment—Rousseau, Diderot, and D'Alembert—all translated him into French. Rousseau admired the historian as a stylist, and he and his contemporaries regarded both Tacitus and Machiavelli as republicans. Diderot loved him as a political thinker and a hater of tyrants, but he was also aware of the danger inherent in these texts; they could be used by one's enemies as well: "Distrust a ruler who knows by heart Aristotle, Tacitus, Machiavelli and Montesquieu."[60]

The leaders of the French Revolution admired Tacitus' passion for freedom, displayed in great dramatic tableaux. He became one

---

58. Gibbon, *Decline and Fall of the Roman Empire*, 1897 ed., edited by J. B. Bury.
59. Bowersock (1977), 33–34.
60. *Principes politiques d'un souverain* Nr. 63, cited in von Stackelberg (1960), 233.

of the authors most cited in the revolutionary press, but the revolutionaries conveniently forgot that Tacitus was as contemptuous of rampaging mobs as he was of despots. Camille Desmoulins used Tacitus to protest against the Terror.[61] His journal printed translations of Tacitus as an attack on the Committee of Public Safety, and he found Tiberius and Nero of the *Annals* to be more merciful than the Jacobins. Desmoulins' journal was burned, and he was executed. The men and women of the Revolution, like Tacitus and his heroes, trusted history to vindicate them and indict their adversaries, be they Bourbons, Jacobins, or Bonapartists.[62] They believed, like the Swiss revolutionary La Harpe, that Tacitus "punished tyrants when he painted them,"[63] and hoped the same vengeance would fall on their own enemies.

The Corsican Napoleon Bonaparte (1769–1821) received a French education which deeply imbued him with a love for the classics. His victories in Italy and over Austria were followed by a successful coup against the Directory. As "first consul" and later as emperor, Napoleon ruled France in Roman trappings, though he often expressed his hostility to Tacitus, as when the Institute of France congratulated Napoleon on his victory at Austerlitz.

> The emperor thanked the Institute and, referring to the mention of the future praise of posterity, spoke of the historians and of Tacitus, who had the privilege to occupy his thoughts. He criticized his writings and his method and then, speaking directly to M. Suard, the Permanent Secretary, he urged him to write a commentary in which he might correct the mistaken judgments and errors of Tacitus. Though Suard was a mild-mannered octogenarian, rather feeble and in delicate health, he had hardly heard the master's order when he straightened up and responded with

61. Quoted in von Stackelberg (1960), 236–237; cf. also Parker (1937), 148.

62. Parker (1937), 149, points out that the reactionary paper *Actes des apôtres* also used Tacitus and linked Jacobin opponents with Tiberius and Nero.

63. Quoted in French in von Stackelberg (1960), 235.

unsuspected energy: "Sire, the fame of Tacitus reaches too high for any writer to attempt to lower it." This answer threw a certain chill over the presence of the emperor, who signaled his chamberlain to show in another delegation and brusquely dismissed the Institute.[64]

In his 1808 meetings at Weimar, the emperor sought an alliance with Tsar Alexander. Once again Napoleon expressed his distaste for Tacitus, on both stylistic and political grounds. His comments to Goethe and Wieland are preserved in the *Mémoires* of Talleyrand:

"I assure you that the historian you are all citing continuously, Tacitus, has taught me nothing. Do you know any greater and more unjust slanderer of humanity? He finds criminal motives in the simplest acts, and he makes all the emperors into the blackest villains just to make us admire him for exposing them. We can rightly say that the *Annals* is not a history of the empire, but a statement of the legal activity of Rome. There are continuously accusations, defendants, and people who open their veins in the bath. The man who speaks endlessly of prosecutions is himself the greatest prosecutor of all. And what a style! What night always impenetrable! I am admittedly not a great Latinist, but Tacitus' obscurity is evident in the ten or twelve Italian or French translations I have read. I conclude that it is peculiar to him, and that it springs from his "genius" as much as from his style. It is only inseparable from his manner of expression because it is in his mode of thought. I have heard him praised for the fear he gives to tyrants, but he makes them afraid of the people. And that does harm to the people themselves. Am I not right, M. Wieland? But I'm bothering you; we are not here to talk about Tacitus. Look how well Tsar Alexander dances!"[65]

64. *Tacite et Mirabeau. La vie de Cn. Julius Agricola traduite par Mirabeau*, edited by Henri Welschinger (Paris, 1914), 175–178.

65. *Mémoires du Prince de Talleyrand publiés par le Duc de Broglie* (Paris, 1891), I 442–446.

Napoleon further complained, as he did on other occasions, of the obscure and difficult style of the historian who wishes "to paint everything in black." But style was only a minor annoyance; the emperor felt himself defamed by this "discontented senator" whose savage portraits of the Roman rulers belied the fact that "the Roman people loved their emperors whom Tacitus meant to have them fear."[66] He expressed his anger most clearly in an outburst to the poet Fontanes: "Tacitus! Don't speak to me about that pamphleteer! He has slandered the emperors!"[67] Perhaps he had.

America

Revolutionaries across the Atlantic also looked to Tacitus for inspiration. Young Ben Franklin had little Latin before he began, at age sixteen, his discussion of free speech in his *Dogwood Papers,* for which he had probably read Tacitus in English translation (although he quoted the Latin).[68] He did master Latin later, not least (like Cato the Elder learning Greek) so that he could help his son learn it. Much later, on July 4, 1776, at the signing of the Declaration of Independence, Franklin drew on Tacitus in his famous bon mot addressed to John Hancock: "We must indeed all hang together, or, most assuredly, we shall all hang separately" (*Agricola* 12: "As long as they fought separately, they were conquered together"). Tacitus' hostility to tyranny, his irreverent wit, and his moral outrage appealed to the colonists in their struggle against the British Crown.

The second and third American presidents, John Adams (1735–1826) and Thomas Jefferson (1743–1826), once bitter political antagonists but reconciled in the learned correspondence of their old age, loved Tacitus above all the other ancients.[69] Each found much in his histories to sustain their long argument about the role

66. Wankenne (1967), 260.
67. Translated by Mellor (1995), 195.
68. Gummere (1963), 126.
69. Ibid., 192.

of an aristocratic Senate, but both agreed that autocratic rule must be avoided. Jefferson, who argued for the place of Tacitus and ancient history in the curriculum of the University of Virginia, wrote to his granddaughter: "Tacitus I consider the first writer in the world without a single exception. His book is a compound of history and morality of which we have no other example."[70] As an agrarian democrat, he admired Tacitus' Germans who lived on the boundary of an empire in native freedom while resisting Roman domination.[71] Both men had absorbed their classics; Adams at Harvard and Jefferson at the College of William and Mary. After a twelve-year silence following Jefferson's defeat of Adams in the election of 1800, Jefferson began the correspondence which was to continue through their remaining years. Their letters are sprinkled with allusions to their wide reading, and the tone is often as classical as the quotations. Neither had much use for the ideal Republic of Plato or for the unruly democracy of Athens; these were practical political philosophers who had seen the French struggle for freedom turn into a Bonapartist tyranny. Jefferson wrote to Adams in 1812 that he had "given up newspapers in exchange for Tacitus and Thucydides, for Newton and Euclid; and I find myself much the happier."[72] Adams in turn proclaimed the morality of Tacitus to be "the morality of Patriotism."[73] They died on the same day, July 4, 1826.

8 | Tacitus in the Nineteenth and Twentieth Centuries

In the early nineteenth century many still read and revered Tacitus, some for his politics, and others for his literary power. Stendhal, also a devotee of psychological analysis, refers more than fifty times

70. Colbourn (1965), 26.

71. Luce (1982), 1003.

72. L. J. Cappon, *The Adams-Jefferson Letters* (Chapel Hill, N.C., 1959), II:291–292. Spelling retained.

73. Ibid., 462.

to Tacitus and even read his works on his deathbed, and his protagonist Julien Sorel in *The Red and the Black* prized his edition of Tacitus.[74] Thomas Babington Macaulay regarded Tacitus as an unparalleled portraitist of character, and John Quincy Adams claimed he read the historian every day.

But through the century the writing of history gradually became professionalized and the universities, especially in Germany, adopted the scientific model for historical seminars and research. Tacitus' passionate approach to history was scorned by a new breed of academic, "scientific" historians such as Leopold von Ranke, who professed to write history "as it actually happened."

Yet as Tacitus' reputation as a historian declined, he continued to be praised as a stylist and thinker. Near the turn of the century Friedrich Leo (1851–1914) in Germany and Gaston Boissier (1823–1908) in France argued the case for him. Leo, perhaps the greatest Latin scholar of his time, delivered the emperor's birthday oration in 1896 in Göttingen on the subject of Tacitus. In it he attempts to rescue the historian's literary and historical reputation from the criticism of nineteenth-century positivist historians; he regarded Tacitus as "one of the few great poets" Rome ever produced, particularly praising his rhetorical skill and comparing his dramatic art to Shakespeare's history plays.[75]

Gaston Boissier wrote on archaeology, history, and a range of literary subjects. The elegance and liveliness of his books brought his learning to a wide audience in France and abroad, and he was elected to the Académie Française, of which he became the permanent secretary. Like Leo, his study of Tacitus (1903) signaled a break with the condescension of nineteenth-century scholars and, in many ways, is the first truly modern appreciation of the historian's willingness to subject even monarchs to moral guidelines. Boissier, like Montaigne, saw Tacitus' greatest value in being a moralist of political life.[76]

74. Janssens (1946).
75. Reprinted in Mellor (1995). Translated by G. Dundas.
76. Boissier (1906).

In the twentieth century, Tacitus, like most Greek and Latin writers, has remained on the fringes of intellectual life. He has surely had an effect, but it has usually been indirect. The *Germania* was a revered text under the Nazis, but its ideas had already been incorporated into the German national consciousness by the German humanists and Reformation polemicists. The recognition of the German habit of obedience, in the postwar words of Meinecke, may be traced back to Tacitus,[77] but no one needed to read the *Germania* to recognize its existence.

There have also been many thousands of scholarly publications on Tacitus in the past sixty years, with the greatest being Sir Ronald Syme's two-volume *Tacitus* (1958), which reintegrates the stylist and the historian. Tacitus speaks to us today about the corruption of power, and the ways in which both rulers and ruled are complicit in that mutual corruption. Lies and dissimulation are intertwined with self-deception until the truth of evil is hidden, even from a Nero himself. Power resides in language, and the corruption of language leads directly to the corruption of political life. Tacitus the politician was not a hero; he admits that his courage failed him. But his language is unsparing in its exposure of evil and its devotion to truth. That, rather than a political program, is his lasting legacy.

In our own time, Tacitus' *Annals* has been banned in Eastern Europe, and a collection of essays about him was movingly dedicated "To the People of Czechoslovakia" in 1969, the year after the Prague Spring.[78] The demons of collaboration, corruption, treachery, and tyranny that inspired Tacitus have not yet been laid to rest. The atrocities of the twentieth century have swept away the smug liberalism of the Victorian era: rulers can be monsters, and something close to pure evil is clearly possible. The Tacitean Tiberius and Nero seem positively benign after Stalin, Hitler, and Pol Pot, who murdered not dozens or hundreds but millions.

---

77. Meinecke (1948), 480.
78. Dorey (1969).

Those horrors have opened the eyes of historians to other cruelties that have long awaited our attention. Massacres in the prairie, in the outback, on the veldt, in slave galleys or prison camps or brothels, from hunger or neglect, using swords or high technology—all now lie naked before us. Tacitus' obsession with evil is once more on the agenda of historians of the twentieth and twenty-first centuries. As long as we do not judge him by the narrow academic norms of nineteenth-century scientific history, Tacitus will once again illuminate the moral and political issues of yet another day.

The Julio-Claudian Family

(Genealogy)

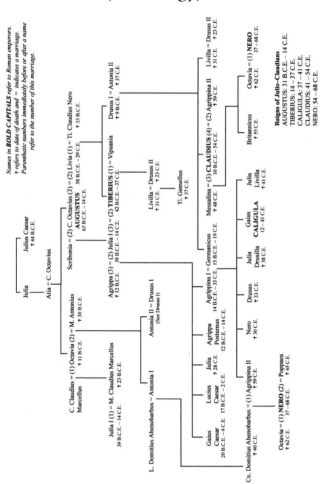

The Julio-Claudian Family

Names in **BOLD CAPITALS** refer to Roman emperors.
† refers to date of death and = indicates a marriage.
Parenthetic numbers immediately before or after a name
refer to the number of this marriage.

Reigns of Julio-Claudians
AUGUSTUS: 31 B.C.E. – 14 C.E.
TIBERIUS: 14 – 37 C.E.
CALIGULA: 37 – 41 C.E.
CLAUDIUS: 41 – 54 C.E.
NERO: 54 – 68 C.E.

Map of the Roman Empire

Prominent Persons

Gnaeus Julius AGRICOLA: native of southern Gaul who served as a successful general in Britain, where he defeated the rebels and extended Roman rule into Scotland. His son-in-law, Tacitus, recounted his career in a laudatory biography. He died in 93 C.E.

AGRIPPA POSTUMUS: exiled to an island by his grandfather Augustus for his violent behavior. He was murdered in 14 C.E. soon after his grandfather's death.

AGRIPPINA I: granddaughter of Augustus, wife of Germanicus, and mother of Caligula. Her stubborn resistance to Tiberius' rule resulted in her exile and death.

AGRIPPINA II: daughter of Agrippina I and fourth wife of the emperor Claudius. She plotted to bring her son, Nero, to the throne; he later had her murdered.

ANTONIA: daughter of Mark ANTONY. She was married to Drusus I, and their sons were Germanicus and Claudius. She revealed to Tiberius, her brother-in-law, Sejanus' conspiracy against him.

Mark ANTONY: legate of Caesar during the Gallic and civil wars. He was triumvir with Octavian and then his opponent in the war at Actium. Antonia, Caligula, Claudius, and Nero were descended from him through his marriage to Octavia.

ARMINIUS: German auxiliary who rebelled against Rome and destroyed the three legions of Varus in 9 C.E.

Gaius Julius Caesar Octavianus—AUGUSTUS: Gaius Octavius was adopted by his great-uncle Julius Caesar and took his name in 44 B.C.E. He fought alongside, and against, Mark Antony 44–30 B.C.E. In 27 he took the name of "Augustus." Thereafter he ruled as emperor until his death in 14 C.E., when he was succeeded by Tiberius.

BOUDICCA: queen of the Britons who led a rebellion against Rome.

BRITANNICUS: son of Claudius. He was installed as joint emperor with Nero but was soon murdered.

Afranius BURRUS: praetorian prefect under Nero and, with Seneca, one of Nero's two chief advisors.

CALGACUS: leader of the Caledonian resistance against Rome until defeated by Agricola.

Gaius CALIGULA: son of Germanicus and Agrippina I. He ruled 37–41 C.E.

Marcus Porcius CATO the ELDER: conservative general and statesman in the second century B.C.E. who argued for the "old values." He died in 149 B.C.E.

Marcus Porcius CATO the YOUNGER: leader of the traditional faction in the Senate who fiercely opposed Julius Caesar. He committed suicide after his defeat by Caesar in 46 B.C.E.

Quintus Petilius CERIALIS: general in command of Lower Germany who put down the Batavian revolt in 70 C.E.

Marcus Tullius CICERO: senator and Rome's greatest orator. He vigorously opposed Mark Antony after Caesar's assassination. He was murdered in 43 B.C.E.

Julius CIVILIS: Roman citizen who led the revolt of his Batavian countrymen 69–70 C.E.

Tiberius CLAUDIUS Caesar: son of Drusus I. Ruled 41–54 C.E. He was murdered by his fourth wife, Agrippina II.

CREMUTIUS CORDUS: historian who committed suicide after his writings were condemned under Tiberius.

DOMITIAN—Titus Flavius Domitianus: the younger son of Vespasian. He ruled from 81 to 96 C.E. He was, for Tacitus, the ultimate tyrant.

Nero Claudius DRUSUS I: son of Livia and brother of Tiberius. He commanded the Roman armies in Germany until his death in 9 B.C.E. His wife, Antonia, gave birth to Claudius and Germanicus.

DRUSUS Caesar II: only son of the emperor Tiberius and heir to the throne until his death in 23 C.E. Sejanus conspired with Drusus' wife to poison him.

Servius Sulpicius GALBA: the elderly governor of Spain who was acclaimed emperor by his troops in 68 C.E. and succeeded Nero to the throne. He ruled for seven months until he was murdered in the Forum in January 69.

GERMANICUS Julius Caesar: son of Drusus who became a favorite of Augustus' and married the emperor's granddaughter Agrippina I. Like his father, from whom he took the honorific name Germanicus, he was enormously popular with the people. Tiberius was forced by Augustus to adopt Germanicus as his co-successor, but Germanicus died in Antioch in 19 C.E. His son Caligula and grandson Nero became emperors.

HADRIAN: born in Spain. Adopted by Trajan, he ruled 117–138 C.E.

HEROD AGRIPPA: grandson of Herod the Great who spent his youth as a hostage at the imperial court. With the support of his boyhood friends Caligula and Claudius, he became king of Judaea and Samaria until his death in 44 C.E.

JULIA I: only child of Augustus, who married, in turn, Marcellus, Agrippa, and Tiberius. Of her five children by Agrippa, only Agrippina I continued the Julian line. Julia was exiled by her father for immorality in 2 B.C.E. and died from violence or starvation soon after his death in 14 C.E.

Gaius JULIUS CAESAR: generally credited with the fall of the Roman Republic. In his will he adopted his great-nephew Octavius (later Augustus) as his son and heir. In 42 B.C.E. he was deified as *Divus Iulius,* setting a precedent for his successors.

LIVIA Drusilla: second wife of Augustus, whom he married in 38 B.C.E. a few days after the birth of Drusus, her second son by her first husband. They remained married for fifty-one years, and she survived until 29 C.E. She supported her son Tiberius' quest for the succession, although their relations were often strained. She seems to have been Augustus' chief advisor.

LIVILLA: daughter of Drusus I who was married to her cousin Drusus II, the son of Tiberius. She was reported to have been seduced by Sejanus into poisoning her husband.

LIVY—Titus Livius: the preeminent historian of the Roman Republic. Although a friend of Augustus', he was thought to have retained Republican sympathies. About a third of his enormous history (in 142 books) survived. He was a tutor of the emperor Claudius.

Valeria MESSALINA: third wife of Claudius. Her promiscuous behavior led to her death in 48 C.E. She was the mother of Britannicus and Octavia.

Tiberius Claudius NARCISSUS: an influential freedman under Claudius who was in charge of imperial correspondence. He intrigued against Claudius' wife, Agrippina II, who had him killed soon after Claudius' death.

NERO Claudius Caesar: son of Agrippina II, he was adopted by Claudius after his mother's marriage to the emperor. Despite a promising beginning, he lost interest in government and reveled in his gifts as a singer and performer. After a rule of fourteen years, he was forced to flee the city and commit suicide in 68 C.E.

NERVA: elderly senator acclaimed as emperor after the murder of Domitian in 96 C.E. He wisely adopted the distinguished general Trajan and was later praised for having established the "adoptive monarchy" that resulted in the "five good emperors."

OCTAVIA I: sister of Octavius and fourth wife of Mark Antony. She always remained close to her brother and was a generous patroness of building projects in Rome.

OCTAVIA II: daughter of Claudius and unhappy wife of Nero as a young girl in 49 C.E. She was later divorced, so that Nero could marry Poppaea; Octavia was then exiled and killed.

OTHO: Poppaea's second husband and friend of Nero's. Nero appointed him governor of the Spanish province of Lusitania. After Nero's death, he succeeded Galba as emperor in January of 69 C.E. and ruled for three months. After his defeat by the troops of Vitellius at Bedriacum, he committed suicide.

Marcus Antonius PALLAS: Greek slave freed by Antonia who came into the service of her son Claudius. He was an ally, and perhaps a lover, of Agrippina II, and helped to arrange her marriage to Claudius. As secretary of the imperial treasury, Pallas became enormously wealthy. He was murdered by Nero, perhaps for his wealth.

Lucius Calpurnius PISO: a member of a distinguished family descended from Julius Caesar's father-in-law. He was sent by Tiberius to serve as governor of Syria and watch over Germanicus. In the aftermath of Germanicus' death, he was tried for various offenses and committed suicide.

PLANCINA: wife of Lucius Calpurnius Piso and friend of Livia's.

PLUTARCH: Greek philosopher and biographer (c. 100 C.E.) whose *Parallel Lives* are the most important collection of ancient biographies.

POPPAEA Sabina: great beauty who became Nero's second wife; he was her third husband.

Lucius Aelius SEJANUS: praetorian prefect and closest advisor to Tiberius. He seems to have plotted to replace the aging emperor; when the plot was uncovered, he was killed.

Lucius Annaeus SENECA: Stoic philosopher, playwright, and statesman who served as tutor of the young Nero and later one of his chief advisors. After being accused of involvement in a conspiracy, he was ordered by the emperor to commit suicide in 65 C.E.

TIBERIUS Claudius Nero: son of Livia and successor to Augustus in 14 C.E. His twenty-three year rule is the subject of the first six books of the *Annals*.

Gaius Ofonius TIGELLINUS: praetorian prefect under Nero.

TITUS Flavius Vespasianus: elder son of Vespasian who commanded Roman forces at the capture and destruction of Jerusalem.

He ruled briefly, 79–81 C.E., and died of a fever at the age of forty-one.

TRAJAN—Marcus Ulpius Trajanus: his father was born in Spain and became an important general and governor of Syria under Vespasian. The younger Trajan was Roman commander on the Rhine when Nerva adopted him as his successor in 97 C.E. After the death of Nerva, Trajan returned to Rome and ruled 98–117 C.E. He was later compared with Augustus as the greatest of Roman emperors.

Publius Quinctilius VARUS: as commander of Roman troops in Germany, he took his army into an ambush in 9 C.E. and suffered the worst defeat since the time of Hannibal. Three legions were destroyed.

VERGIL: Rome's greatest poet, whose epic poem the *Aeneid* recounted the quest of Aeneas, a Trojan hero, to found the Roman people. His poem had immense influence on all later Latin authors, whether they were writing in poetry or in prose.

VESPASIAN—Titus Flavius Vespasianus: descended from relatively humble Sabine stock, he was commander in Judaea when the civil wars of 69 C.E. broke out. He successfully established a new dynasty (known as the Flavian dynasty) and, after his death in 79, was succeeded by his sons, first Titus and then Domitian.

Gaius Julius VINDEX: a senator of Gallic background who, as governor of Gaul, led the first revolt against Nero. He was defeated by the German army, who remained for a time loyal to Nero.

VITELLIUS: commander of armies in Germany who successfully defeated Otho in 69 C.E. He then ruled for eight months before being killed by the Flavian troops.

Further Reading

The most obvious book for further exploration of the *Annals* is Tony Woodman's excellent translation (Indianapolis, IN, 2004). As I say in the acknowledgments, Woodman's English version provides a very accurate sense of both the content and the Latin style of Tacitus. His introduction is extremely helpful. For Tacitus' other historical works, the best easily available translations are: *Histories*, translated by K. Wellesley revised with a new introduction by Rhiannon Ash (London, 2009); *Agricola* and *Germania*, translated by A. Birley (Oxford, 2009). For those who know some Latin and wish to read Tacitus in the original with the help of a bilingual edition, the five volumes of the Loeb Classical Library are excellent—volumes 3–5 are devoted to the *Annals*.

The most important modern book on Tacitus remains after a half-century Ronald Syme's magisterial two-volume *Tacitus* (Oxford, 1958). Shorter introductions to Tacitus in English include R. Martin, *Tacitus* (London, 1981 [rev. 1994]), and R. Mellor, *Tacitus* (New York, 1993). For other accessible books on the *Annals,* I recommend B. Walker, *The Annals of Tacitus* (Manchester, 1952); P. Sinclair, *Tacitus: The Sententious Historian* (University Park, PA, 1995); and E. O'Gorman, *Irony and Misreading in the* Annals *of Tacitus* (Cambridge, 2000).

Readers who wish a detailed account of the historical background of the Julio-Claudian era might examine the relevant chapters of Volume 10 of the *Cambridge Ancient History* (Cambridge, 1996, 2nd ed.). Recent biographies of the emperors or empresses discussed by Tacitus include those by A. Barrett (*Livia*; *Agrippina*), E. Champlin (*Nero*), M. Griffin (*Nero*), and B. Levick (*Tiberius*; *Claudius*). All provide a historical antidote to the more polemical Tacitus and the more salacious Suetonius. For a lively version of Suetonius' *Lives of the Twelve Caesars,* the old translation by Robert Graves is available from Penguin Classics in a 2007 revision by J. Rives.

For the impact of Tacitus since the Renaissance, there are many books and articles mentioned in the footnotes of chapter 10. A conference volume dedicated to Sir Ronald Syme contains a good collection of essays about both Tacitus and the tradition: T. J. Luce and A. J. Woodman, eds., *Tacitus and the Tacitean Tradition* (Princeton, N.J., 1993). A compendium by R. Mellor, *Tacitus: The Classical Tradition* (New York, 1995), contains excerpts by dozens of authors from the sixteenth to the twentieth centuries.

Works Cited

This bibliography of scholarly works does not include citations of earlier literary authors—e.g., Boccaccio, Machiavelli, Thomas More, Montaigne, Ben Jonson, and Racine—whose references are contained in the footnotes of Chapter 10.

Allott, T. 1980. "Tacitus and Some Late Plays of Corneille." *Journal of European Studies* 10: 32–47.

Auerbach, Erich. 1953. *Mimesis.* Princeton, N.J.

Barish, J. A., ed. 1965. *Ben Jonson: Sejanus.* New Haven, Conn.

Barrett, A. A. 1996. *Agrippina: Sex, Power, and Politics in the Early Empire.* New Haven, Conn.

———. 2001. "Tacitus, Livia and the Evil Stepmother." *Rheinisches Museum* 144: 171–175.

———. 2002. *Livia: First Lady of Imperial Rome.* New Haven, Conn.

Bartsch, S. 1994. *Actors in the Audience: Theatricality and Doublespeak from Nero to Hadrian.* Cambridge, Mass.

Benario, H. W. 1976. "Gordon's Tacitus." *Classical Journal* 72: 107–114.

Boissier, G. 1906. *Tacitus, and Other Roman Studies.* Translated by W. G. Hutchison. London.

Bolgar, R. R., ed. 1976. *Classical Influences on European Culture* a.d. *1500–1700.* Cambridge.

Borchardt, F. L. 1971. *German Antiquity in Renaissance Myth.* Baltimore.

Bouwsma, W. J. 1968. *Venice and the Defense of Republican Liberty: Renaissance Values in the Age of the Counter Reformation.* Berkeley, Calif.

Bowersock, G. W. 1977. "Gibbon on Civil War and Rebellion in the Decline of the Roman Empire." In Bowersock, Clive, and Graubard, 27–35.

Bowersock, G. W., J. Clive, and S. R. Graubard, eds. 1977. *Edward Gibbon and the Decline and Fall of the Roman Empire.* Cambridge, Mass.

Bradford, A. T. 1983. "Stuart Absolutism and the 'Utility' of Tacitus." *Huntington Library Quarterly* 46: 127–155.

Braund, D. C. 1985. *Augustus to Nero: A Sourcebook on Roman History 31 b.c.–a.d. 68.* London.

Brownley, M. W. 1977. "Appearance and Reality in Gibbon's History." *Journal of the History of Ideas* 38: 651–666.

Burke, P. 1966. "A Survey of the Popularity of Ancient Historians, 1450–1700." *History and Theory* 5: 135–152.

———. 1969. "Tacitism." In Dorey, 149–171.

———. 1995. "Tacitism, Scepticism and Reason of State." In J. H. Burns, ed., *The Cambridge History of Political Thought: 1450–1700.* Cambridge. 479–484.

Butler, P. 1959. *Classicisme et Baroque dans l'Oeuvre de Racine.* Paris.

Cameron, A. 1976. *Circus Factions: Blues and Greens at Rome and Byzantium.* Oxford.

Champlin, E. 2003. *Nero.* Cambridge, Mass.

Clive, J. 1977. "Gibbon's Humor." In Bowersock, Clive, and Graubard, 183–192.

Colbourn, H. T. 1965. *The Lamp of Experience: Whig History and the Intellectual Origins of the American Revolution.* Chapel Hill, N.C.

Coleman, K. M. 1990. "Fatal Charades: Roman Executions Staged as Mythological Enactments." *Journal of Roman Studies* 80: 44–73.

Croll, M. 1966. *Style, Rhetoric, and Rhythm: Essays.* Princeton, N.J.

Damon, C., and S. Takács, eds. 1999. *The Senatus Consultum de Cn. Pisone Patre: Text, Translation, Discussion*, special issue of *American Journal of Philology*, 120.1.

Dawson, A. 1969. "Whatever Happened to Lady Agrippina?" *Classical Journal* 64: 253–267.

Davies, S. 1981. 'Triumph and Anti-Triumph: Milton's Satan and the Roman Emperors in *Paradise Lost.*" *Etudes Anglaises* 34: 385–398.

Dorey, T. A., ed. 1969. *Tacitus.* London.

Eck, W., A. Caballos, and F. Fernández. 1996. *Das Senatus Consultum de Cn. Pisone Patre.* Munich.

Edwards, C. 1993. *The Politics of Immorality in Ancient Rome.* Cambridge.

Evans, R. 1992. *Jonson, Lipsius, and the Politics of Renaissance Stoicism*. Wakefield, N.H.

Feldman, L. H. 1993. *Jew and Gentile in the Ancient World: Attitudes and Interactions from Alexander to Justinian*. Princeton, N.J.

Fumaroli, M. 1980. *L'Age de l'éloquence: rhétorique et "res literaria" de la Renaissance au seuil de l'époque classique*. Geneva.

Gay, P. 1974. *Style in History*. New York.

Gill, C. 1983. "The Question of Character-Development: Plutarch and Tacitus." *Classical Quarterly*, n.s., 33: 469–487.

Ginsburg, J. 2006. *Representing Agrippina: Constructions of Female Power in the Early Roman Empire*. New York.

Grafton, A. 1987. "Portrait of Justus Lipsius." *American Scholar* 56: 382–390.

Griffin, M. T. 1982. "The Lyons Tablet and Tacitean Hindsight." *Classical Quarterly*, n.s., 32: 404–418.

Gummere, R. M. 1963. *The American Colonial Mind and the Classical Tradition: Essays in Comparative Culture*. Cambridge, Mass.

Heller, W. 1999. "Tacitus Incognito: Opera as History in *L'incoronazione di Poppea*." *Journal of the American Musicological Society* 52: 39–96.

Holborn, H. 1937. *Ulrich Von Hutten and the German Reformation*. New Haven, Conn.

Hopkins, K. 1983. *Death and Renewal*. Cambridge.

Isaac, B. H. 2004. *The Invention of Racism in Classical Antiquity*. Princeton, N.J.

Janssens, E. 1946. "Stendhal et Tacite." *Latomus* 5: 311–319.

Joshel, S. R. 1997. "Female Desire and the Discourse of Empire: Tacitus' Messalina." In J. P. Hallett and M. B. Skinner, eds., *Roman Sexualities*. Princeton, N.J., 221–254.

Kelley, D. R. 1993. "*Tacitus Noster:* The *Germania* in the Renaissance and Reformation." In Luce and Woodman, 152–167.

Ker, J. 2009. *The Deaths of Seneca*. New York.

Ketterer, R. C. 2009. *Ancient Rome in Early Opera*. Urbana, Ill.

La Penna, A. 1976. "Vivere sotto i tiranni: un tema tacitiano da Guicciardini a Diderot." In Bolgar, 295–303.

Lessing, G. E. 1984 (German original 1766). *Laocoön: An Essay on the Limits of Painting and Poetry*. Translated by E. A. McCormick. Baltimore.

Levick, B. 1990. *Claudius*. New Haven, Conn.

Levy, F. J. 1967. *Tudor Historical Thought*. San Marino, Calif.

Lomas, K. 1993. *Rome and the Western Greeks, 350 BC–AD 200*. London.

Luce, T. J., ed. 1982. *Ancient Writers: Greece and Rome*. New York.

Luce, T. J., and A. J. Woodman, eds. 1993. *Tacitus and the Tacitean Tradition.* Princeton, N.J.

Marañón, G. 1956. *Tiberius: A Study in Resentment.* With a foreword by Sir Ronald Syme. London.

Martin, R. 1981. *Tacitus.* London.

Meinecke, F. 1948. "The Year 1848 in German History." *Review of Politics* 10: 475–492.

————. 1957. *Machiavellism: The Doctrine of Raison d'Etat and its Place in Modern History.* Translated by Douglas Scott. New Haven, Conn.

Mellor, R. 1995. *Tacitus: The Classical Heritage.* New York.

————. 2004. "Tacitus, Academic Politics, and Regicide in the Reign of Charles I: The Tragedy of Dr. Isaac Dorislaus." *International Journal of the Classical Tradition* 11: 153–193.

————. 2008. "*Graecia Capta*: The Confrontation between Greek and Roman Identity." In K. Zacharia, ed., *Hellenisms: Culture, Identity, and Ethnicity from Antiquity to Modernity.* Aldershot, England, 79–126.

Millar, F. 1992. *The Emperor in the Roman World: 31 b.c.–a.d. 337.* 2nd ed. London.

Momigliano, A. 1966. *Studies in Historiography.* New York.

Mullinger, J. 1911. *The University of Cambridge.* Vol. 3. Cambridge.

Nolhac, P. de. 1892. "Boccace et Tacite." *Mélanges d'Archéologie et d'Histoire* (Ecole Françaises de Rome) 12: 125–148.

O'Gorman, E. 2000. *Irony and Misreading in the* Annals *of Tacitus.* Cambridge.

Oliver, J. H. 1953. *The Ruling Power: A Study of the Roman Empire in the Second Century after Christ through the Roman Oration of Aelius Aristides. Transactions of the American Philosophical Society,* n.s., 43.4: 871–1003.

Orwell, G. 1954. *A Collection of Essays.* New York.

Parker, H. T. 1937. *The Cult of Antiquity and the French Revolutionaries: A Study in the Development of the Revolutionary Spirit.* Chicago.

Petrochilos, N. 1974. *Roman Attitudes towards the Greeks.* Athens.

Raaflaub, K., and L. J. Samons. 1990. "Opposition to Augustus." In K. Raaflaub and M. Toher, eds., *Between Republic and Empire: Interpretations of Augustus and His Principate.* Berkeley, Calif., 417–454.

Riggs, D. 1989. *Ben Jonson: A Life.* Cambridge, Mass.

Rowe, G. 2002. *Princes and Political Cultures: The New Tiberian Senatorial Decrees.* Ann Arbor, Mich.

Rudich, V. 1993. *Political Dissidence under Nero: The Price of Dissimulation.* London.

———. 1997. *Dissidence and Literature under Nero: The Price of Rhetoricization.* London.

Rutland, L. W. 1978. "Women as Makers of Kings in Tacitus' *Annals.*" *Classical World* 72: 15–29.

Rutledge, S. H. 2001. *Imperial Inquisitions: Prosecutors and Informants from Tiberius to Domitian.* London.

Sailor, D. 2008. *Writing and Empire in Tacitus.* Cambridge.

Salmon, J. H. M. 1980. "Cicero and Tacitus in Sixteenth-Century France." *American Historical Review* 85: 307–331.

Santoro L'hoir, F. 2006. *Tragedy, Rhetoric, and the Historiography of Tacitus' Annals.* Ann Arbor, Mich.

Schäfer, P. 1997. *Judeophobia: Attitudes toward the Jews in the Ancient World.* Cambridge, Mass.

Schellhase, K. C. 1976. *Tacitus in Renaissance Political Thought.* Chicago.

Shay, J. 1994. *Achilles in Vietnam: Combat Trauma and the Undoing of Character.* New York.

Sherwin-White, A. N. 1967. *Racial Prejudice in Imperial Rome.* Cambridge.

Sinclair, P. 1992. "*Deorum iniurias dis curae* (Tac. *Ann.* 1. 73. 4)." *Latomus* 51: 397–403.

Sinclair, P. 1995. *Tacitus the Sententious Historian: A Sociology of Rhetoric in Annales 1–6.* University Park, Pa.

Smuts, M. 1994. "Court-Centred Politics and the Uses of Roman Historians, c. 1590–1630." In K. Sharpe and P. Lake, eds., *Culture and Politics in Early Stuart England.* London, 21–43.

Syme, R. 1958. *Tacitus.* Oxford.

———. 1960. "Roman Historians and Renaissance Politics." In *Society and History in the Renaissance: A Report of a Conference Held at the Folger Library on April 23 and 24, 1960.* Washington, D.C., 3–12.

———. 1974. "History or Biography: The Case of Tiberius Caesar." *Historia* 23: 481–496.

Tenney, M. F. 1941. "Tacitus in the Politics of Early Stuart England." *Classical Journal* 37: 151–163.

Toffanin, G. 1921. *Machiavelli e il tacitismo.* Padua. 2nd ed., Naples, 1972.

Turpin, W. 2008. "Tacitus, Stoic *exempla,* and the *praecipuum munus annalium.*" *Classical Antiquity* 27: 359–404.

von Stackelberg, J. 1960. *Tacitus in der Romania: Studien zur literarischen Rezeption des Tacitus in Italien und Frankreich.* Tübingen.

Walker, B. 1952. *The Annals of Tacitus: A Study in the Writing of History.* Manchester.

Wankenne, A. 1967. "Napoléon et Tacite." *Les Etudes Classiques* 35: 260–263.

Watson, P. 1995. *Ancient Stepmothers: Myth, Misogyny, and Reality.* Leiden.

Weinbrot, H. D. 1978. *Augustus Caesar in "Augustan" England: The Decline of a Classical Norm.* Princeton, N.J.

———. 1993. "Politics, Taste, and National Identity: Some Uses of Tacitism in Eighteenth-Century Britain." In Luce and Woodman, 168–184.

Wells, P. S. 2003. *The Battle That Stopped Rome: Emperor Augustus, Arminius, and the Slaughter of the Legions in the Teutoburg Forest.* New York.

Williamson, G. 1951. *The Senecan Amble: A Study in Prose Form from Bacon to Collier.* Chicago.

Wirszubski, C. 1950. *Libertas as a Political Idea at Rome during the Late Republic and Early Principate.* Cambridge.

Womersley, D. 1991. "Sir Henry Savile's Translation of Tacitus and the Political Interpretation of Elizabethan Texts." *Review of English Studies* 42: 313–342.

Woodman, A. J. 1988. *Rhetoric in Classical Historiography: Four Studies.* London.

———. 1989. "Tacitus' Obituary of Tiberius." *Classical Quarterly*, n.s., 39: 197–205. Reprinted in Woodman 1998, 155–167.

———. 1992. "Nero's Alien Capital: Tacitus as Paradoxographer (*Annals* 15. 36–37)." In A. J. Woodman and J. Powell, eds., *Author and Audience in Latin Literature.* Cambridge, 173–188, 251–255. Reprinted in Woodman 1998, 168–189.

———. 1993. "Amateur Dramatics at the Court of Nero (*Annals* 15. 48–74)." In Luce and Woodman, 104–128. Reprinted in Woodman 1998, 190–217.

———. 1995. "A Death in the First Act (*Annals* I. 6)." *Papers of the Leeds International Latin Seminar* 8: 257–274. Reprinted in Woodman 1998, 23–39.

———. 1998. *Tacitus Reviewed.* Oxford.

———, trans. 2004. *Tacitus: The Annals.* With an introduction by Woodman. Cambridge, Mass.

Woolf, G. 1998. *Becoming Roman: The Origins of Provincial Civilization in Gaul.* Cambridge.

Index